Blessed Ambiguity

Blessed Ambiguity: Brothers in the Church

Michael F. Meister, FSC, Editor

The Brotherhood Seminar
Sponsored by the
Christian Brothers Conference,
Conference of Major Superiors of Men, and
National Assembly of Religious Brothers

Cover photo: PhotoDisc, Inc.

Published by Christian Brothers Publications, Landover, MD 20785

Copyright © 1993 by Christian Brothers Conference, Landover, MD 20785

Printed by Saint Mary's Press, 702 Terrace Heights, Winona, MN 55987

ISBN 1-884904-00-9

Contents

Introduction

John Paige, CSC

Most of us have had the experience of sailing along gracefully on a project, in a relationship, in life, when suddenly we were jolted senseless by events not only unexpected, but incomprehensible. In experiences like these, we soon learn in our fragility that unsolved and unsolvable questions must be lived a while before they begin to make sense to us, if indeed they make sense at all. When the sudden jolt involves a paradigm shift, creation itself seems adrift. The poet Yeats would say a cog has slipped in the universe; the center is not holding together.

The world, the church, religious life, and brothers have been jolted. Struggling to regain composure seems a logical move, yet some attempts to attain a remembered equilibrium involve definitions and codification that brothers resist. New paradigms do not come easily or rapidly.

Brothers live "on the edge"; we tend to resent definition. We freely choose to eschew the facile groundedness of official function, status, or place in the church. By so doing, we keep company with prophets and live an intuitive experience that defies easy codification. Living this freeing, creative, prophetic experience of being a brother renders our lives liable to more than one

---

BROTHER JOHN PAIGE, CSC, is currently President of Bishop McNamara High School in Forestville, Maryland. Prior to this assignment he was Director of Novices for the Congregation of Holy Cross, and has served in educational apostolates for the Holy Cross community as teacher, coach, Athletic Director, Director of Studies, and Principal. He has an MA in Mathematics from Wesleyan University and an MA in Applied Theology from the Graduate Theological Union in Berkeley. As recent President of the National Assembly of Religious Brothers, John was instrumental in the initiation of the Brotherhood Seminar leading to the publication of this book. Brother John may be addressed at 6800 Marlboro Pike, Forestville, MD 20747-3270.

interpretation. Yet that is an ambiguity we revere, a "blessed ambiguity," for it captures the reality of what we experience in the church.

This book, *Blessed Ambiguity: Brothers in the Church*, documents that experience and explores the shift to a new paradigm for religious brotherhood. This shift necessarily involves the search for a new language that allows us to express ourselves and our reality in a variety of ways: monk, creator, brother, prophet. In our explorations here, we use a cosmological approach, we vision new ways of relating in clerical orders, we explore Hebrew and Christian Testament foundations, we approach the topic from psychological, systemic, and creational perspectives, and we consider various spiritualities. Our reflections here are organized into a Prologue, a section Exploring Foundations, articles Exploring Futures, and an Epilogue, all of which beckon the reader to join us in the quest of forming a new vision of brotherhood.

Bruce Lescher's Prologue sets the stage for a new vision outlining the possibilities of various brotherhoods considered within the church's own view of itself. His article speaks clearly of issues and gives concrete examples, noting that charisms have always functioned outside hierarchical structures and have often challenged and confronted such structures.

Thomas Maddix begins the section Exploring Foundations by considering archetypes through which we name and claim our uniqueness. If our life as brothers is to continue, there has to be an archetype in human nature that nurtures that experience. Robert Berger's reflection, cast in the tradition of the Hebrew Scriptures, urges us to speak to each other about our personal vision as brothers. His point is that if we articulate our vision among ourselves, then other people will also begin to understand what that vision is about. He notes the difficulty in speaking of the unsure waters of the present versus the ease in talking about the past. Joel Giallanza contends that our vision of brotherhood is an unfinished conversation. Motivated by the mission of Jesus portrayed in the Christian Scriptures, he challenges us not to give up asking questions that will frame any new paradigm for brotherhood.

David Werthmann's article relates a collective personal experience of being a brother in a clerical community. He contends that brothers bring a giftedness to clerical communities, and that much needs to be done for that giftedness to be recognized and accepted. Reflecting on his personal experience, Brian Henderson suggests new ways of looking at the evangelical counsels, a necessity in a time of shifting paradigms. In the closing article of this Foundations section, Sean Sammon takes a conscious psychological approach to the issue of loss of identity. His description of the journey along the path to adult maturity includes guideposts for responding with integrity and fullness to the quest for a new vision of brotherhood. All who search to recognize the unfolding of God's will in their lives will find this article refreshing and comforting.

The section, Exploring Futures, is initiated by Edward Coughlin who coined the phrase "blessed ambiguity," a term that redeems what we presently experience as brothers. Coughlin maintains that brothers' experience is caught up in some of the larger ambiguities of religious life, and that the exploration of this yet unnamed experience manifests the timeless struggle of faith seeking understanding. Francis Presto's sensitive article documents experiences that have led him to view ministry and leadership in the Christian community beyond the traditional role and definition of the presbyterate. His contribution makes a soulful cry for paradigmatic change in the church. Bernard Spitzley, while writing from the context of brothers in a clerical community, calls on all to recognize the need to create right relationships in community. His thesis is proactive: where there is injustice, name it, and work for change.

In Thomas Grady's view, the paradigm shift has already taken place. He describes the experience of being a brother in ways that transcend the traditional language, outlining what we are in light of the new vision of the cosmos. Joseph Martin's article, influenced by the men's movement and creation spirituality, describes who we can be in light of these contemporary insights. He makes connections in terms of community and spirituality which we share in common with men who are searching for new definitions and new roles. Using an approach often foreign to discussions of religious life, Louis DeThomasis incorporates social and cultural models in exploring futures. Knocking down walls that shield us from the pluralism and diversity of the world, he imagines a brotherhood that involves continual transformation into an integrated, healthy, sexual, holy, celibate life at the service of others and the church.

The Epilogue is written from the experience of a wise elder and sage. Thomas More Page notes, in discussing renewal and refounding, that unless everything we do is geared to the creation of a new world community, then it is all sounding brass and tinkling cymbal. He views the history of brotherhood as an evocation, not an obituary; daring, not dying; in its spring, not winter. Ours is a story of things passing, and yet vibrantly present, a story of blessed ambiguities.

In reading this book, we hope you will be imbued with the spirit of the prophet Habakkuk that motivates our work.

> Write down the vision clearly on tablets, so that one can read it readily. For the vision still has its time, precious unto fulfillment, and will not disappoint. If it delays, wait for it. It will surely come. It will not be late. (Hab 2:2-3)

As you read these articles, listen and wait; the vision is unfolding. Join us in the quest for the vision.

Note: The Summary at the end of this book captures the discussion about each of the articles at our Seminar. The reader may wish to read the summary of an article before or after reading the article itself.

A Prologue to Brotherhood

Bruce H. Lescher, CSC

In her novel, *Beloved,* Toni Morrison relates the story of an African-American woman preacher named Baby Suggs. On Saturday afternoons Baby Suggs would meet with her congregation in the Clearing, "a wide-open space cut deep in the woods," and here she would invite them to laugh, dance, and cry. Morrison says:

> She did not tell them to clean up their lives or to go and sin no more. She did not tell them they were the blessed of the earth, its inheriting meek, or its glorybound pure.
>
> She told them that the only grace they could have was the grace they could imagine. That if they could not see it, they would not have it.[1]

This insight into the necessity of vision and imagination illumines the situation of brothers in the church today. Brothers' lack of theological imagination contributes to their marginalization. They often remain invisible and unheard because they have lacked the imagination to envision grace-full alternatives.

An integrated theological vision of religious brotherhood, however, seems premature at this time. Brothers themselves, still

---

BROTHER BRUCE H. LESCHER, CSC, is a Brother of Holy Cross, Midwest Province. Born in Corpus Christi, Texas, he was raised in northern Ohio and currently resides in Austin, Texas. He joined the Brothers of Holy Cross in 1963 and professed final vows in 1970. He has a BA from the University of Notre Dame, an MA from the University of Michigan, an MAS from the University of San Francisco, and a PhD from the Graduate Theological Union in Berkeley. He is presently an Assistant Professor of Religious Studies at Saint Edward's University. He has served as a high school teacher, province coordinator of social justice, formation director, and provincial councillor. Brother Bruce may be addressed at Saint Edward's University, 3001 South Congress Avenue, Austin, TX 78704.

reeling from the ferment brought on by Vatican II, do not agree on what it means to be "brother." Furthermore, they have lost the attention of both theologians and the Catholic popular press. The brother's vocation received more coverage in the 1950s than it does in the 1990s.[2] A prologue to religious brotherhood, an exploration of conditions that would have to be met before a theology of brotherhood could be articulated, is the most that can be hoped for at this time.[3] A suggested approach follows.

What prerequisites would assist the development of a coherent theology of religious brotherhood? I suggest the following five:

1. a renewed effort by brothers to articulate their own experience;
2. an analysis of the varied spiritualities which animate religious brothers today;
3. an appreciation of the unique position of the religious brother within the institutional structure of the church;
4. a theological reformulation of religious life beyond the "lay" and "clerical" categories of canon law; and
5. a renewed ecclesiological vision of religious life in general.

Brothers' Own Experience

Brothers' reflection on their own experience constitutes a necessary first step toward articulating a theology of brotherhood. Essentially, brothers have dropped out of sight in the church's reflection on ministry and vocation. I do not say this to cast blame, for whatever damage has occurred resulted from unconscious neglect rather than malicious intent. Ultimately, brothers have only themselves to blame. As a group they have not paid attention to the forces which have been shaping their vocation (and, perhaps, subtly destroying it).

Historically, brothers, more than priests or women religious, have been a pragmatic lot. They have attended to their daily ministry: showed up at the office, taught their classes, visited the sick of the parish, run youth retreats, administered high schools and universities, kept the buildings in working order, counseled students and parishioners, cooked a million meals. This pragmatic focus served them well as long as the basics of religious life were defined, as they pretty much were from the Council of Trent until Vatican II. Brothers knew the meaning of poverty, chastity, and obedience; they knew what to expect of community life; they knew their obligations for prayer. Thus, they could get on with the daily work of the apostolate or the daily life of the monastery.

The value of this pragmatic approach collapsed somewhere in the late 1960s, about a quarter century ago. It collapsed because the basics of religious life were no longer given: they became (and, I would argue, still are) open to question and discussion.[4] In general, brothers continued to go about their daily ministry, only now they didn't know what the vows entailed, they didn't know what to expect of community, and sometimes they no longer knew what prayer meant. They went on with their daily business even though their meaning system had collapsed, and often enough they didn't even acknowledge that it had. A great deal of grief probably lies beneath this surface of denial, and releasing the grief promises to be as painful as it is healing. Brothers know better how to repair wiring or plumbing than how to rebuild meaning.

The presence of younger brothers, who entered their congregations after the mid-70s, compounds the situation even further, for these men did not live through the changes following Vatican II. They did not experience firsthand the collapse of a pre–Vatican II subculture and may not identify with the past shared by their elders. The dialogue between older members and these younger confreres is particularly important both for passing on a community's tradition and for finding a new vision for the present. But the discrepancies in experiences of the past complicate the dialogue.

Brothers need to develop the skills for talking about what has happened to them and, more importantly, how they feel about what has happened. To my knowledge, very little hard data exists about either.[5] These conversations ought to take place both within and between congregations.

Who Are the Brothers?

The second step toward articulating a theology of brotherhood is a mapping of what is "out there." Who are brothers anyway? How do they understand "the brother's vocation"? My experience leads me to conclude that religious brotherhood is multifaceted and pluralistic.[6] Though my data is informal and anecdotal, I would like to suggest some distinctions which could serve as starting point for further reflection, discussion, and analysis. More rigorous studies certainly need to be carried out.

One basic distinction between brothers flows from their vision of ministry. Some brothers understand their ministry in relation to priesthood. They joined a community to work with priests and to provide services which assist priests in carrying out their sacramental duties. These brothers often serve as bookkeepers, secretaries, maintenance workers, farmers, housekeepers, etc., within their congregations. These auxiliary services assist the congregation in carrying out its sacerdotal functions. While this differentiation of roles could be perceived in a hierarchic manner, in most communities of priests and brothers it was intended to be organic: different members performed different roles in order to sustain the life of the group. Canonically, this distinction usually resulted in the exclusion of brothers from the community's decision-making roles, an exclusion which usually did not trouble the brothers, since they never joined the community to serve as superiors. I have argued elsewhere that this understanding of religious brotherhood developed from the monastic reforms of the eleventh century.[7] Even within this category of "ministry as ancillary service," further distinctions could be made, particularly between monastic brothers and those who belong to an apostolic congregation.

Other brothers understand their service as the primary ministry of their congregation, unrelated to the priesthood. Congregations of brothers whose primary apostolate has been health care or education provide examples. These brothers share their gifts with the people of God through teaching, social work, or health care. They seek certification in their fields, as do other professionals, and participate in the organizations which serve their discipline. Within this category of "ministry as profession" further distinctions could be made. Holy Cross Brothers, for example, have tended to branch out from educational ministry and diversify their apostolates more than Christian Brothers (both De La Salle and Irish).

Both understandings of brothers' ministry have become problematic within the last decade. Ministry as ancillary service clashes with the democratic, egalitarian milieu of North American society. This model of ministry has undoubtedly led many men to holiness, but will young people still be attracted to it? Perhaps more to the point, what kind of person would be attracted to it today? Ministry as professional service runs the risk of becoming co-opted by professionalism. How is a brother who is a social worker or a teacher different from any other person in that profession? Furthermore, brothers are beginning to move into new forms of parish ministry, whether as directors of religious education, members of pastoral teams, or parish administrators. This move toward parochial ministry blurs the ancillary/professional distinction because both "types" of brothers are involved.

These broad strokes only suggest the diversity found among brothers, even within the same congregation. It may be more accurate at this time to speak of "brotherhoods" rather than "brotherhood." Research into this diversity is needed to establish a clearer picture of what is "out there."

Brothers: Unique in the Ecclesial Community

Since the 1960s, brothers have lost the attention of both theologians and the popular Catholic press. Vatican II's *Perfectae Caritatis,* the Decree on the Renewal of Religious Life, stated that religious communities should "return to . . . the primitive inspiration of the institutes" and also adapt to "the changed conditions of our time."[8] The resulting ferment has led to two developments which have unintentionally obscured the brother's vocation.

First, religious life, at both the practical and theoretical levels, has become increasingly homogenized. At the practical level, religious communities, whether male or female, increasingly share similar challenges: dwindling numbers in the active apostolate, rising health care and retirement costs, fewer people in formation. This has led to a rich sharing of resources through joint ventures like internovitiate programs, the pooling of financial assets and stock portfolios, and intercommunity personnel offices. At the theoretical or theological level, members of religious institutes have had to re-vision their role precisely as religious within the ecclesial community. Consequently, contemporary studies tend to speak of "religious life" as a generic lifestyle.[9] Brothers, priests, and sisters are placed in the same category.

While understandable, this homogenization runs counter to many trends in theology. Ours is an age of theological pluralism. Schneiders, for example, suggests

> it is unlikely that we will ever again have the theology of religious life in the univocal sense that was once embodied in The Catechism of the Vows. Just as we have today various ecclesiologies, christologies, and soteriologies, so we will have various theologies of religious life.[10]

While we accept that different cultures may give rise to different christologies (so that Sobrino's Christology will differ from that of Schillebeeckx), we seem to assume that "male religious life" is a monolithic ecclesial culture. Homogenization obfuscates the brothers' unique position within the church's institutional structure. Brothers, as religious, unquestionably share a great deal with sisters and priests. Yet they also face issues which are uniquely their own, issues flowing from their unique position as male vowed religious whose ministry is exercised through non-sacramental service.

Since Vatican II, for example, brothers have faced a greater loss of identity than have their ordained confreres. This constitutes a pastoral problem which has not been adequately addressed. Priests have had sacramental ministry to provide some stability in the midst of the dizzying changes which have buffeted religious life, whereas brothers (like women religious) have not had this ministerial stability. Most statistics of which I am aware indicate that proportionally more brothers than either priests or sisters have left religious life.[11] The superior general of my congregation has expressed concern about the "increasing disparity" between the number of priests and brothers.[12] In some congregations, brothers' identity has been radically altered in the name of renewal. The Trappists provide one example of this; they did away with the category of lay brother as part of their renewal, a move which still does not sit well with many former lay brothers.[13]

As another example, brothers have somehow become lost in the current discussion of ministry within the church. This is understandable because most discussions of ministry focus on the parish, and brothers have often ministered in institutions other than parishes. For example, the Cushwa Center for the Study of American Catholicism recently published a study with a revealing subtitle: *Transforming Parish Ministry: The Changing Roles of*

Catholic Clergy, Laity, and Women Religious.[14] The title reflects ministerial issues which are rightfully receiving a great deal of attention: the changes occurring within the priesthood, the expanding role of lay ministry, and women religious' adaptation to the post–Vatican II era. Yet these topics bypass brothers, who are neither clergy, laity (a point I will develop below), nor women. As full-time male ministers, brothers could make an important contribution to the ongoing discussion of ministry, but generally they are not doing so.

Second, to the extent that a differentiation has taken place within the generic treatment of religious life, this differentiation flows from the reflections of women religious. Many sisters (at least in the United States and Canada) have been deeply affected by the women's movement and challenge the Catholic Church's exclusion of women from ordained ministry. The awareness that women need to reflect on their own experience constitutes a fundamental step in both the women's movement and the critical consciousness of women religious. This differentiation of women's experience nuances the homogenization mentioned above. Men and women religious, as religious, work together to articulate their place in the ecclesial community; but fewer and fewer of us would assume that women's experience of church is the same as men's.

This important and necessary differentiation of women's experience within religious life has also served to inadvertently obfuscate brothers' distinctiveness. Many feminist writers (not only theologians) connect male consciousness with dualism and hierarchy.[15] Men tend to be inherently hierarchic; women tend to be inherently communitarian. The Roman Catholic Church plays into this analysis because only males can be members of the hierarchy, while females are excluded. This assumption about men and hierarchy influences a wide range of religious authors. In her recent book on celibate relationships, for example, Sheila Murphy writes:

> Inherent in male system perspectives are dualisms and hierarchies, so if males must be masculine, which is normative
> . . . then females must be feminine, a state embodying all the opposite traits, which, hierarchically, are deemed less valuable but complementary. Thus, the nonrelational, logical, unemotional masculine requires a relational, illogical, emotional feminine female. As the antithesis of masculine,

feminine is cast as compliant, passive, nurturing, weak, dependent, and emotional, and the female's upbringing and training are nonconsciously designed to prepare her to assume these characteristics.[16]

As a male I have a problem with stereotyping "male system perspectives" as inherently dualistic and hierarchic, but as a brother I have a special problem with it. Brothers are full-time male ministers who have chosen a nonhierarchic lifestyle.[17] The very title "brother" implies an egalitarian relationship with other brothers and sisters. Inasmuch as brothers are males, it is true, they have benefitted from sexism in the culture and the church. But inasmuch as brothers are not members of the hierarchy, they can be as marginalized as women in terms of decision-making in the church. Indeed some of the words which Murphy applies to the stereotypic feminine (compliant, passive, dependent) have at times been generically applied to brothers. The brother's lifestyle poses a challenge to some of the gender stereotyping which has been a part of the differentiation of women's consciousness.

Both the homogenization of religious life and the differentiation of women religious' experience have, then, unconsciously obscured the uniqueness of religious brothers within the ecclesial community.

Beyond "Clerical" and "Lay"

A theological reformulation of religious life in categories which are not drawn from the 1983 Code of Canon Law constitutes the fourth facet of this prologue. The Code speaks of religious life in clerical/lay categories: "The state of consecrated life by its very nature is neither clerical nor lay."[18]

Prior to Vatican II, religious understood themselves in terms of a very structured ecclesiology. Catholics were divided into three states of life: clergy, religious, and laity. The priesthood and religious life were states of perfection, while the laity were (in the words of the 1950 Constitutions of the Congregation of Holy Cross) "mere Christians."[19] Furthermore, these states were hierarchically arranged, with the priesthood being the highest and the lay state the lowest.

Vatican II left these basic categories intact; that is, the Council documents still speak of three states of life. *Lumen Gentium,* the Dogmatic Constitution on the Church, for example, defines the lay state in this fashion:

> The term "laity" is here understood to mean all the faithful except those in Holy Orders and those who belong to a religious state approved by the Church.[20]

However, *Lumen Gentium* also significantly altered the meaning or interpretation of these three states in at least two ways.

First, in Chapter III the Council affirmed the hierarchic nature of the church, thus dividing all members into clergy (those who hold office) and laity (those who are served by the clergy). The third state, religious life, does not fit into this schema.

> The state of life, then, which is constituted by the profession of the evangelical counsels, while not entering into the hierarchical structure of the Church, belongs undeniably to her life and holiness.[21]

Religious life is

> not . . . a kind of middle way between the clerical and lay conditions of life. Rather it should be seen as a form of life to which some Christians, both clerical and lay, are called by God.[22]

These statements leave religious life somewhat "stateless" because "clerical" and "lay" are the foundational categories for discussing Christian vocation.

Second, Chapter V of *Lumen Gentium* speaks eloquently of the universal call to holiness: "The forms and tasks of life are many but holiness is one."[23] This universal call does away with the notion that the religious life constitutes a state of greater holiness than lay life. While I do not favor the hierarchical ranking of the old "three-states-of-life" ecclesiology, a ranking which smacks of elitism, I do suggest that the old system expressed an important truth: religious life demands a commitment to holiness which differs from both the clerical and lay lifestyles. The Council documents seem ambiguous on this point. On one hand, they describe religious life as "neither clerical nor lay," but on the other they suggest that religious are either clerical (ordained to office) or lay (not so ordained). The focus should rather be: what commitments typify a lifestyle structured by the vows of religious life?

In my own experience, brothers have reacted to "stateless-ness" in two ways. Those who tend to identify with the "state-of-perfection" ecclesiology seek to transcribe some of that system's values into post–Vatican II religious life. Such brothers might emphasize the importance of wearing identifying garb, of living in community, of attending daily liturgy, and so on. Those who tend to identify with Vatican II ecclesiology see themselves as laymen with religious vows. They might emphasize the wearing of "secular" clothing, of living in residential homes or apartments, and of greater flexibility in the practice of communal prayer and liturgy. It is the concerns of this latter group which I would like to address.

Section 3 of Canon 588 states:

> An institute is called lay if recognized as such by church authority, by virtue of its nature, character, and purpose it has a proper function defined by the founder or by legitimate tradition which does not include the exercise of sacred orders.[24]

This canon establishes the category of lay religious life, the term "lay" here obviously meaning nonordained (as opposed to lay meaning neither ordained nor a member of a religious order).

The term lay religious life has prompted some brothers to define themselves primarily as laity. One example of this is the definition of brother worked on by an intercongregational group of 12 brothers meeting at Maryknoll, New York, in September of 1989.

> Brothers are men who choose to respond to their Baptismal call to ministry as laity in the Church with vows/oaths according to a rule of life in a religious community or a society of apostolic life.[25]

This definition was circulated to all brothers in the United States, inviting their further reflection.

The phrase "lay religious life," I suggest, contains so many internal contradictions that it needs to be scrapped. It attempts to unite two different lifestyles: lay and religious. Chapter IV of *Lumen Gentium* discusses the role of the laity in the ecclesial community and points out the importance of their involvement in society's everyday concerns.

> By reason of their special vocation it belongs to the laity to seek the kingdom of God by engaging in temporal affairs and directing them according to God's will. They live in the

world, that is, they are engaged in each and every work and
business of the earth and in the ordinary circumstances of
social and family life which, as it were, constitute their very
existence.[26]

This involvement in temporal affairs contradicts the "flight from
the world" which has always characterized religious life, as
Schneiders has noted.

> Separation from the world, renunciation of the secular,
> even a certain cultivated distance from the so-called "secu-
> lar" members of the Church itself, has been characteristic of
> religious life since the days of the desert fathers and moth-
> ers. This separation has taken various forms in the course of
> history ranging from the actual flight from the city to the
> desert in the fourth century, through the separation by
> monastic enclosure, to the distance created by means of
> practices such as dressing differently, living in convents,
> and following a pattern of life that could not be assimilated
> into ordinary contemporary life.[27]

Brothers who understand themselves as laity have mistakenly applied the lay/clerical distinction of canon law. The laity
are intimately connected to the social and economic order: they
have mortgage and car payments, sit on corporate boards, work
in all manner of occupations, usually live in families, worry
about schools and taxes and health care. Religious are separated
from the routine socioeconomic order, not so they can escape
the challenges of adult living, but so that they can provide an alternative lifestyle to that order. One needs an alternative view in
order to call into question the cultural "givens" which can lull
people into spiritual death.

Brothers need to understand themselves as religious, not as
laity. In some cases those who see themselves as laymen with religious vows have become indistinguishable from the laity; they
run the risk of being co-opted by the materialism and individualism of North American culture. Brothers need to recover and
re-interpret the ancient tradition of flight from the world. Of
course one cannot totally leave the world, and of course all people are called to love this world which comes from the gracious
hands of the Creator. But flight from the world does not have to
be world-denying, as Thomas Merton often insisted; rather it can
become a means of loving the world enough to critique it.

Flight from the world may, for example, be re-interpreted as a countercultural lifestyle. Brothers embody a masculinity which is egalitarian and fraternal in a culture which has experienced males as domineering and even violent. They live a commitment to poverty in a society dying from its addiction to consumption. They assert the centrality of the spiritual quest to a culture which has often feminized this quest and relegated men to the "real world" of corporate competition.

A theology of religious brotherhood must begin with religious life, not clerical/lay life, and must make separation from the world intelligible to our contemporaries.

Renewed Ecclesiological Vision

Finally, a theology of brotherhood can be articulated only in the context of a renewed ecclesiological vision of religious life in general. The uniqueness of the brother's vocation has been obscured in the decades following Vatican II, and brothers' potential contributions to the discussion of both ministry and vocation in the church have not been realized. In the final analysis, though, brothers must understand their unique vocation in the context of religious life. They thus need to explore, at both the practical and theoretical levels, the commonalities they share with their ordained confreres and women religious.

This exploration of commonalities constitutes an ongoing project and cannot adequately be addressed here. I would, however, like to make one last suggestion: a crucial question facing male religious life at the brink of the twenty-first century is the relationship between ordination and religious profession within a religious community, a relationship in desperate need of re-visioning. The foundational canonical categories of cleric and lay have been imposed on a lifestyle which ought to be marked by brotherly (in the generic sense) love, and a lifestyle in which men should he appointed or elected to community service or office on the basis of their gifts and talents. In the history of religious life, the relationship between profession and ordination has often been debated, and one can hardly expect the debate to be settled now. But the question needs once again to be raised so that new alternatives can be imagined.

The limitations of rooting religious life in canonical categories become apparent in a document like *Lineamenta,* the working paper for the 1994 Synod on Religious Life. The document gives brothers a positive treatment, affirming that brotherhood "is today the most visible form of consecration" and "represents consecration in its utter simplicity," simplicity apparently meaning that brotherhood is not mixed with ordination.[28] But overall the document attempts to place religious life under the control of the hierarchy.[29] The charismatic nature of religious life becomes subsumed under a clerical agenda. Such an approach ignores the historical reality that new forms of religious life have often challenged the canonical categories endorsed by the hierarchy.[30]

Conclusion

I offer this as a prologue to a theology of brotherhood. I am conscious of many topics which have not been addressed: the vows, community living, prayer, service in either active apostolate or monastery. All of these comprise indispensable elements of each brother's life; they all deserve further prayer, reflection, and study. But the questions facing brothers today, I believe, go deeper than these specific elements; they go to the very meaning of this vocation in the ecclesial community. Brothers need to reflect on their own experience, analyze the varied spiritualities which animate them, appreciate anew the uniqueness of their vocation, and participate in a reformulation of religious life beyond clerical/lay categories. If they begin with these steps, they will eventually arrive at a new vision of the vows, community life, prayer, and ministry. Rainer Maria Rilke wrote to the aspiring poet Franz Xaver Kappus:

> . . . I want to beg you, as much as I can, dear sir, to be patient toward all that is unsolved in your heart and to try to love the questions themselves like locked rooms and like books that are written in a very foreign tongue. Do not now seek the answers, which cannot be given you because you would not be able to live them. And the point is, to live everything. Live the questions now. Perhaps you will then gradually, without noticing it, live along some distant day into the answers.[31]

For brothers, too, perhaps, now is a time for living the questions so as to later live into the answers.

Notes

1. Toni Morrison, *Beloved* (New York: Alfred A. Knopf, 1987) 87ff.

2. I attempted to explore this theological silence systematically in "Brothers in the Church Today: Probing the Silence," *New Blackfriars* 71 (Oct. 1990) 445-455. One survey, taken between 1971 and 1982, yielded the following count of articles printed in Catholic periodicals: 925 on the topic of priesthood, 250 on religious women, and 25 on brothers (Adrian Gaudin, "The Identity of the Religious Brother in America Today" [MAT Thesis: School of Applied Theology, Berkeley, California, 1982] 9). By my count, the *Catholic Periodical and Literature Index* lists 16 articles dealing with the brother's vocation between 1983 and 1992. The CMSM has published a helpful study: Philip Armstrong, ed., *Who Are My Brothers? Cleric-Lay Relationships in Men's Religious Communities* (New York: Alba House, 1988).

3. This insight came to me in a series of discussions with Joel Gial-lanza, CSC, and in fact he first suggested it. I am indebted to Joel for his insights and helpful suggestions throughout the writing of this article.

4. In 1983 the Congregation for Religious and Secular Institutes published the document "Essential Elements in the Church's Teaching on Religious Life as Applied to Institutes Dedicated to Works of the Apostolate." This document argued that the period of experimentation after Vatican II had come to an end. I disagree. Does law follow life or life follow law? I would argue that law must follow life and that, in fact, experimentation is still going on.

5. In August 1991, the Center for Applied Research on the Apostolate (CARA), completed a study of vocations to 18 provinces/congregations of teaching brothers. The data from this study might provide a good starting point for a statistical picture of at least some brothers.

6. My conclusions are based upon two workshops given at the Brothers' Institute at Catholic Theological Union, Chicago: "Historical Development of Religious Life" (February 1989) and "Spiritualities of Brotherhood" (March 1990); two presentations ("Trends in Religious Life" and "Focus on Brothers") at a meeting of the English-speaking Redemptorist Brothers of North America at Sainte Anne de Beaupré, Quebec (May 1989); participation in a group of brothers assembled at Maryknoll, New York, in September 1989 to formulate a definition of brotherhood in order to begin a national process of reflection (see *Brothers* [newsletter of the National Assembly of Religious Brothers] 10 [Sept.-Oct. 1990]); and participation as a delegate at the 1986 General Chapter of the Congregation of Holy Cross. This Chapter devoted considerable attention to the status of brothers within the congregation.

7. "Laybrothers: Questions Then, Questions Now," *Cistercian Studies* 23:1 (Spring 1988) 63-85.

8. Austin Flannery, ed., *"Perfectae Caritatis,"* in *Vatican Council II: The Conciliar and Post Conciliar Documents,* vol. 1, rev. ed. (Northport, NY: Costello Publishing, 1988) 2, 612.

9. This statement applies to most contemporary studies of religious life, but for some examples see Marcello Azevedo, *Vocation for Mission: The Challenge of Religious Life Today,* John W. Kiercksmeier, trans. (New York/Mahwah: Paulist Press, 1988); Barbara Fiand, SNDdeN, *Living the Vision: Religious Vows in an Age of Change* (New York: Crossroads, 1990); and John M. Lozano, *Life As Parable: Reinterpreting the Religious Life* (New York/Mahwah: Paulist Press, 1986).

10. Sandra M. Schneiders, *New Wineskins: Reimaging Religious Life Today* (New York/Mahwah: Paulist Press, 1986) 22. Author's emphasis.

11. I have quoted these statistics in the *New Blackfriars* article mentioned in Note 2: worldwide, between 1980 and 1985, the number of brothers dropped by 11 percent. For the same period the number of women religious dropped by 4.5 percent, and priests (both religious and diocesan) by 2 percent. See John A. Weafer, "Vocations—A Review of National and International Trends," *Furrow* 39 (August 1988) 501-502. The decreases are even greater if one goes back to years closer to Vatican II. For example, in 1964, there were 22,707 religious priests in the United States; in 1985 there were 22,265, a drop of 2 percent. For the same time period the number of brothers went from 12,271 to 7,544, a drop of 39 percent. Sisters went from 179,954 to 115,386, a drop of 36 percent. See the *Official Catholic Directory* (Wilmette, IL: P.J. Kenedy and Sons) for 1965 and 1986. In Ireland the number of brothers dropped from 2,195 to 1,230 between 1970 and 1986, a loss of 44 percent. During the same years religious priests went from 4,019 to 2,789 (a loss of 31 percent) and women religious from 15,145 to 11,397 (a loss of 25 percent). See Weafer, "Vocations," 502.

12. Claude Grou, "Holy Cross in 1991" (Circular Letter of the Superior General, no. 10, Dec. 1, 1991) 7.

13. For an allusion to this tension see Thomas Merton, *A Vow of Conversation: Journals 1964–1965* (New York: Farrar, Straus, Giroux, 1988) 39. For letters from Trappist brothers relating to the issue see *Brothers* 8 (May–June 1989) 4.

14. Jay P. Dolan, R. Scott Appleby, Patricia Byrne, and Debra Campbell, *Transforming Parish Ministry: The Changing Roles of Catholic Clergy, Laity, and Women Religious* (New York: Crossroads, 1989).

15. See, for example, Rosemary Radford Ruether, *Sexism and God Talk: Toward a Feminist Theology* (Boston: Beacon Press, 1983) 47–71.

16. Sheila Murphy, *A Delicate Dance: Sexuality, Celibacy, and Relationships Among Catholic Clergy and Religious* (New York: Crossroads, 1992) 74.

17. I base the term "nonhierarchic lifestyle" on a literal reading of the word "hierarchy," which derives from the Greek word *hieros,* "sacred" or "holy." In the Roman Catholic Church a member of the hierarchy has sacred authority derived from God. Communities of brothers govern themselves hierarchically (in the generic sense of subordinated ranks) in a democratic manner. Superiors are elected to office and return to the ranks when their time in office is through. Unlike priests or bishops, they do not possess a sacred authority for the duration of their lives.

18. Canon 588. James A. Cordien, Thomas J. Green, and Donald E. Heintschel, eds., *The Code of Canon Law: A Text and Commentary* (New York/Mahwah: Paulist Press, 1985) 460.

19. Constitutions of the Congregation of Holy Cross (1951) 75.

20. *Lumen Gentium,* 31; Flannery, *Vatican Council II,* 388. These distinctions are maintained in *Lineamenta,* the working paper for the 1994 Synod on Religious Life prepared by the Vatican Synod Secretariat. See "Consecrated Life in the Church and the World," Origins 22 (Dec. 10, 1992) 435 (Lineamenta, Section 20).

21. *Lumen Gentium,* 44; Flannery, *Vatican Council II,* 405.

22. *Lumen Gentium,* 43; Flannery, *Vatican Council II,* 403.

23. *Lumen Gentium,* 41; Flannery, *Vatican Council II,* 398.

24. Canon 588. Coriden, *Code,* 460.

25. *Brothers* 10 (Sept.–Oct. 1990) 1.

26. *Lumen Gentium,* 31; Flannery, *Vatican Council II,* 389.

27. Schneiders, *New Wineskins,* 25.

28. "Consecrated Life in the Church and the World," 441 (*Lineamenta,* Section 21).

29. This bias pervades the whole document but comes to clearest expression in Sections 36 and 37; see "Consecrated Life in the Church and the World," 447–448.

30. In his sociology of religion Max Weber notes the tension between charism rooted in personal call (prophecy) and charism rooted in office (priesthood): ". . . fully developed office charisma inevitably becomes the most uncompromising foe of all genuinely personal charisma, which propagates and preaches its own way to God and is prophetic, mystic and ecstatic." (Max Weber, *Economy and Society: An Outline of Interpretive Sociology,* Guenther Roth and Claus Wittich, eds., vol. 1 [Berkeley: University of California Press, 1978] 1165.)

31. Rainer Maria Rilke, *Letters to a Young Poet,* M. D. Herter Norton, trans. (New York: W. W. Norton, 1934) 34.

Blessed Ambiguity

Exploring Foundations

An Enduring Archetype: Naming and Claiming Our Uniqueness

Thomas D. Maddix, CSC

The German poet, Rainer Rilke once wrote:

> I want to unfold
> I don't want to stay folded anywhere,
> because where I am folded
> There I am a lie.[1]

These words point to the challenge of brothers not only to claim their historical roots but also to live fully from the depths of their being. But in grappling with the identity of any group, its historical origins and the forces which formed, shaped, and defined its identity need careful consideration.

In existence almost from the beginning of Christian culture and rooted in the ancient archetype of the monk, the historical evolution of the brother within the Catholic tradition has suffered from clericalization, near extinction, suspicion, and conflicting identities and images over which we brothers have had little control. In addition to these factors, various historical, religious,

---

BROTHER THOMAS D. MADDIX, CSC, a member of the Brothers of Holy Cross, Midwest Province, Notre Dame, presently serves as Director of Mission Services for the Alberta Catholic Hospitals Foundation and teaches a course in Christian Spirituality at St. Stephen's Theological College, University of Alberta, Edmonton. A Holy Cross Brother since 1965, Brother Thomas has a BA from St. Edward University, Austin, Texas, an MA in English from Notre Dame University, an MA in Organizational Ethics from the Pacific School of Religion, Berkeley, California, and a DMin from the Pacific School of Religion, Berkeley, California. Brother Thomas may be addressed at P.O. Box 460, Notre Dame, IN 46556.

canonical, and educational situations have greatly impacted our identity as well as our ability to shape the world in which we minister either as individuals or as members of a religious congregation.

The descriptive words "brother" and "monk" will be used interchangeably in this article. They refer to the inner urge to give all of ourselves over to Christ and his mission within a vowed religious community of men. While the expressions of being a brother/monk differ today from yesterday, the inner call remains constant as well as the invitation to live "unfolded lives."

Some Basic Questions

Monks and brothers. Brothers and monks. What do these descriptive terms mean? What relates them to each other, the world, God, the Christian experience, and the depth of the human soul? For over 25 years, my experience as a Holy Cross brother has forced me to ask the question many times, not only for myself but also in response to others' queries. In recent years, however, the importance of the questions has grown within me and in other brothers as we struggle to grasp our basic identity as brothers in the church. A critical reflection on the relationship between the core personality of the brother or monk is necessary not only to illuminate the roots of this vocation shared by men from various religious traditions throughout the world, but also to reclaim, revitalize, and celebrate the enduring archetype that compels people to live their lives as brothers.

The process of illumination demands the use of intuition[2] as well as willingness to pose questions of the historical bias and ideology used in writing the history of monks throughout the Christian era.[3] The process also seeks a fresh awareness of the symbolic dimensions of this archetype within the Christian tradition. Furthermore, in trying to understand both the anthropological and Christian roots of this way of life within the Christian Church, a survey of historical records and discussions necessitates a clear understanding of the brother. Yet, this study cannot be done without acknowledging that as a brother, I write from that perspective and interpretation.

Intuitions

Over the years, the historical significance and connectedness of the vocation of the brother has continually intrigued me. While a graduate student in English at the University of Notre Dame, I was continually amazed when Christian, Marist, and Xaverian Brothers would use the term "monk" to describe fellow members of their religious communities. To me, at that time, monk meant Trappist or some other person who lived in a monastery and separated himself from the affairs of society. Brothers, on the other hand, represented a group of men, like the group to which I belong, called together to do ministry through a shared vision of life and mission.

Later, as Director of Vocations for the Brothers of Holy Cross, and today, as I explain the brother's vocation I constantly find myself hearkening to a vision of a "contemporary monk" to illustrate how the vocation of the brother has emerged throughout history and different cultures. With the term, "contemporary monk," a connection started to exist between my present experience and a whole heritage of men choosing a life of celibacy, shared poverty, and attentive obedience to the Word of God. Moreover, inner stirrings and intuitions impelled me to wonder: what relationship does exist between the vocation of the brother and the monk? This forced me to speculate: are we talking about the same calling, but with different expressions?

When I did research for a paper entitled, "Focusing the Issue: Toward a Liberation Theology for Brothers," a number of brothers submitted responses to questions about their experience of being a brother. A response by Frank Englert, CSC, especially interested me since his vision of brother resonated with mine. Englert, in fact, captures my intuition about the lost connectedness between brother and monk when he writes:

> As brothers we need to rediscover the ancient monk within, who with all his heart, is rooted in the depths of what it means to be human, and then discovers that this leads into the deepened mystery of God.[4]

He continues: "Brothers need to preserve that vocation with a single heart . . . in a variety of ways."[5]

By listening to the various clues within people's speech and descriptions of themselves and their way of life, as well as to my own intuitions and inner connections between early Christian monks and brothers, the desire to discover the energizing link between brother and monk grew within me.

Enduring Monastic Archetype

Any attempt to discuss the enduring power and quality of the monastic archetype in one of its contemporary expressions, the vowed life of brothers, requires a clear understanding of archetype.

One definition of archetype rooted in Jungian psychology states that it constitutes the "contents of the collective unconscious; primordial images, and patterns of symbol formation which recur throughout [hu]mankind."[6] In discussing the power of myth to give shape and meaning to the life of a person and a group, Gerald Slusser states that Jung uses the term archetype to represent the "visual or verbal symbols of psychic components," which "represent the deep structures of the human psyche."[7] Later he writes: "Archetype symbols are the primary structuring elements of human experience and are remarkably similar in many cultures."[8]

The significance of archetypal symbols or images for Slusser, Jung, and others lies in the fact that the appearance of the archetype, like the monastic one within a person, molds, shapes, and gives direction to an individual as well as a group. Moreover, the shared irruption of the archetype of the monk within religious traditions and cultures brings persons into relationship with the deepest elements of their soul and binds them to others who share the ongoing manifestations of this unique archetypal energy.

Myriam Dardenne in an essay entitled, "Who is the Integrating Subject: A Response from a Western Point of View," emphasizes that contained within the archetype of a monk lies not only "the emergence of the human soul," but also "the impulse to put one's life orientation under the sign and primacy of God, both Immanent and Transcendent." She notes that this option displays itself

> in a vow to accept, partner, shoulder, serve, and celebrate the Transcendent mystery in and with creation. In each case, the result is a unifying process of the personality, an encompassing simplicity of life and attitude. . . .[9]

By identifying the common call (and its roots) to be a brother or monk within the archetype of a monk, a fresh perspective to view the evolution of both monasticism and the brother's troubled identity and history with the Roman Catholic tradition emerges. Likewise, awakening the archetype of a monk as the core identity of the contemporary brother's vocation provides a refreshing way of examining that vocation. Finally, by awakening and reclaiming ancient roots stripped of cultural interpretation, the monk archetype attests to the persistent vitality of the brother's vocation within history and culture.

Basic Definitions, Experiences, and Tensions

Louis Bouyer defines the early monk as simply a "Christian . . . a devout layman who limited himself to taking the most radical means to make his Christianity integral."[10] Bouyer further elaborates, "The primitive monk in no way appeared to be a kind of specialist, his vocation was not a particular vocation, considered by himself or by others as more or less exceptional."[11]

Raimundo Pannikkar captures the intuition of Englert and myself. In attempting to offer a description of what constitutes the archetype of the monk, whether alone or as part of a group, Pannikkar writes:

> By monk, *monachos,* I understand that person who aspires to reach the ultimate goal of life with all his being by renouncing all that is not necessary to it, i.e., by concentrating on this one single and unique goal.[12]

Pannikkar continues his discussion by distinguishing this "singlemindedness"[13] as core to the vocation. In trying to grasp the mystery that transforms, motivates, and lures the monk, he says:

> The monk ultimately becomes monk not by a process of thinking, or merely desiring, but as a result of an urge, the fruit of an experience that eventually leads him to change and, in the final analysis, break something in his life for the sake of that "thing" which encompasses or transcends everything.[14]

By grounding the essence of the call in experience and the singlemindedness that flows from that context, Pannikkar identifies both the source of our call as brothers as well as the wellspring of our rejuvenation.

Pannikkar's identification of an urge that moves a person speaks also of the experience of the "holy men" in ancient Syria and Egypt who sought to live the Gospel in a more radical fashion. The motivation of many people who left Egyptian cities certainly contained elements of a flight from responsibilities, civic or domestic. Yet, among these "anchorites" also existed men who followed an inner urge to abandon all in search of the living God. Whether they wandered the hills and villages of Syria or settled by the fertile banks of the Nile, their desire to know and experience the living God produced within the early Christian culture the archetype of the brother. He lived outside family ties and economic interests, and through his life and contact with society, preached a life of penance and conversion. In writing about the holy man's experience and cultural uniqueness, Peter Brown comments:

> The holy man carried the burden of making such a distant God relevant to the particularity of human needs. In his person, the acute ambivalence of a Christian God was summoned up in a manageable and approachable form: for the holy man was both easily moved to tears of compassion, and, at the same time, the heir of the Hebrew prophets.[15]

The terms monk and holy man have their origins in early Christendom, and the term brother also appears about this time. Like his counterparts, the monk and the holy man, the brother also responds to a call from within and without to meet God in all people, events, and creation. The dual lines of development are clearly captured by Jesuit Philip Sheldrake when he writes:

> Consequently, the "single ones," (the *monachos:* meaning the "single one" or the one who adopts singleness) remained a visible challenge near human habitation . . . the Egyptian ascetics tended to recreate the habits of normal village community while the Syrians . . . adopted a life-style which contrasted more strongly with "the world."[16]

Characteristics of a Monk

In trying to identify the various characteristics that embody the life of the monk, writers do not always agree. However, a short survey of identifiable descriptions provides a means of looking at the commonality of experiences of monks or brothers, whether they be Buddhist, Zen, or Christian.

Mircea Eliade identifies four basic characteristics of all monks. The first trait displays itself in the "distinctive social status and pattern of social relationship." Thus monks select a deliberate way of life that marks them as different from their peers in society. Second, Eliade identifies the specific rule or discipline as a formative element in this unique pattern of social interaction both within the monastic group and its relations within a given culture. The third characteristic uses ritual to celebrate and publicize the monastic commitment. For instance, the tonsure, the clothing in the habit, or receiving the Buddhist staff and begging bowl establish formative and distinctive rituals within the tradition. A fourth attribute requires the participation within a larger religious tradition and a set of traditions. Thus, brothers find their core identity within the Christian as well as Catholic and congregational traditions.[17]

Frank Houdek, SJ, distinguishes the Christian vocation of brother with five characteristics. First, as a lay movement it finds expression rooted in the common experience of people. Second, a charismatic versus an institutional framework dominates its early history and originating inspiration. Third, as a prophetic witness, the vocation is geared toward the recognition of God's power and presence in all of creation. Fourth, a tendency exists within its originating framework to be anti-intellectual. Fifth, it expresses itself in a celibate lifestyle.[18]

Both Eliade and Houdek identify characteristics that also belong to certain expressions of the monastic experience: voluntary poverty, and solitude, or some type of withdrawal from society for the purpose of study, meditation, and aloneness with God. Finally, a way of discipline or rule that gives meaning and direction to the followers of a particular way of life allows them to open themselves and thus the entire community to decipher God's voice and presence in their midst.

Responding to the Call

To choose brotherhood as a means of escaping responsibility and consciousness not only damages the individual but also weakens the entire vocation and its perpetual charismatic and prophetic witness within the church and society. Furthermore, the very nature of the brother's vocation contains in its unique essence a way of encountering the living God.

Brothers do not exist to provide various functions or services. Instead, action within this vocation springs from discernment and attentiveness to the often subtle voice of God on the part of the individual and the religious institute. This realization holds significant importance for groups of brothers founded in the sixteenth century and afterward. They carry the archetype of a monk—lay, charismatic, and prophetic—but find themselves divorced from their origins due to juridical and historical developments within vowed religious life and church history. Thus, at the core of the archetype of a brother is the energizing image of pilgrimage and attentive obedience to God's voice.

Kenneth Leech, by drawing on a variety of contemporary and ancient sources, employs a number of images to heighten the description of the monk. The monk as "watchman, a person of vision," portrays the role of the monk as the "eyes of the Church." Another description of the monk centers around the paradox that "the holy is common and the common is holy." A third portrays the monk as a marginal person who by his very profession draws to the edge of society and identifies with other marginalized people. A fourth attribute lies in the freedom to avoid social convention and respond wholeheartedly to the voice of God. Finally, a fifth quality, conflict, identifies the monk as experienced in spiritual warfare and wrestling with the inner and outer "demons" that seek to dehumanize culture and humanity as well as to distort the voice and experience of God as the core of the monastic calling.[19]

Leech's observations basically find their substance in the prophetic and charismatic roles as outlined by Houdek. Likewise, Leech's humanly demanding characteristics dispel the image of the monk as a recluse, uninvolved and incapable of participating creatively and responsibly within society. Finally, the development of these prophetic and charismatic markings strengthen the rootedness of the archetype of monk within society and religious culture. They challenge the contemporary brother to deepen his commitment to his primordial roots as an epiphany of God's invigorating and transforming presence within humanity and culture.

Historical Considerations

Christian Beginnings

Jean Gribomont, in his article, "Monasticism and Asceticism," quotes from early Christian papyri in Egypt to trace the roots of the Christian monastic tradition. He writes:

> In about 324 and then again in 334 and in the subsequent period there appeared in Christian papyri . . . the term *monachos* [monk] with its derivatives and synonyms: *apotaktikos* [he who denies himself], anchorite [recluse, hermit], or simply brother.[20]

The origins of the Christian experience of monasticism or brotherhood find their roots in the hills of Syria and the deserts of Egypt. According to Gribomont, Syrian fraternities, "sons [or daughters] of the covenant," appeared. At baptism these people committed themselves to a life of celibacy, lay ministry, and prayer. They then created the nucleus of small Christian communities in Syria. Their way of life developed from contacts with itinerant prophetic teachers.[21] Likewise, wandering ascetics appeared in upper Mesopotamia and were often a concern of the local bishops who accused them of a lack of discipline. The power of their charismatic and prophetic appeal reveals itself in the following description of Gribomont.

> Under their influence wives frequently freed themselves from their husbands, and children from their parents; slaves and soldiers refused obedience; ecclesiastic laws were disregarded; and the economic rights of the clergy were ignored. Still, by helping the poor and nursing the sick, they earned fervent love and devotion.[22]

Popularized by Athanasius's book, *The Life of Anthony*, the Egyptian version of monasticism continues to be the most studied, understood, and accepted expression of monasticism within the Christian experience. From Anthony's life, early themes of monastic spirituality and lifestyle develop. Through manual labor, prayer, reflection on the Word of God, battling with their inner demons, and fasting, these early monks opened themselves to the transforming power of a living God.

According to Bouyer, these men represented not an escape from humanity and Christian responsibility, but an asceticism that "is a liberation necessary to awaken a consciousness of self which will be truly human and Christian."[23]

In writing about the importance of the early expressions of monasticism, Bouyer emphasizes that the monk "in no way appeared to be a kind of specialist." The primitive monk existed as a "devout layman who limited himself to taking the most radical means to make his Christianity integral." Cassian, according to Bouyer, sums up the entire tradition of the Egyptian desert experience by "making discretion, that is, the gift to discern the path of God's will for us, a gift essential to the solitary but one which is not acquired except in docility to proved masters."[24]

Although expressed differently, the archetype of the monk emerged within Christianity: in Syria in the primitive experiences of the holy men, wandering ascetics, and various fraternities; in Egypt in the lives of the desert fathers. The latter were modeled by Anthony offering consultation to people seeking a more radical commitment to God and by Pachomius developing the roots of common living. Whether in Syria or in Egypt, all point to the underlying archetype of lay people answering an inner urge to devote their entire life to listening to God's voice.

These people sought to express a personal intuition by responding to the archetype of the brother. Their responses demonstrated the variety of ways in which God invited them to live their deepest calling: meditation on the Word of God, spiritual direction, prayer, a distinctive celibate lifestyle—solitary, group, or inter-related—for which manual labor provided the economic basis.

Monastic Clericalism

While Benedict's Rule changed the structure of monasticism, Augustine's revisions had already altered the very identity and mission of the monastic vocation. Based upon an experience of living with some friends in a semi-solitude monastic situation at Cassiciacum, Augustine decided upon his return home to Tagaste to form a similar community. When he was ordained in 391, he realized he could no longer be part of this lay movement, so he decided to change the texture of the monastery in order to accommodate clerics.

With this alteration in the monastic character, new trends emerged within the church. In later years, the East chose most if not all of its bishops from the celibate monastics. In the West, the ascetical practices of the monastery and the value of celibacy became dominant features. Thus, based upon the success of Augustine at Hippo and the earlier attempts of Ambrose in Milan and Eusebius of Vercelli in 363, where clerics were invited to live a monastic lifestyle in the cathedral, the lay identity of monasticism started to erode.

Bouyer, a monastic cleric, speaks of "an accidental clericalization of monasticism," called for by the needs of evangelizing a still pagan country lacking clergy in Gaul and Syria. He insists that a "monasticizing of the clergy was being attempted," [25] but within the same vein a clericalizing of monasticism was also occurring. He concludes:

> There is no doubt that what the clerical monasticism desired by St. Augustine tended toward was the "religious," in the sense that the Later Middle Ages were to give to the term; and this is no longer in any way the monk in the primitive and Eastern sense.[26]

Eventually, the clericalization of monasticism within the West became dominant if not complete. Moreover, its lay origins faded from memory and experience. Nonetheless, in the twelfth century it formally emerged again through the appearance of lay brothers.

While the twelfth century saw the formal development of the lay brother movement, traces of its development can be seen as early as the sixth century. Lay people started moving into the vicinity of the monasteries. According to Bruce Lescher, while these people did not belong to the monastery proper, they were often

> pious people seeking spiritual direction and wanting to live in proximity to the monks; some were artisans whose skills in crafts were needed by the monks. These people comprised the monastic family, the *familia*.[27]

Without delving into the historical development of the lay brother movement within church history, certain patterns emerge.

First, the movement, like its forerunners in Syria and Egypt, flowed from lay people. Second, the movement re-emerged when the clericalization of the monasteries had dominated, if not completely eliminated, its originating lay charism. Third, the group arose in response to an inner urge for conversion and obedience to God's voice, as implied by the name often associated with it, *conversi*. Finally, the archetype reappeared when monasticism had become dominated by liturgical practices and separated from its early emphasis on the integration of prayer and service.

Emergence of Lay Charismatic and Prophetic Groups

The lay brother movement within monasticism represented an institutional development. Nonetheless, lay movements rooted in a prophetic and charismatic living of the Gospel attempted to present another pattern of living the archetype of a monk prior to, during, and after the emergence of monastic lay brothers. Part of the development of these charismatic and prophetic groups stemmed from the rapid "ordering" of the life that marked the Carolingian revival. Leclercq describes the ordering this way:

> On the ascetic level the layman is bidden care for the "common people," particularly the poor; to reverence the clergy and respect their liberty.[28]

At the end of the eleventh century, an "eremetical movement" re-emerged within the church. According to Leclercq, it was a movement of "some complexity in which women played a part."[29] Lay people again appeared as the originators of this movement which stressed either life alone as hermits or as small clusters of groups coming together. These individuals had a strong desire for poverty; they selected their prayer "either from the liturgies of the canons or the monks, or from the vocal prayers of some groups of lay ascetics and penitents." Because of their life of prayer, fasting, penance, and labor, many left their hermitages to beg and travel through the countryside as itinerant preachers. Their preaching focused on church reform and was rooted in the Bible. According to Leclercq, often "their preaching was incorrect," and the monks and clergy "justly accused these people of being vagabonds, but they at least bore witness to the fervor of the generation they benefitted." Leclercq finishes his observations by acknowledging the eventual benefits of these movements, often called *pataria,* had upon the church. He writes:

> This "lay movement" had its dangers and was to meet with failure, but to the clergy and religious too it brought a sense of the responsibilities inherent in each state of life, and so was one of the results of the crisis in monasticism that bore fruit.[30]

Contemporary Issues

With the emergence of the lay brother vocation and the subsequent blight or incorporation of various lay groups into the church, the juridical description of a lay brother as someone less than a priest who is destined to serve clerics dominated church life. Not until the 1600s and the emergence of groups of all lay religious like the Christian Brothers of John Baptist de La Salle does the life of the brother in the church separate itself somewhat from clerical domination and definition. Despite the emergence of separate orders of brothers, the primordial richness of the archetype of a monk as expressed in the life of the brother often remains hidden if not repressed by the wording of church law as well as written and historical expression.

The misunderstanding of the brother's identity is demonstrated in the following current definition found in *The Catholic Encyclopedia.*

> Generally, those members of a religious community or society of men who are not priests are called "brother." . . . There are also religious communities of men whose members do not intend to enter the priesthood but who serve a special purpose.[31]

This definition also demonstrates the inability of some writers to describe the brother without a clerical reference point. They define the brother by *what he is not* rather than by *who he is.* This type of definition places the brother in a defensive posture and in a situation of always having to demonstrate his identity. Furthermore, by relegating the enduring archetype of a brother to the monastic orders, the symbolic and anthropological base of the brother's vocation remains hidden. The long-term impact of this situation has had devastating results in terms of the identity and ministry of brothers, especially those in mixed communities of brothers and priests.

Even today, official church law neither acknowledges nor respects brothers as equal members with their clerical counterparts when they form one community. Thus, canon law decrees that if an institute has a large number of clerical members, the institute "is said to be clerical and . . . it is under the supervision of clerics."[32]

Unfortunately, this classical vision of the lay brother continues to be the dominant motif of brothers living in mixed communities, their lives defined and described through a clerical prism. Moreover, canon law does not acknowledge the presence of lay men in a religious congregation defined as clerical. Yet, the lay members exist with faces, histories, and experiences of ministry, leadership, and prayer. Carol Pearson describes the human tragedy of ignoring the experiences of others.

> Women, minority men, and the working class all have been culturally defined as inferior, and as such, their role is to serve. To the degree that these groups have internalized such ideas, much of the giving and serving is linked unconsciously to their belief that they do not have a right to exist, to be here unless they do serve—that they do not have a right to exist for their own sake.[33]

Michael McGinniss, in a challenging article entitled, "Being Forgotten and Forgetful: A Subtle Clericalism," captures the experiences of many brothers who repeatedly hear or read about priests, sisters, and lay people, but who rarely hear their experience of life and ministry being mentioned. McGinniss notes: "being forgotten will seem a familiar experience to brothers who frequently hear people list the celibate vocations in the church as priests and sisters."[34]

In the same article, McGinniss recounts a noted woman theologian's address on the state of ministry at a major Catholic university campus to a group of men and women engaged in theological and ministerial education. In the course of her address, she never once mentioned brothers and their ministerial role within the church, even though many brothers were present in her audience. After the lecture, McGinniss mentioned her exclusion of brothers to her. "She was momentarily taken back," he writes. Yet, his reflection upon the implications of this exclusion of brothers from the ministerial discussion points to the second class or forgotten situation often assigned to them. McGinniss concludes:

> Her silence on the matter spoke volumes about her unconscious perceptions and her lived experience of the ways that brothers typically have not impacted on the structures of the church, especially here in the United States.[35]

Some Sociological Insights

Sociologist Peter Berger writes on the relationship between people and the society or societies in which they live and affiliate. He captures the interrelatedness between consciousness and social structures in these words.

> Society not only controls our movements, but shapes our identity, our thought, and our emotions. The structures of society become the structures of our own consciousness. Society does not stop at the surface of our skins. Society penetrates us as much as it envelops us.[36]

Berger opens the path to understanding the dynamism of the monk archetype. In considering this dynamism as a lay phenomenon, the role of prophecy and social control dominate the discussion. Likewise, the interrelatedness between consciousness and social system demonstrates what happens to people, movements, and organizations when their symbol system collapses or remains unacknowledged.

Gregory Baum, writing about the power of symbol in a discussion on the contributions of Freud and Durkheim, notes that for Freud the "symbol is the proper mode of a person's self-manifestation, and it is the encounter with these symbols that may lead to self-knowledge and eventual psychic transformation."[37]

In discussing the insights of Durkheim, which hold tremendous potential for brothers and the reawakening as well as rediscovery of their original archetype, Baum summarizes Durkheim by noting that "religion unifies people; it links them to their common history and strengthens them in their common task." He goes on to say that not only does religion exist as a means of social identification, but that it is also "the symbolic representation of the vision and values immanent in society."[38]

In discussing groups like brothers who seek to rediscover their forgotten history and roots, Baum writes, "It is through the symbolic representations that a society discovers its hidden potentials, its richest resources, and its most daring dreams."[39] Then, borrowing from Durkheim, he adds that "religion is, in a word, a system of symbols by which society becomes conscious of itself."[40]

Contemporary brothers, traditionally devoid of a recognized symbolic structure that not only supports their inner urgings and intuitions but also firmly connects them to the liberating energy of the archetype of the monk, need to not only rediscover but also reclaim their ancient roots. This reawakening and revitalizing invite a commitment to a lay vocation defined by celibacy, an attentiveness and obedience to the voice of God, and a charismatic and prophetic lifestyle conversant with the heritage of the church and responsive to the needs of particular cultures and situations. In fostering this renewal, brothers touch the enduring symbolic energy that provides the pathway for further individual, collective, and church transformation.

The Cost of Reawakening the Ancient Archetype

The difficulties of touching these powerful symbolic and archetypal energies is captured by Slusser when he writes:

> Any advance in spirituality begins with an individual, one who is conscious of isolation from collective beliefs, one who dares to find a new pathway to unknown territory.[41]

By reappropriating the archetype of the monk as the underlying symbolic energy of our vocation as brothers within the church and society, we ground ourselves not only in a Christian archetype but also in a universal archetype and symbol system found in all major religious traditions. Likewise, the liberation of the brother's life as a vocation in itself and not in reference to priesthood, forces the brother and others to appreciate and value his unique calling. It also frees the brothers who respond to this calling from the classical church and juridical definitions which use either negative terms, defining who they are not, or functional terms, describing them by the work they do.

While this change of definition may threaten those who view life within a juridical and hierarchical system, the shift brings dignity, groundedness, and an enduring inner and outer vitality to the vocation of the brother. Yet, reclaiming the archetype of a monk will cost since it invites the liberation of those caught in a system of repression, isolation, hiddenness, and dependency; it offers them responsibility and consciousness as a way of living in relationship to their inner call, God, and their neighbor.

In describing the impact of this inner and outer shift upon a structured society that cherishes and protects the status quo of power and privilege, Slusser quotes Erich Neumann who believes that the "first step in sociological wisdom [is] to recognize that the major advances in civilization are processes which all but wreck the societies in which they occur."[42] Slusser elaborates by reminding those who choose the path of conscious responsibility versus a path of dependency and unconsciousness that "novelty is always met with suspicion by those forces who most benefit by the status quo both in culture and psyche."[43] Those would be harbingers of the renewed paradigm of the monk archetype and seek the awakening of the archetype within their brothers must recognize that suffering constitutes a necessary part of the journey. Again, Slusser quotes Neumann: "It is only through suffering that the person fully arrives at an awareness of a new ethic."[44]

Example of Jesus

As followers of Jesus, brothers find their model and hope in one who was also called to a life of obedience to the voice of God. In Jesus we discover someone who likewise recognized the "cost" of saying yes to the intuitions of his vocation. John Desrochers, CSC, captures the transforming nature of Jesus's identity.

> By vocation, one is as much an agent of change as a custodian of tradition. . . . Jesus was supremely free from social pressures. Yet, he did not follow his whims and fancies. . . . Jesus showed that a person's vocation is not to submit passively to existing institutions, but to create a more human and just world. Giving us the power to dissent and disobey, Jesus invited each one of us to become free and to exercise

a prophetic identity in our daily activities. It is in this way that we can work for God's kingdom and humanity's liberation.[45]

Desrochers further elaborates on God's role in redemption and liberation when he writes about prayer, suffering, and God's intervention in history. To Desrochers, prayer was the secret way in which Jesus discovered the "non-conformity, [and] struggle for change," which led him into his clash with the existing religious traditions and social conventions of his era.[46] Writing about change and how God works through people, he says:

> It is not God's intention to protect people of good will through miraculous interventions; God will not establish God's glorious kingdom on earth. Yet, God wants us to persevere in the struggle and to work for this world's liberation through Jesus' values.[47]

Thus, the reappropriation of the monk archetype and the symbolic system of the brother demand that a person be willing to open himself to the transforming power of Jesus in whatever way that develops. By grounding himself in the experience of Jesus, the brother paves the way for a transformation not only of his inner reality but also of the culture in which he lives. To live and minister as Jesus did becomes the life-giving energy of the brother as it does for all Christians.

Conclusion

The enduring archetype of the monk provides the way for us brothers to reclaim and revitalize our ancient roots within religious archetypal and symbolic experience. While we may have felt an inner connectedness to the archetype through intuition and casual conversation, now the intuition has an opportunity to flower in both word and gesture. Rooted in a lay charismatic movement, nourished by the Word of God, we brothers potentially provide the world an image of persons seeking with all our energy and talent to recognize and manifest the diverse faces of God.

Like our ancient brothers living in the desert or wandering the cities and countrysides, we need to ask questions. Within the church, culture, and ourselves, what are the "demons or issues" that need to be wrestled with today? Where and how will this battle be waged? What type of spirituality, community support, relationships, and lifestyles will nourish us for this mission? Also, what kind of help do we need to shape, define, and symbolize the re-discovery of our ancient calling? Finally, as brothers, how are we going to find our buried history and reclaim as well as awaken the ancient symbols that provide vision, unity, and energy to our life and identity?

Questions prevail now. However, in raising the questions, living them, and encouraging their development, new consciousness and hope will flourish. To avoid the questions, or even worse, to repress or deny them, results only in broken people, "folded" lives, and a diminished relationship with our deepest selves and with God. Even worse, avoidance allows us to continue hiding our vitality, gift, and vision for church and society.

As brothers, we need to reclaim our collective memory of who we are and how God has continually sought to work through us. Likewise, we need to awaken our collective vision within the church today. Like Elhanan, the main character in Elie Wiesel's novel, *The Forgotten*, we need to pray continually:

> God of truth, remember that without memory truth becomes only the mask of truth. Remember that only memory leads man back to the source of his longing for You. Remember, God of history, that You created man to remember. . . . What sort of witness would I be without my memory?[48]

Notes

1. Rainer Maria Rilke, *Selected Poems*, quoted by Paula Ripple in *Growing Strong at Broken Places* (Notre Dame: Ave Maria Press, 1986) 21.

2. Throughout this discussion, the use of the term intuition refers both to the idea of a "hunch" or more formally, the type of "knowledge discerned directly by the mind without reasoning or analysis." *New Webster's Dictionary of the English Language*, college edition (Chicago: Consolidated Book Publishers, 1975) 794.

3. For a more detailed study please refer to a work by Philip Sheldrake, SJ, *Spirituality and History: Questions of Interpretation and Method* (London: Biddles, 1991).

4. Francis Englert, CSC, quoted in "Focusing the Issue: Toward a Liberation Theology for Brothers," unpublished paper by Thomas D. Maddix, CSC (May 8, 1986) 6.

5. Ibid.

6. Radmila Moacannin, *Jung's Psychology and Tibetan Buddhism: Western and Eastern Paths to the Heart* (London: Wisdom Publications, 1986) 121.

7. Gerald H. Slusser, *From Jung to Jesus: Myth and Consciousness in the New Testament* (Atlanta: John Knox Press, 1986) 25.

8. Ibid., 32.

9. Myriam Dardenne, "Who is the Integrating Subject: A Response from the Western Point of View," in Raimundo Pannikkar, *Blessed Simplicity: The Monk as Universal Archetype* (New York: Seabury Press, 1982) 181.

10. Louis Bouyer, *The Spirituality of the New Testament and Fathers: A History of Christian Spirituality* (New York: Seabury Press, 1963) 317.

11. Ibid.

12. Raimundo Pannikkar, *Blessed Simplicity: The Monk as Universal Archetype* (New York: Seabury Press, 1982) 10.

13. Ibid., ii.

14. Ibid.

15. Peter Brown, *Society and the Holy in Late Antiquity* (Berkeley: University of California Press, 1982) 153–154.

16. Sheldrake, *Spirituality and History,* 111.

17. Mircea Eliade, ed. *The Encyclopedia of Religion,* Vol. 10 (New York: Macmillan, 1987) 36–37.

18. Frank Houdek, SJ, class presentation, Jesuit School of Theology at Berkeley, Graduate Theological Union, Berkeley, California (Oct. 8, 1987).

19. Kenneth Leech, *Experiencing God: Theology as Spirituality* (San Francisco: Harper and Row, 1985) 141–149.

20. Jean Gribomont, "Monasticism and Asceticism," *Christian Spirituality: Origins to the Twelfth Century* Bernard McGinn et al., eds. (New York: Crossroads, 1985) 90.

21. Ibid.

22. Ibid.

23. Bouyer, *The Spirituality of the New Testament,* 309.

24. Ibid., 318–320.

25. Ibid., 499.

26. Ibid.

27. Bruce Lescher, CSC, "Laybrothers: Questions Then, Questions Now," unpublished paper (April 29, 1985) 3.

28. Dom Jean Leclercq, "The Carolingian Renewal" in *The Spirituality of the Middle Ages* (Minneapolis: Winston Press, 1968) 101.

29. Leclercq, "The New Orders" in *The Spirituality of the Middle Ages* (Minneapolis: Winston Press, 1968) 129.

30. Ibid., 130.

31. Robert Broderick, *The Catholic Encyclopedia* (Nashville: Thomas Nelson) 81.

32. James A Cordien et al., eds., *The Code of Canon Law: A Text and Commentary* (New York: Paulist Press, 1985) 460.

33. Carol Pearson, *The Hero Within: Six Archetypes We Live By* (San Francisco: Harper and Row, 1986) 75–76.

34. Michael McGinniss, FSC, "Being Forgotten and Forgetful: A Subtle Clericalism," in *Who are My Brothers: Cleric-Lay Relationships in Men's Religious Communities* (Staten Island, NY: Alba House, 1988) 152.

35. Ibid., 153.

36. Peter Berger, quoted by Gerhard Lenski in *Power and Privilege: A Theory of Social Stratification* (Chapel Hill: University of North Carolina Press, 1966) 26.

37. Gregory Baum, *Religion and Alienation: A Theological Reading of Sociology* (New York: Paulist Press, 1975) 117.

38. Ibid., 130.

39. Ibid., 131.

40. Emile Durkheim, quoted by Gregory Baum in *Religion and Alienation,* 131.

41. Slusser, *From Jung to Jesus,* 42.

42. Ibid., 61.

43. Ibid.

44. Ibid., 76.

45. John Desrochers, CSC, *Christ the Liberator* (Bangalore, India: Centre for Social Action, 1977) 58–59.

46. Ibid., 83.

47. Ibid., 214.

48. Elie Wiesel, *The Forgotten* (New York: Summit Books, 1992) 12.

Your Old Brothers Shall Dream Dreams and Your Young Brothers Shall See Visions

Robert C. Berger, FSC

Religious brotherhood. How do we brothers tell the story? How do we let the world in on its secret? Is it possible to describe religious brotherhood in words? Certainly, a great story might come out of the lives of ordinary brothers in schools, parishes, hospitals, and other ministries, but are the brothers who are involved in these ministries writing it? The story, the whole story, tends to be complex; its contentments and joys emerge out of doubt, pain, and change. The question is: how do we tell the story in a North American church where our brotherhood, for the most part, remains unknown or somewhat confusing—even to those who know directly?

Like many who write about religious life, I am invigorated by the variety of gifts to be found in brotherhood, and I feel a need to tell part of its story. Writing is a solitary act, and, ideally, religious life should provide a brother with ample solitude and quiet.

BROTHER ROBERT C. BERGER, FSC, is a De La Salle Christian Brother. He is a native of, and presently lives in, New York City. He joined the Christian Brothers in 1973 and professed final vows in 1981. He has a BS from Manhattan College (1973), an MSEd from Monmouth College (1978), an MDiv from Princeton Theological Seminary (1988), and a DMin from Drew University (1990). He is presently an Assistant Professor in the Department of Religious Studies and a Director of a student residence hall at Manhattan College, Bronx, New York. Brother Robert's previous ministries have included high school teaching, college campus ministry, spiritual direction, and retreat work. Brother Robert may be addressed at 4415 Post Road, Bronx, NY 10471.

But the frantic pace of an active ministry conspires to silence a person. There are far fewer men religious than jobs to fill. Someone must be found to teach the history course, to lead the parish youth group, to coach the baseball team or moderate the debate club, to run a hospice program or social justice committee. Many jobs are vital: the director of the community, the brother who handles the house accounts, the brother who coordinates the kitchen, the brother who quietly volunteers to do the 101 small, but necessary, tasks behind the scenes of community life. All too often a kind of workaholism takes over and makes of religious life a series of tasks to be performed and duties to be undertaken. Imagine spending the rest of your life going from one activity to another!

It is not at all facetious to suggest that religious brothers today are in serious danger of becoming overwhelmed by ministry. Indeed, the threat is great. Furthermore, it is not the same danger experienced in the past when many brothers were overwhelmed by ministry, because they were really convinced that "this is what is needed!" Instead, this contemporary sense of being overwhelmed is like running away from not knowing what to do. One facet of our present reality as men religious is that deep down we are not convinced that we are where the action is. Not being sure, we double our activity. The less sure we are, the harder we work, and this frantic activity puts blinders on us. We tell ourselves that since we are working we are doing God's will. The question is are we running away in our work? Are we hiding ourselves from each other and from the fact that we are not facing the issues?

One reason why some brothers are overwhelmed in ministry is that when push comes to shove they do not really believe in collaboration, in lay leadership in their particular ministry. On an unconscious level we still define ourselves by the tasks we are involved in and so we take on all this work. As a result, we identify more with the work we do than with what we are supposed to be about in a given situation.

In ministry today many people need our prayerful attention and loving response. Yet, in the midst of these urgent needs, brothers must remain focused on the action of God, pray with the Scriptures daily, and reflect on how their collective past will shape tomorrow's vision.

In this article, then, I hope to speak to the action of God and to the common concerns that brotherhood and the Hebrew

Scriptures have for our times. I hope to demonstrate that there is much common ground between brotherhood and the Hebrew Scriptures, and that brothers who are open to the great challenges and needs of today will profit by taking counsel from those Scriptures.

Exodus

In beginning this conversation with the Hebrew Scriptures, we must remember the community God called to be Israel through the actions of figures like Moses, Aaron, and Miriam. In this formation of a people we see a struggling group of unnamed men and women who, in almost every way, were far from the initial excitement given in Yahweh's promise to Abraham and Sarah, Isaac and Rebecca, Jacob and Rachel. Even physically, they found themselves far from the land held out in promise to them and their children. With experience of nothing but disappointment and despair in a lifetime of slavery and oppression, these people lead us—as they themselves were led—to an important biblical event: the Exodus. On one level, we have here the story of a people who moved from Egypt through the desert into the promised land. On a deeper level, however, the Exodus represents a lesson that must be learned and passed on to countless generations in the future: *people who strive to follow the living God move from sureness through uncertainty into newness.*

In this story there is good and bad news. First, the bad news. The Exodus experience assures us that all three movements—sureness, uncertainty, newness—will be very uncomfortable and, at times, downright painful experiences. The good news is that throughout the whole process God is always faithful.

The first element in this story is the notion of sureness or certainty, represented by the nation of Egypt. Egypt saw itself as powerful; people of various nations experienced its dominance through war and conquest. For the Hebrews, however, the land of Egypt was also a familiar world where "we sat by our fleshpots and ate our fill of bread" (Ex 16:3). This sense of sureness came at a heavy price. The Hebrews' experience of familiarity was mixed with the deadly combination of oppression and persecution. They faced two alternatives: continue to live in sureness as slaves, or break out of the cycle of persecution and death to seek freedom.

To embrace the ambiguity of the latter choice involved the unknown realities of the desert: the harsh home of uncertainty, where everything familiar was stripped away, where life as it was lived in the past could not be sustained. The starkness of the desert afforded no pretenses, for there all lay exposed before God. There the Hebrews experienced brokenness as never before in their history. In the desert they were totally dependent on God; all they could do was hope that the faithfulness of God would sustain the promise made to them through their ancestors.[1]

From this hope, however, sprang the possibility of new life as the Hebrews struggled to claim their promised land. Even though entrance into this land was fraught with a new set of life and death problems, in the act of acquiring it the people came to see the newness of God. Courage and strength were reborn as they remembered the promise of God and saw it fulfilled.

> I will bless you abundantly and make your descendants as countless as the stars of the sky and the sands of the seashore; your descendants shall take possession of the gates of their enemies. (Gn 22:17)

Finally, the land was theirs. Their experience of God was practically inseparable from the reality of land. God became known in the gift of land. Over the centuries this awareness of a God who dwelled among them gradually took on the quality of sureness in the form of the Temple as a guarantee of God's presence among them. Newness of the land faded into the certainty of the Temple.

Exile

Once again, the notion of "sureness" intruded darkly into the history of the community. In 587 B.C.E., as the powerful Babylonian nation destroyed Jerusalem and deported its leaders, the people of Judah struggled with the notion of how God was with and for them. The certainty of God's presence as the exclusive possession of the Judean community gave way to confusion. If God dwelled in the Temple, why this total destruction? Why were royal families killed and influential leaders deported? Had God turned away from the chosen people? Or, perhaps, was God bringing forth newness from what was once thought to be certainty? Years later, the community would hear another word from God.

For surely I know the plans I have for you, says the Lord, plans for your welfare and not for harm, to give you a future with hope. Then when you call upon me and come and pray to me, I will hear you. When you search for me, you will find me; if you seek me with all your heart, I will let you find me, says the Lord, and I will restore your fortunes and gather you from all the nations and the places where I have driven you, says the Lord, and I will bring you back to the place from which I sent you into exile.

(Jer 29:11–14)

In the Babylonian exile the pattern of sureness, uncertainty, and newness was replayed in the community as it was shaped by God into something intended by God. From the sureness of God's presence in the land since the time of Joshua to the uncertainty of entering into exile in the time of Jeremiah, the people had to enter into a new way of understanding God's action in their lives. Exile led to one thing: a new understanding of God. Finally, as a new Jewish generation left its captivity in Babylon to return to Jerusalem, they took with them a re-conceived understanding of God and of God's relationship to them.[2]

Today we brothers are re-conceiving our idea of God, and this process is threatening to everyone. It will surely change the church and religious life as we rethink the whole world, our place in it, and our relationship with God.

Exodus and Exile: Shaping Community

What we see in the desert experience of the exodus and the exile ordeal in Babylon are two events, separated by several centuries, which teach the same lesson. The years lived in the desert and the equally long experience of exile were, first and foremost, a period of struggle and bewilderment. Both desert and exile needed to be experienced as completely as possible because they were pivotal times. There was no escape other than death. Though they were extremely difficult situations, one thing was definite: in those pivotal times God spoke clearly. People were formed by these experiences in ways that could not be compared to any other way of shaping a community.

Both in the desert and in exile people were exhausted and despairing. Many could only recall a partial picture of the past. Faced with life-threatening situations, some were unable to cope and go on. This was unfortunate, but understandable. Parts of the community were capable of tolerating just so much ambiguity and change. Yet despair showed no partiality; it permitted no option. The present moment of extreme challenge overwhelmed some of the community. In terms of the future, these people saw, hoped, and spoke nothing new. For them, hopelessness became the central theme of life.

However, God's shaping of the community was not to end with a despairing and disconsolate people. These years of desert and exile also brought forth a remnant of the community able to speak about newness. Among these people were found visionaries like Moses and Joshua as well as hopeful prophets like Isaiah, Jeremiah, and Ezekiel. These leaders and prophets, with the men and women who heeded their authentic voices, are key to any discussion of newness as a result of God's action. Their story in the Hebrew Scriptures is also our story today. In many ways brothers in the late twentieth century are experiencing wilderness, exile, and the loss of meaning. But this has happened before in the history of God's people, and previous experiences can enlighten the present moment. Right now, our task as brothers is to articulate our grief as we experience loss, breakdown, and wandering.

Vatican II: Shaping Community

Enriched by memories of the exodus and exile experiences, the Roman Catholic Church also found itself at a pivotal moment in the story of its development as a people of God: the Second Vatican Council. Often our limited memory recalls a pre–Vatican II church which clearly presented itself as a unified organization having an equally clear sense of its teaching and mission. Within this church religious orders of sisters and brothers declared with equal clarity what they were about and how they would grow in the future. Questions were few and precise answers abounded. Today, more than a quarter of a century later, questions abound and answers seem far off, if not totally unreachable.

With the present challenges facing our world come new questions, needs, and responses. Once again the pattern which started with sureness—a pre–Vatican II church—is moving through uncertainty during these latter years of the twentieth century; key to this process is the recognition that we are a church called into newness.

To focus this process we need only mention the topic of religious vocations to know that we are in a desert experience. In this situation we must continue to talk with each other about its implications for today as well as tomorrow. But once we brothers recognize the crisis of the times, how do we deal with the ramifications that accompany this desert experience? Once we know ourselves to be in the muddy conditions of exile, how do we live in the present without some of our past securities? What many of us took for granted in religious life is now gone. Other dimensions of the life seem headed in the same direction. Today nothing short of our genuine struggle with the harsh aspects of life and death can be called brotherhood. However, this very struggle is the source of our hope. There is no hope without struggle. No hope drops from heaven through the intervention of God. Hope lies within the struggle.[3] But all too often our conversations lack the energy needed to address the present crisis. "Like those of other men, our conversations tend toward endless rehearsal of the safely remote past rather than testing the unsure waters of the present."[4]

Fortunately there are always a number of brothers who dare to dream dreams and see visions. By their actions they acknowledge our task today: to test the unsure waters of the present. But this is never done with timidity and fear. Like the countless men who went before us in brotherhood, who responded courageously and imaginatively to the needs of their contemporaries, who experienced the barrenness of the desert and the deprivations of exile in their own times, we too are called by God to deal with the dryness and concerns of dramatic change and upheaval. This is no easy task.

Relinquishing and Receiving

What does it mean for brotherhood to be in exile at the close of the twentieth century? We can look to the original exile experience, recalling its starting and closing movements—sureness and newness—and remember that these characteristics were crucial and difficult periods in the lives of the Israelites. When the community of Jerusalem entered into exile they left behind the sureness of the land and the Temple. The single most difficult aspect of that initial experience of exile was the lived reality of relinquishment.

For us brothers, relinquishment has been a basic reality of life in the last 25 years since Vatican II. Today we find that many community structures which we knew and perhaps loved are no longer part of religious life. Even more dramatic and heart-breaking is the fact that many of our confreres have left us either through dispensation or death. Symbols, attachments, structures are quickly destroyed.[5] But Vatican II did not leave brotherhood with only the relinquishment of sureness. It also pointed to the equally challenging task of receiving newness in our brotherhood.[6]

From the memory of the exodus and exile, with its people of vision and prophets of hope, Vatican II calls us to receive a new church given by God through key people. In religious communities we need brothers who are men of vision brave enough to face the dangers of the desert, to live with its unknowns, and to have the courage to enter into a new land. We need hopeful prophets who are willing to enter into exile themselves and help others enter into it; brothers who are willing to be part of that exile, trusting that at the right time God will call us into newness. In short, we need brothers who are open to the gift of receiving. This is risky.

Like the Hebrews out of Egypt and the Judeans out of Jerusalem, we have a wide variety of brothers today who span the entire spectrum of energy levels, from disheartened to encouraged. At one end of the spectrum we have brothers who are exhausted and despairing. They can be identified by their need for excessive mastery, control, and security. At the other end of the spectrum we have among us brothers who are visionaries and prophets who can see and respond to the realities of human hurt and human hope among us. The former group views exile in terms of aging, numbers, institutional commitments, and the lack of vocations. The latter group strives to see exile in terms of faith, hope, vision, possibilities, and dreams. For brothers in these two extremes and for the vast majority of brothers in between, it is most important to remember one thing: this transformation is God's action. God is doing it.

Power of Choice

As we experience the power of God today we must also acknowledge the powerlessness of brotherhood: the same sense of powerlessness we can see at two pivotal moments in biblical history. In the desert the people had two choices: they could wander aimlessly as nomads or they could journey ahead to the promised land. They were cut off from the familiar (though oppressive) world they once knew in Egypt, and they found that their freedom had its own price. In this crisis, the people were powerless to select any alternatives other than those presented by God. Their "gift" was the freedom of choice. They had to chose between "life and prosperity, [or] death and doom" (Dt 30:15b). Exile was also an experience of powerlessness, the sharpest point of discontinuity known in the history of Judah. The people living in captivity were cut off from their homeland with no immediate way back. They found themselves powerless and could only wait to understand their new relationship to God.

In these two scenarios of desert and exile we must be mindful that there is much common ground. The people who entered the desert and those who went into exile did not find newness. They only experienced the pain of seeing sureness disappear before their eyes. All they could do was hope that God would remain faithful. It was the next generation that found newness. Are we, as brothers, willing and able to endure this pain as we relinquish sureness? Are we willing and able to be brothers to each other now *and also* for the next generation? We are faced with a choice, and once again it is not an easy one. But whether we like it or not, this is our task historically (and this is our historic task).

Moses can serve as an example of a transitional generation. He led the people of God, but he himself never entered the promised land. Like Moses, many of us will most likely not see the full flowering of future religious brotherhood. We are part of a transitional generation. But to accept this belief should not depress us. The question is whether we, as leaders of our generation, will take responsibility for the future with no promise to see it, as Moses did. One way to do this is to carry out our present role. It is not enough to say, "It should be different," or to ask, "Why was I born in this time?" By carrying out our role in the present we will insure the future, however it evolves. This is God's work for brothers today.

Signs of Certainty and Risk

If we opt for sureness and security, for whatever reasons, we can expect the following results in our lives. We will not take risks; we will experience a minimum of pain because we will pay only modest prices for what we do and how we live; there will be little newness to be faced or even hoped for in our lives; institutions, rather than persons, will be honored, and then with empty rituals; old times and places will be seen as more assuring, simple, and manageable; and the years will bring numbness as we speak less and less to each other about vital topics, succumbing to the great desire to "tell" what is rather than what could be.

However, we have another choice: newness. As men of faith supported by one another in community we must have the courage to criticize constructively and energize the situations in which we involve ourselves. We must continue to remember that we are made in the image of God and together, as brothers, discern that image. We must acknowledge that "the Lord will reign for ever and ever," and not Holy Redeemer School! We need to trade security for responsible freedom, to cut through the numbness as we listen to the prompting of the Spirit among us.[7] With God's grace we must continue to encourage gifted brothers who have the ability to resist the numbness while naming the signs of hope that come out of darkness. Only then will our communities grow in the realization that God's new actions hinge on our discernment of traditions. Only then will we experience the great desire to "trust" what will be.

The Courage to Be Hopeful

It takes courage to approach God in exile, to be receptive to the reality that God intends for us. This courage expresses itself in many ways. How much of our fear and brokenness is covered up by busyness in ministry? Brothers must have the courage to give public expression to the fears and brokenness they have denied for so long and suppressed so deeply. Brothers must have the courage to imagine new possibilities. This is a daring and dangerous part of our tradition because *brothers who have dreams have power.* Like bees to pollen, people are attracted to a dream. Nothing is more powerful than a group of people who work together for the realization of a common vision. But to do this, brothers need to be able to mourn the death of things they took for granted in the past, so that eventually they may be comforted by newness. This mourning might take the shape of embracing endings in order to permit beginnings.

Like all members of the church, we brothers praise God through our ability to work and to love. We also have the task to live in such a way that people notice God as the source of our energy, an energy not generated among us but given to us.[8] All brothers share the responsibility to look at our traditions seriously and critically. Hopeful brothers spread an awareness of this hope to others. Brothers of vision are called to imagine in the midst of the community. This task is so urgent and necessary that it is probably more important than most one-to-one situations of concern, or even the implementation of institutional goals.[9] Last, but not least, hopeful brothers know old memories and discern new realities.

Brothers who are hopeful prophets engage in battle for the public imagination of the community. Imagine what our communities would be like if we talked about the newness of God in the midst of the shambles of brokenness. The ultimate question is: do we believe that we can come full circle from this terminal illness to God's powerful healing? Psychology tells us that a healthy sense of grief allows us to move on in life and to embrace newness. Can men living with other men grieve? If so, how? Grief that is nothing but an analysis of a current lifestyle only serves to maintain the status quo. Unfortunately the world highly values the status quo. Contemporary North American society gives us a powerful message: "Don't grieve. Pretend nothing is wrong." These underlying attitudes become powerfully vested interests that can keep the grief unnoticed.[10]

In reality, where does this consideration of "hopefulness, grief, and imagination" lead to? Does it become part of an empty God-language that all too often means nothing when it comes to action? The answers to these questions can be found in the experiences of ordinary brothers who know the power of God in their lives. Like Israel who saw land as a gift, these men see life as a gift. These men stand against those who insist on sureness or continuity, who grasp life as a right and fail to see it as a gift. To see life as a gift is to remember that newness comes in discontinuity and to those who have no claim. The people of Jerusalem discovered that land and institutions were expendable, and when lost, newness came. The God who tears down, builds up; the God who plucks up, plants (Jer 1:10). Instead of asking, "Will God squeeze some more history out of the old forms?" courageous brothers ask, "Will God speak a new word that will take on a new shape from what has ended?" "Will God come from some other direction and give us a new gift?" "Are we even ready to look in other directions for the purposes of God?" Here is the good news: God transforms.

Danger of Amnesia

If we want brotherhood to be the same as it was in the past, then we are asking for guaranteed security, which does only one thing: it dulls the memory. Guaranteed security erodes the capacity to maintain the distance and the linkage between "how it really was" and "how it actually is now," and it deadens the capacity to be open to "how it might yet be." Israel's chief temptation was to forget, to cease to be open either to the God of history or to God's blessings yet to be given. Forgetting leads to amnesia.

When brothers settle into what appears to be an eternally guaranteed institution or ministry, they silence the voice of history which gives gifts and makes claims. If we are unaware of being addressed, then we do not answer. If we do not answer, then we are free not to care, not to decide, not to hope, and not to celebrate. If brothers do not dream, then they are easy to control. Without a dream there is no attraction for others to join in their ministry. A chief temptation of contemporary brothers is to make a common twentieth-century choice: a life of private well-being, which leads only to death.

Gift of Discontinuity

Before the Israelite community went into exile they were no longer recipients of the land as a gift; rather they were under the illusion of being its controllers. As we re-evaluate our needs and purposes, we brothers have a choice just as real and just as critical. Are we to be creatures of grace or managers of achievement?

The only way we brothers can sustain our gifted existence is to stay singularly with the Gift Giver.[11] We must never allow the mystery of our brotherhood to be reduced to a manageable size. If we do, then transcendence is domesticated. When our institutions and ministries are fully controlled, it is easy for us to imagine that we have generated these places of service and can use them for our own objectives. The marvel is that God can remind the church, through brotherhood, that institutions are not *from* us but are gifts *to* us.

It takes courage to realize that our ministries are not fully our own, that they are not for our benefit. It takes courage to know a God who challenges us to a new and formidable task: to be holy before God in the formation of the future.

For the men and women who left Egypt, for those who entered into exile in Babylon, and for us after Vatican II, the radical announcement of discontinuity must be seen and understood as an initiation into a new history of anticipation. Newness begins with discontinuity and initiation. So a new chapter has begun in the history of brotherhood which has a twofold thrust. First, we are challenged to go from a positive work into a new dimension within that work. Second, we are summoned to leave and go somewhere we might not otherwise choose. This involves a radical breaking off and departure. Briefly, it means to become a brotherhood that we have not yet been, but which God fully intends.

As we look at the history of the Hebrews in the desert, we see their buoyant trust rapidly turn to grim resentment. In situations of landlessness, faith rapidly erodes. But that is precisely where we are called. The Hebrews left a secure barrenness in Egypt for the sake of a risky future of promises. But God is the Lord of all things new, and God's partners in history are pilgrims who believe God will do what God says. Are we brothers men who believe and rely on God's power and fidelity to bring freedom out of slavery, rivers out of deserts, fertility from barrenness, joy from sorrow, life out of death? Isaiah tells us:

> Remember not the events of the past, the things of long ago consider not. See, I am doing something new! Now it springs forth, do you not perceive it? In the desert I make a way, in the wasteland, rivers. (43:18–19)

As the twentieth century comes to a close, we brothers are called to wait and wonder, to look and not yet know.[12]

Trust versus Doubt

What is the message of the Hebrew experience for us? It is a very difficult one: God is not present to assure continuities; rather, God is present to work newness out of discontinuities.[13] This is scary! God's presence is evident in God's intervention not to keep some ministries going, not to do business as usual, but to bring life out of death, to make us promise-trusters in the midst of promise-doubters. In Hebrew history the story of the manna in the desert was just such a theme: promise-trusters became promise-doubters. We have all been promise-trusters at one time or another. God gave us the answer for that day's question or need. But today, because we live in an ever-involving world, we have new questions and needs which demand new solutions and purposes. The promises of old take on new forms.[14]

Pause for Hope and Action

As the Israelite community was about to enter the promised land it paused. Today that pause is known to us as the book of Deuteronomy.[15] It was a long and reflective pause. Israel listened and the traditions of Moses spoke. Israel knew that hard, disciplined reflection was never more needed than at that particular moment when the new situation of land required a new Israel with a renewed faith. Issues of self-identity had to be addressed again and again. Life had to be redefined if it was to be one of promise.

No less serious is the situation of brotherhood as it enters the twenty-first century. Brotherhood has paused for the past 25 years in an attempt to renew and redefine itself. That pause today is revealed in our new Rules and renewed interest in the charisms of our founders. Brotherhood listens, and the traditions of our individual founders speak. Like the Hebrews who left Egypt, promoters of hope within our brotherhood intensely believe that things can and will be different from the way they are now. These brothers boldly act with that hope.

Where can we find these promoters of hope among us? They can probably be found living and working with the marginalized of our society, among the very least.[16] In that position they are able to envision a different shape for life. They proclaim that a power for life is indeed available, and that God is the one who provides that power for life. This power is never possessed *by* the community; it is a gift *to* the community. This power to hope is the attracting dream of the community.

Remember, in exile God had no final commitment to the present order of things, least of all to the continuation of institutions. The community of Judah was drastically displaced; the new order of the Jewish people in Babylon was not established by human plan, human knowledge, or human power. It was the inscrutable, irresistible work of God.[17]

Today, more than ever, we need to remind ourselves as brothers in community and as members of the larger church, that our hopes, dreams, and visions are powerful ways in which God communicates to us. Nothing in them is private, romantic, or otherworldly. Their power is always communal, social, historical, and thisworldly. We must remember that the dream of God and the hope of Israel were for the establishment of a new social order which would embody peace, justice, freedom, equality, and well-being. Our tradition as brothers has always been hope-filled, and the substance of our hope is clear: we proclaim by our lives a new social order. We proclaim it to each other in community and to those with whom and to whom we minister on a daily basis.

There is no way to avoid this. God asks us as communities of brothers to live in a passionate and profound hope that the world will become the world God intends, the world for which our founders once yearned and for which we yearn today. This tradition of hope means following the vision of Christ as we learn to relinquish control over life: not in the sense of life being out of control, but in the sense of governance entrusted to this God who eludes our explanations. Hope does not consist of losing control, but of relinquishing it to God in trust.

Finally, there is the story of a small boy who surprised his father one day by saying, "I want to tell you something I've never told anybody." "Tell away," said the father, who expected a secret about a friend or a toy or school. "Love," said the child, "is a thing you have to take care of." Brotherhood, like love, is a thing we have to take care of. We brothers must take care not to surrender our imaginative powers to any pretense of absoluteness. Our hope must remind us not to absolutize the present, not to take it too seriously, not to treat it too honorably, because it will not last. The essence of our vocation is to dream large dreams and to see equally impressive visions about God's powerful purposes. Our vocation is an immense human act that stands as an alternative to the dominant society. It is an invitation to realize a critical dream. It is a vision to engage in risky imagination. As brothers, the heart of our call is to nurture with faith and love a hope rooted in God's word.

> After this I shall pour out my spirit on all humanity. Your sons and daughters shall prophesy, your old people shall dream dreams, and your young people shall see visions. (Joel 3:1)

Notes

1. Walter Brueggemann, *The Land* (Philadelphia: Fortress Press, 1977) 53-56.

2. William Holladay, *Jeremiah: A Fresh Reading* (New York: Pilgrim Press, 1990) 2.

3. Dorothee Soelle with Shirley A. Cloyes, *To Work and To Love* (Philadelphia: Fortress Press, 1986) 161.

4. Terrence J. Moran, "Risking the Distance: Religious Men and Friendship," *America* 167 (Dec. 12, 1992) 469.

5. Sean Sammon, "The Transformation of Religious Life," *Origins* 21 (August 29, 1991) 188–189.

6. Walter Brueggemann, *Hopeful Imagination: Prophetic Voices in Exile* (Philadelphia: Fortress Press, 1986) 31.

7. Walter Brueggemann, *The Prophetic Imagination* (Philadelphia: Fortress Press, 1978) 47–48.

8. Soelle, *To Work and To Love*, 89.

9. Brueggemann, *Hopeful Imagination*, 96.

10. Walter Brueggemann, *Hope within History* (Atlanta: John Knox Press, 1987) 72–91.

11. Brueggemann, *The Land*, 57.

12. Brueggemann, *Hopeful Imagination*, 90–108.

13. Ibid., 43.

14. Brueggemann, *The Prophetic Imagination*, 44–46.

15. John Bright, *Jeremiah*, The Anchor Bible, (Garden City: Doubleday, 1985) lxxxvi.

16. Brueggemann, *Hope within History*, 55.

17. Terence E. Fretheim, *The Suffering of God* (Philadelphia: Fortress Press, 1984) 29–33.

Continuing the Mission of Jesus: Some Unfinished Business for Brothers

Joel Giallanza, CSC

> As Jesus and his disciples were leaving Jericho, a large crowd was following. Two blind men who were sitting by the road heard that Jesus was passing by, so they began to shout, "Son of David! Have mercy on us, sir!" The crowd scolded them and told them to be quiet. But they shouted out even more loudly, "Son of David! Have mercy on us, sir!" Jesus stopped and called to them, "What do you want me to do for you?" (Mt 20:29–32)

Here is a simple yet significant question which exemplifies the heart of the apostolic person. Simple, because it directly seeks to uncover the immediate situation to be addressed. Significant, because it conveys no conditions, only a desire to serve. I have no doubt that brothers in the church, yesterday and today, are quite

---

BROTHER JOEL GIALLANZA, CSC, is a member of the Congregation of Holy Cross. He is a native of New Orleans, Louisiana and presently lives in Rome, Italy. He entered Holy Cross in 1967 and made perpetual profession in 1976. He has a BA from Saint Edward's University in Austin, Texas, and an MA from the University of San Francisco. He is presently a member of the General Council of the congregation. His previous ministries have included teacher, parish director of religious education, formator, Constitutions writing committee member, provincial councillor, retreat director, and spiritual director. His publications have appeared in *Review for Religious, Spiritual Life, Human Development, Mount Carmel,* and *Living Prayer.* He has served as a board member of the National Assembly of Religious Brothers and is currently on the editorial board of Human Development. Brother Joel may be addressed at Generalizia di Santa Croce, Via Framura, 85, 00168 Rome, Italy.

fluent in the experience of asking this question. Brothers have been and continue to be people of the mission.

Mission stands as a centerpiece around which religious life has identified itself in recent years. Revised constitutional texts and recent general chapters reflect the importance assigned to mission. The efforts that have been made toward formulating an apostolic identity reflect the sensitivity of religious in responding to situations in our world which desperately need the healing presence and power of the Gospel. Without that response, those situations—and the human lives within them—might be summarily dismissed as hopeless. Every dimension of religious life is touched by the mission; thus, we speak of the apostolic character of prayer, community, and the vows or the various forms of commitment. Those in authority emphasize that effective governmental procedures and practices facilitate the priority of mission over maintenance. Formators note that programs of initial and continuing formation must be designed for and in the mission, not isolated from it.

This relationship between the mission and the dimensions of religious life is precisely where I see some unfinished business. Unfinished, not because nothing has been done, but because much more needs to be done. The perspective frequently operative in the initial formation of years past tended to emphasize the personal, salvific character of ministry, prayer, community, and the vows. A classic example of this is articulated in a little work which was used as a basic reference manual in many religious institutes, *Catechism of the Vows*.

> The religious state is wherein one makes profession of tending to perfection by the best means, or, to develop this definition a bit, it is a form of life approved by the Church, wherein some of the faithful, joined in a society, establish themselves in order to tend to perfection by means of the three vows of poverty, chastity, and obedience, which they make according to the Rule. . . .
>
> A religious therefore does more for God and for self-sanctification by entering the religious state than if he were to stay in the world, even with the intention of there practicing the Christian virtues.[1]

The same emphasis could be found implicitly or explicitly in constitutional texts and rule books of many communities prior to the recent revisions.

A different emphasis operates today which gives mission a major identifying role. Even the Code of Canon Law points to the apostolic character of religious life.

> Life consecrated by the profession of the evangelical counsels is a stable form of living by which the faithful, following Christ more closely under the action of the Holy Spirit, are totally dedicated to God who is loved most of all, so that, having dedicated themselves to His honor, the upbuilding of the Church and the salvation of the world by a new and special title, they strive for the perfection of charity in service to the Kingdom of God and, having become an outstanding sign in the Church, they may foretell the heavenly glory.[2]

Revised constitutional texts are more exact and more eloquent in the priority assigned to mission. General chapters have stressed the importance of the apostolic dimension of religious life as a means to respond to current and emerging needs in our world. This emphasis has not diminished the truth that religious life is a means to salvation; rather, it seeks to link more directly salvation to our presence and activity in the mission.

In this article, I hope to identify some aspects of this unfinished business, and to encourage continuing reflection and discussion on the apostolic character of religious life. These reflections need the expansion and refinement provided by the heritage, perspective, and experience of each religious institute and of brothers in particular. One distinction is important to note for these reflections. I will use *mission* when referring to the mandate to proclaim the Gospel and continue the work which Jesus began. I will use *ministry* in reference to the wide spectrum of services provided by brothers as an expression of that mission.

Attentiveness:
"Look around you, look at the fields"

> "You have a saying, 'Four months more and then the harvest.' But I tell you, look around you, look at the fields, the crops are now ripe and ready to be harvested!" (Jn 4:35)

Among the basic building blocks for continuing the mission of Jesus is an attentiveness to the world around us. Jesus' statement implies the need to look up from our own concerns so we can look around at the world of needs which surrounds us. To be effective, this attentiveness must be sensitive, adaptable, and willing to be involved. In practice, it is an active vigilance.

Sensitivity is attentive to the finer points of a situation; it is able to distinguish between the possibility of responding in many ways and the limitation of responding in a way purported to be the only one viable. Such sensitivity is particularly important in multicultural settings where we must first be observers before being commentators. Adaptability flows from this sensitivity and is attentive to providing an appropriate and sufficient response. Such adaptability forestalls patterned responses, disconnected from the situation they seek to address. Willingness to be involved is attentive to the needs which, realistically, can be addressed. Such willingness takes the necessary steps for formulating a response based on what is learned from the sensitivity and adaptability which shape it.

Attentiveness is not a new quality among brothers; nevertheless, it is especially important today given the rapid changes in the world around us and in the demographic trends within religious institutes themselves. Discernment about future ministries or continuing institutional commitments, discussion about the identity of brothers within the church, and deliberation about the quality of our community and our prayer life will be supported by the sensitivity, adaptability, and willingness marking our attentiveness to influences within and without religious life.

This attentiveness must also scrutinize the church itself. If we use the *Lineamenta,* written in preparation for the 1994 Synod of Bishops on "The Consecrated Life and Its Role in the Church and in the World," as a barometer of the church's awareness of and interest in brothers' experiences of life and ministry, then the forecast for the future is decidedly low. The document's three paragraphs on brothers do not reflect the rich deliberations on identity and role that brothers have undertaken in recent years. Nor does the document reflect the probing and prophetic language incorporated into revised constitutional texts. Brothers must embrace wholeheartedly the responsibility of reflecting on, clarifying, and articulating their identity and role in the church. They must take up this responsibility since it is doubtful that significant guidance and support, or even questions, will come from the church in the near future. Brothers will have to be educators in and of the church concerning their present experiences and their future hopes.

"Look around you, look at the fields." Look at our world, look at the needs to be met, look at the church, look at the transformation which must take place. The capacity for our attentiveness is not self-manufactured; it is generated by compassion, by the urgency to respond to that world, those needs, and the church. Compassion is attentive, but ever an active attentiveness. Compassion never merely observes; it initiates, interacts, and challenges. This is the place of compassion in Jesus' own life, to initiate a healing, a teaching, a practical example, to interact with the people, to challenge injustices. It will be no different for us. The same compassion will urge us to respond by initiative, interaction, and challenge.

Planning: "Sit down first and consider"

> "If you are planning to build a tower, you sit down first and consider what it will cost, to see if you have enough resources to finish the project." (Lk 14:28)

Attentiveness provides us with valuable material for making decisions; without planning, that material may never be focused enough to be used effectively. In his teaching on discipleship Jesus is practical: it will cost something. If we do not consider what that cost involves for us, we run the risk of responding by half-measures, unacceptable by Jesus' standards. Similarly, what we do in response to what we learn once we "look around" will cost something. Planning enables us to determine what resources we will need and what resources we already have at our disposal.

Planning is a continuum, effective only to the degree that we engage its components, four of which will be noted here.

1. Planning begins with information-gathering about the situation we want to address.
2. Analysis will assist us in determining the meaning and the usefulness of that information.
3. From this determination we begin to design the action that will best respond to the situation. The action itself corroborates or contradicts the effectiveness of planning. Planning, however, is not complete once the response is determined and action is taken.

4. The effects of that action must be evaluated, which in turn provides new information for further planning. The planning cycle continues with information, analysis, action, evaluation.

The timeline for each component of this continuum is affected by the situation being addressed. The urgency of some situations may speak so loudly that the information to be gathered, the analysis to be made, and the action to be taken are immediately evident. Other situations may require years of planning to address them effectively. In both cases, though, the evaluative component serves as a door to the future.

Brothers have become increasingly fluent in the principles and practices underlying these basic components of planning. Our congregations continue to develop strategies for addressing the quality of individual and communal life as it is affected by the demographic trends within the membership. Brothers must engage those principles and practices to explore and articulate their relationship with and role within the church. Brothers must also continue their efforts to configure that relationship and role or, as has happened in the past, it will be done for them. To the degree that brothers do not make these efforts, to that degree they will simply be forgotten. One example happens regularly in presentations on church vocations. Very often, the focus of such presentations and related prayers is priests and religious sisters; the audience may depart without even knowing that religious brotherhood is a possibility. Brothers must continue their efforts to raise their visibility and vocality; it is simply unrealistic to assume this recognition will happen on its own.

"Sit down first and consider." The quality of productive planning does not flow primarily from the skills needed nor even all its components. Primarily, quality planning finds its source in hope, hope in new life, in the endless possibility for growth and development. This hope accepts God's loving presence and activity even when they are least evident; it assigns value on the basis of God's love, not human expediency.

Competence:
"Let your light shine before others"

> "Let your light shine before others, so they may see your works and give glory to God in heaven." (Mt 5:16)

Attentiveness to changing life situations and planning for our response posture us for implementation. The immediate effectiveness of what will be implemented is affected if not determined by our competence. Jesus' images of salt and light represent dimensions of our presence and activity among others. One dimension, like salt, is quiet and hidden, yet noticeably adept in its influence. The other dimension, like a brilliant light, is bold and visible. Our competence in the mission, in religious life, must be bold and visible like the light that shows the way for others.

Competence includes but goes beyond the acquisition and mastery of the knowledge, skills, and resources necessary to engage in a particular activity or to complete a specific task. Competence reaches beyond this to include the personal dimension; that is, our awareness of the personalities, preferences, and predicaments of those who will benefit from our use of knowledge, skills, and resources. Disregard for this personal dimension quickly blurs the dividing line between competence and control.

Competence takes time and energy, both from the perspective of acquiring and mastering what is necessary, and from the perspective of knowing and respecting the persons and situations we are called to serve and to which we bring our knowledge, skills, and resources. Since all this continues to evolve, competence is never the accomplishment of a moment, but the development of an approach to mission throughout life.

A chronicle of the myriad ministries in which brothers have demonstrated competence would constitute a book in itself. The emphasis here, however, is not to rest content with past accomplishments, but to discover which avenues lead to the future. Brothers can draw upon the vast storehouse of their experiences to shape the future. It is insufficient merely to state that brothers have done a good job; they have, in fact, shaped the lives of countless people. Their experiences give them a unique perspective on the church and place them in a unique relationship with people. Brothers' view from inside the church yet outside its hierarchical structure provides the opportunity to objectively observe the church's gifts and challenge its sins. It is an opportunity which brothers must take. Their relationship with men and women, as brother and believer, places them in a position of knowing and sharing the daily aspirations and frustrations of God's people. It is a place which brothers must maintain.

"Let your light shine before others." The foundation for competence is justice, the justice of responding to those situations we are capable of addressing and available to address. This is also the justice of self-knowledge, of knowing our capabilities and our limitations, of knowing when we can respond and when we cannot. Anything less compromises the mission, and dims the light we bear.

Decisions: "Do not . . . keep looking back"

> "Do not start plowing then keep looking back. Anyone who does that is of no use for the reign of God." (Lk 9:62)

However perceptive our attentiveness, precise our planning, and professional our competence, decisions must be made and sustained. Jesus is unimpressed with second-guessing, "looking back," missing opportunity because of preoccupation with possibilities and probabilities. A former provincial used to say during extended meetings, "All this discussion and planning eventually has to degenerate into actually deciding and doing something!" Eventually, we have to start plowing somewhere because the issues we confront in religious life are endless; they will never be lined up just waiting to be plowed.

Decisions about ministry or prayer or community can be delayed or bypassed endlessly under the guise of needing yet one more piece of data, one more study by a task force, one more committee. Possibly the opposite of making and implementing a decision is not so much blatant indecisiveness as mistaking more discussion or study or analysis for the decision itself. Since something is going on, a decision must have been put in operation. The seductiveness of this course is to forget that discussion, study, and analysis usually take place in a closed system, that is, having limited or no effect beyond the immediate participants until the point of presentation and implementation.

Decisions are rarely single-subject events because no one aspect of life can be conveniently and neatly isolated from another. Quality of community life will affect and be affected by the ministries of the members, continuing institutional commitments will affect personal and financial resources available for emerging needs, individual and communal prayer will be affected by all these. This process becomes even more complex when nostalgia or second-guessing are ingredients in decision-making. The risk is that decisions may never be made; then there is no need to look back since the plowing never begins.

Brothers have made some difficult and painful decisions in the face of declining personnel and financial resources. Residences and ministries with which they had long been associated have closed, been sold, or passed on to others, sometimes for purposes other than the original ones. Increasing ages and decreasing numbers combined with current trends of fewer vocations set the stage for more difficult and painful decisions yet to come. Brothers have had to decide that they want a future. The challenge now is to reaffirm that decision since clear external supports, from the institutional church and society, are not evident and may not be present at all. The danger is discouragement which compromises the conviction that there is a future for this way of life. The temptation is to stop plowing and look back nostalgically. Given their rich history of fidelity, it is unlikely that brothers will succumb to the temptation. Nevertheless, its siren call will echo as brothers make their way into the future.

"Do not start plowing then keep looking back." Decisions come to life by faith. We need only a "mustard seed" of faith (Lk 17:6), but it will enable us to trust that God's grace can transform whatever inadvertent deficiencies preceded the decision. The challenge lies not so much in making the decision as it does in moving forward from that point, without looking back, trusting in faith that our efforts can truly be a reflection of the Lord's own.

Fidelity: "Set your hearts on the reign of God"

"Set your hearts on the reign of God, and you will have all things besides." (Lk 12:31)

We have to know where we want to go and which direction we are taking now for our future. We must shape the future quality of our life or incidental and random happenings in our life will shape it for us. Jesus instructs his disciples to remain fixed on and faithful to the reign of God. He does not devalue material goods, but he teaches that they must be kept in perspective so God's reign remains the priority. It is a matter of fidelity, to assure that our time and energy are expended first on the mission.

Fidelity thrives on purpose and passion, on why we do what we do and the intensity with which we do it. Our purpose is to continue the mission of Jesus. Fidelity to that mission touches every dimension of religious life: ministry, prayer, community, vows. These are the means through which we continue the mission and live the example of Jesus. Our understanding of that purpose does not come with a warranty to cover neglect; it can be obscured by legalism or fundamentalism which assigns higher priority to "doing" the means than to using and adapting them according to the exigencies of daily life. Our passion communicates the mission's importance for us and its urgency for our world. Fidelity to that mission animates and sustains our efforts, so ministry never becomes maintenance, community never convenience, prayer never performance, and the vows never vacuous. As the mission becomes central to our life, we tap its transforming power and become a sign to others.

Fidelity is undone by passivity, which means our approach to religious life will be neither proactive nor reactive, but inactive. In this case, attentiveness gives way to apathy, planning to procrastination, and competence to compromise. Purpose and passion become too costly to maintain and so are laid aside for less demanding ways to constitute the quality of our life and ministry.

Maintaining purpose and passion is costly. Brothers today are challenged to move into the future without a map of where the journey is leading and without seeing the effects of their efforts. Brothers must live by faith because their lifestyle in the church does not come equipped with whatever clarity, clout, and certainty are usually associated with a definite position on the hierarchical ladder. This lack of definition could diminish a willingness to take risks and move toward the future; however, brothers have used it as a stimulus for creativity. They have continued to search for new ways to continue Jesus' mission. Brothers have transformed a dimension of life which could have weakened their ministerial efforts into a wellspring of apostolic passion. Brothers must live by faith to have a future marked by creativity and passion. The alternative is a programmed certitude which leaves little room for passionate responses to the demands of Jesus' mission.

"Set your hearts on the reign of God." The impetus for fidelity is nothing less than love. Love for the Lord, for one another in community, and for the people to whom we minister are clear expressions of fidelity. This love is vibrant and versatile, ever developing and deepening the mission within our religious life. It is love that will keep our hearts fixed on the reign of God, love that can transform our world into the reign of God.

Way of Living

Attentiveness, planning, competence, decision, fidelity, and the compassion, hope, justice, faith, and love which animate them cannot be limited solely to those activities and attitudes by which we describe our involvement in ministry. The mission of Jesus must touch every dimension of our religious life. The alternative is to approach ministry, prayer, community, and the vows as separate and possibly unrelated elements, presuming they will integrate themselves into a unified way of life.

These aspects of continuing Jesus' mission work together to assure integrity in maintaining the primacy of that mission. Attentiveness assures that neither maintenance nor minimalism displaces mission; compassion activates a response as pressing needs emerge. Planning assures that our response does not drift without aim or effort; hope seeks a direction and directs the search. Competence assures that the appropriate resources are coordinated toward the effectiveness of our response; justice probes until priorities are configured by decision and confirmed by action. Decision assures that action is taken and monitored; faith sustains our efforts. Fidelity assures that our response is attentive to emerging needs; love opens us to the transforming grace by which the possibilities and probabilities of God's reign become inevitabilities.

Continuing Jesus' mission is nuanced by the rich history and heritage of each religious community. The mission does not ignore the diversity which has been born of that richness. Brothers must continue to explore both the common ground in their diverse experiences and the different approaches to life and ministry among their congregations. With the grace and strength of that exploration, brothers can accept the challenges of continuing the mission of Jesus, clarifying their own identity and role within the church and society, and living the pattern of Jesus' life and the promise of new life.

Living the Pattern and the Promise

Religious life is rooted in the mission of Jesus. In continuing that mission through our ministry, prayer, community, and vows, we bear the pattern and the promise of Jesus as a guide and a light along the way. Even more, we are called to live that pattern and promise.

The pattern is clear: "If any want to become my followers, let them deny themselves and take up their cross and follow me" (Mt 16:24). As Jesus was crucified and is risen from the dead, so too will we know the cross and new life through our religious life. Encounters with the cross are inevitable; no life of ministry, prayer, community, and vows can be long without them. We will meet the cross through difficult and distressing situations in ministry, dry and dark periods of prayer, awkward and painful issues and incidents in community, times when the vows seem all conflict and no comfort. The cross will come as we face our own inability or unwillingness to address these experiences.

We will meet the cross. We need not search for it; the cross will come to meet us. We need only embrace it; that action is requisite for discipleship because it is the pattern of Jesus. Embracing the cross also empowers us to support others during their encounters with the cross, through our presence, without pretense or platitude. If we are people of the pattern established by Jesus, then we will be fluent in the language of the cross.

Brothers have felt the probe of this pattern in their congregations and in the church: through a persistent clericalism and hierarchicalism which either dismiss the value of their presence and contribution or simply ignore it altogether; through structures and attitudes which identify and define brothers more by *what they are not* than by *what they are*. More examples could be added from the peculiarities of each congregation. While such experiences have made brothers particularly sensitive and responsive to the oppressed, the forgotten, and the powerless, they also raise a question. How do we continue to work for the church, be hopeful about the church, and even love the church, given our experiences within the church? Brothers must ask and answer the question because the church itself cannot.

The promise is equally clear: "I am the resurrection and the life. Those who believe in me, even though they die, will live, and everyone who lives and believes in me will never die" (Jn 11:25–26). This promise demands faith, for Jesus asks immediately,

"Do you believe this?" If our response is affirmative, then we must live accordingly. We must live that hope which acknowledges the loving presence and activity of God even when observation and perception give us no evidence of them.

This acknowledgement creates the link between the pattern and the promise. It is precisely our encounters with the cross which must be met with hope in God. Such hope is no mean task in and for our world today; despair or devaluation is much more convenient. It is quicker and neater to abandon the situation after some initial efforts, pronouncing it unresponsive and unsalvageable, or to ignore it altogether, claiming it unworthy of any time and energy. The challenge for brothers is to seek and strengthen that hope within themselves, for it may never be offered from without.

Brothers can and will bring many gifts to the world and church of the twenty-first century. Hope will stand among the most significant, for we can bear witness that God has not abandoned creation. Despair and devaluation are not the only ways of responding to situations which have been judged intractable. Hope can explore once again for signs of movement toward change and conversion, encouraging, supporting, guiding. Hope is no fanciful, frivolous thinking without design or direction, but a conviction that the promise of new life can transform all situations. If we are people of Jesus' promise, then we live and proclaim hope in the goodness of humanity, the renovation of our world and church, and the constancy of a God who knows only how to love.

Brothers at Work on the Lord's House

After Jesus cleared the temple, the Jews demanded to know what sign he could possibly give to justify his actions. Stunned by Jesus' reference to a rapid rebuilding project, "the Jews exclaimed, 'This temple has been under construction for forty-six years, and you will raise it up in three days?'" (Jn 2:20). The Jews missed the point, as John comments immediately: "He was speaking about the temple of his body." Given the work involved in maintaining, renovating, and refining the temple, it was no doubt perpetually "under construction," even to the day of its destruction. But Jesus lays the foundation for a new temple, built by love, entered through faith, and sustained in hope. We are the stones for that temple because "in the Lord we are being built together into a dwelling place of God in the Spirit" (Eph 2:22). We are still "under construction."

It would be tempting to have some prefabricated principles to quick-construct a relationship between the mission and the various dimensions of religious life, a model which would be applicable to all situations in all cultures for all needs. But this would be a momentary panacea at best since it fails to recognize that the unfinished business of Jesus' mission is shaped by the context in which it operates. The mission of Jesus takes into account the culture of the people being served, the priority of the needs to be addressed, the practices of the local church and society, and the heritage of the religious community. The presence and activity of brothers in the church and society, enriched by their international and multicultural experiences, give them an insider's knowledge of that culture, priority, practice, and heritage. From that knowledge, brothers have developed a practical wisdom for building a realistic relationship between the mission and their religious life.

The mission of Jesus, like the former and present temples, is always under construction and unfinished precisely because the example and work of Jesus unfold in differing and changing settings throughout our world. The ministry, prayer, community, and vows of religious are touched by those settings insofar as we seek a prophetic presence and activity. The apostolic character of religious life, then, while founded firmly on the mission of Jesus, must have myriad expressions for that attentiveness, planning, competence, decision, and fidelity which shape it. The apostolic character of religious life remains unfinished even as the mission of Jesus itself is unfinished.

"Unless the Lord builds the house, those who build it labor in vain" (Ps 127:1). Undoubtedly, reflection and discussion on the apostolic character of religious life will continue, influenced by the continuing reflection and discussion among brothers on the identity of religious life and by the variety of perspectives on future directions to be taken. The apostolic character of religious life must be more than an academic house built solely by human works and words. The Lord, too, must build that house through our willingness to explore the horizons and challenges which open before us in life and ministry. Together with the Lord, through our attentiveness, planning, competence, decision, and fidelity, we can build a house of compassion, hope, justice, faith, and love.

"Jesus stopped and called to them, 'What do you want me to do for you?'" This question is not likely to become obsolete. Immense needs surround us, their urgency made even more stark by poverty, attitudes toward internal and external refugees, oppressive governments, civil wars, and domestic economic policies, to name a few. The list could be expanded almost indefinitely and each need shouts, like the blind men in the gospel, "Have mercy on us!" We want to respond but we also want to transform these situations. Not easy tasks now and unlikely to become so! For the present and for the future, how will we maintain the priority of Jesus' mission in our life and ministry? How will we reinforce our ability and willingness to ask, "What do you want me to do for you?" For the good of our church and our world, brothers must continue their work on building the Lord's house.

Notes

1. Peter Cotel, SJ, *Catechism of The Vows*, Emile Jombart, SJ and William McCabe, SJ, eds. (New York: Benzinger Brothers, 1945) questions 17, 18.

2. *Code of Canon Law* (Washington, DC: Canon Law Society of America, 1983) Canon 573, §1.

Bibliography

Commission of Superiors General of Lay Institutes of Religious, "Brothers in Lay Religious Institutes" (Rome: Union of Superiors General, June 1991).

Claude Desbron, "L'Eglise et La Mission," *Christus* (Oct. 1992) 156–55F.

"The Consecrated Life and Its Role in the Church and in the World," *Lineamenta* (Vatican City: Libreria Editrice Vaticans, 1992).

David Nygren, CM and Miriam Ukeritis, CSJ, "Future of Religious Orders in the United States, *Origins* 22:15 (Sept. 24, 1992).

David O'Connor, ST., "Seeking a Sense of Direction in a Time of Transition," *Review for Religious* 51:5 (Sept.–Oct. 1992).

Richard Rohr, OFM and Joseph Martos, "Important Virtues in Short Supply," *Human Development* 13:1 (Spring 1992).

Louis Sintas, SJ, "Contemplation et Mission," *Christus* (Oct. 1992) 156–55F.

Joseph Thomas, SJ, "La Mission: un débat," *Christus,* (Oct. 1992) 156–55F.

Patricia F. Walker, OP, "Religious Life in Church Documents," *Review for Religious* 51:42 (July–August 1992).

Brothers in Clerical Institutes: A Hidden Gift

David Werthmann, CSsR

Throughout history the basis of religious community life for men has been a fraternity, that is, a group of persons banded together for a common purpose. In the first centuries of the church, religious life was predominantly a lay movement. Early monks and nuns lived apart from the world for the purpose of contemplation. On the other hand, the purpose of priesthood was evangelizing and providing the sacraments. Thus, in those early times priesthood was considered incompatible with the ascetical nature of religious life. However, from the fifth century on, male religious life gradually became clericalized and lost its nature as a lay movement.[1] Most orders and congregations retained lay members, but as a distinct minority class within their ranks. In more recent times, congregations consisting only of brothers (for example, the Christian Brothers, the Brothers of the Sacred Heart) have appeared for specific ministries, such as teaching.[2]

The universal call to holiness introduced by Vatican II caused church members to reconsider the relationship between clergy, religious, and laity. This, in turn, affected the relationship

---

BROTHER DAVID WERTHMANN, CSsR, is a native of Davenport, Iowa, and has been a Redemptorist for 16 years. He holds a BS in biology (1975) from Marycrest College, and an MAPS with a concentration in spirituality (1990) from The Aquinas Institute of Theology, St. Louis, Missouri. His ministries have included education, parochial ministry, and parish mission preaching. Currently he is part of the novitiate formation team for the western US (vice-)provinces of Redemptorists. He has also served on the national board for the National Assembly of Religious Brothers, and on the international Permanent Commission for Brothers of the Redemptorist Congregation. Brother David may be addressed at 120 North Elizabeth, St. Louis, MO 63135.

between priests and brothers living together in the same community. Although clerical religious congregations have begun to struggle with the renewal of community life, previous attitudes toward their lay members, have, in many cases, impeded a true renewal for brothers. Their image is still that of auxiliary members of institutes centered on ordained ministry.

The premise of this article is that brothers in clerical congregations are not accessories, but must be considered vital to the life of those institutes if those brothers are to maintain their identity. Brothers are a gift to clerical congregations because they connect these institutes with the original roots of religious life as a fraternity. Unfortunately this essential gift of brotherhood is often largely ignored in congregations today.

What follows is a brief historical review of the situation for brothers in clerical communities before and since Vatican Council II. I will then examine differences of approach to the religious vocation between clerical and lay members of the same community. Finally, I will present a vision for the future of clerical religious life as a more faithful brotherhood, with brothers playing a significant role in its development.

Brief Historical Perspective

Before Vatican II religious brothers in all types of clerical institutes led a life distinctive from, and often even totally separated from, the life of the priest members of their order. This arrangement was by design, as can be seen in this brief description of Trappist life in 1960.

> Notwithstanding this wonderful unity of purpose and spirit, there do exist within the monastic family two distinct vocations: the vocation of the Brother Religious and the vocation of the Choir Religious.[3]

Separate Formation Programs

Formation programs for brothers were starkly different from those of clerical candidates. Separate schools were set up for brother candidates, apart from the minor seminary; often the education was inferior. In these schools basic classes in math and the humanities were taught, but significant portions of time were spent on vocational skills such as carpentry, plumbing, and cooking. The young brother was trained to be proficient in the sacristy, the rectory office, and in caring for the upkeep of the house.

Seldom were these schools accredited by an educational agency, and whatever diploma or certificate of completion they awarded was not the equivalent of a typical high school diploma. This formation prepared brothers for only certain types of jobs, usually within the community. These kinds of schools continued to exist through the late 1960s.

Despite their shortcomings, however, these schools provided a deep bondedness among the young men who attended. Brother candidates learned to look out for each other and to pick up the slack so their comrades would not get into trouble. Those who attended such schools developed a true sense of community and continue to maintain a strong sense of fraternity though they now live miles apart, and may strongly disagree on issues.

Distinct Work and Prayer

Because brothers tended to the domestic chores of the house and were not schooled in Latin, they did not participate in the prayer life of the community. In apostolic congregations brothers rose from sleep earlier than the priests and seminarians in order to tend the boilers and prepare the sacristy and altar for Mass. They left morning prayer early to prepare breakfast for the community. In monastic communities the brother religious worked on the farm or in the factory while the choir religious prayed in chapel. Note the following schedule, again from a Trappist monastery in 1960.

> The monk rises from his couch at 2:15 AM to begin Vigils, and a series of other prayers including *Lectio Divina* and Mass. Then a light breakfast of bread and coffee is taken before Prime, which is sung at 6:15. *At this time the brother religious begin their daily work.* Prime is followed by the daily chapter, during which the monks gather to receive spiritual instruction from their Father Abbot. After chapter there is another period of Lectio Divina followed by Tierce and the Conventual High Mass.[4]

Notice that the brothers did not participate in any spiritual activities after breakfast because they were out working.

Later in the day, "manual labor ended at 3:30 PM for the Choir Religious, and at 4:30 for the Brother Religious."[5] In some communities brothers could not join the evening common recreation until all was cleaned up and put away in the kitchen, which meant that even those brothers not assigned to kitchen duty worked in the kitchen to help those who were.[6]

Brothers also had no voice in the governance of the institute. They could never be appointed superior; they could not be elected to a chapter; they had no say in the structure or schedule of their communities. They were virtually voiceless in determining even their own lives.

In apostolic congregations a brother was often assigned to a mission where he was the only member of the community who was not a priest. In some places the separation was taken to such extremes that the brother ate dinner by himself at a small table in the corner of the dining room, with the priests gathered around the main table a few feet away! The brother seldom participated in recreation because the recreation period would be over by the time he finished doing dishes and cleaning the dining room.

Though essential to the smooth operation of the rectory or monastery, brothers were often forgotten and neglected community members. A priest told me the following story. Because he was new to that city he asked the lone brother in the community to go for a ride with him and point out things around town. While on the short excursion the brother began crying. It was the first time in two years that anyone had invited him to go somewhere outside the house.

Whether in contemplative or apostolic settings brothers lived very much a contemplative lifestyle. Their total function in the institute was work and private devotional prayer. Their spiritual lives were sustained by the rosary, stations of the cross, visits to the Blessed Sacrament, meditation, and whatever forms of mental prayer they had learned to practice while working. They did attend daily Mass, but it was usually one of the priests' private Masses offered very early in the morning. Seldom did they participate in the community's solemn High Mass because it took too long and they had other tasks to tend to. Because brothers came to chapel only when they could get away from their chores, and left whenever needed somewhere else, they sat in pews farthest back in chapel so as not to disturb the priests, novices, and seminarians.

In the apostolate, brothers almost always stayed home while the priests went on mission. The only contact brothers had with the public was in the sacristy, at the rectory office window, or possibly while shopping for the house. Even in these limited situations brothers significantly affected those they encountered. Countless priests testify that a sacristan brother was the major influence in their vocation; troubled persons coming to the rectory were greeted by the warmth and compassion of a brother at the door. Yet for the most part brothers were never allowed to move beyond a well-understood position in the community and in ministry.

Separation Legislated

A separation in the sense of apartheid was very real and formally prescribed in typical Rules of clerical congregations.

> Our brothers should keep in mind that they are members of a Clerical Religious Congregation...in such a congregation the Chorists should always have precedence over the lay-brothers. . . . The Rule says, indeed, that all should be uniform in everything, but this should be understood of each in his own rank, that is, of the Fathers amongst themselves, and of the brothers amongst themselves, but not of uniformity between the Fathers and the brothers, because of the difference of state and duties.[7]

The brothers' rank in community was also defined by subliminal regulations. In many orders the brothers' habit differed in color or in length, or was missing some article, such as the mission cross.[8] Many institutes labeled brothers as "coadjutors," a word which means assistants.[9] Even today publications of the Dominican Order refer to "cooperator brothers."[10] These titles seemed (and in groups like the Dominicans continue) to serve as constant reminders that brothers are merely less important helpers in the mission of the institute.

Results of Vatican II

Vatican II brought with it the age of the laity: ordinary lay persons were invited to take their rightful role in the mission of the church, to become involved in most of the ministries previously performed by lay religious. Following shortly on the heels of the

Council was the renewal of religious life based upon the Vatican document, *Perfectae Caritatis,* which called for those who were lay brothers to be "brought into the heart of [the community's] life and activities" (PC 15).

The result was that brothers, without warning, were suddenly thrust into full membership in the life and work of the community, with little or no preparation. Their initial formation had instilled in them a sense that they were not responsible for ministry. Their spirituality advocated staying in the background as a virtue: always assisting the priests and preparing the necessary articles for the priests to carry out the mission of the congregation. With Vatican II, the traditional role of brothers was pulled from under their feet.

Brothers advanced in age and those with little or no higher education were lost. They had never anticipated moving into public ministry, and at this point in their lives, they did not desire to go back to school for pastoral training. Because of their poor educational formation, many, in fact, could not return to school because they did not possess the undergraduate credentials needed to admit them for more studies. Most of these older brothers would have found it necessary to start from the beginning to acquire adequate ministerial skills.

Thus, rather than placing brothers in a position of equality and fraternity with their priest confreres, renewal attempts only reinforced and compounded the low self-image that earlier programs had instilled in them.

A few brothers sought the permanent diaconate as a means of lifting their status in life. But the role of deacon remains unclear in the United States. The newly ordained "deacon-brother" continued to perform auxiliary services only, and found himself in much the same role as before. Though ordained, he was still not "equal" to the priests, and some congregations were uncertain about which category these brothers belonged in. Much vocation confusion ensued.

Unfinished Business from the Past

While many brothers adapted and found niches for themselves in ministry, many others left religious life during those years after the Council. Among those who remain, however, are many who continue to struggle inwardly with anger and bitterness. Though radical in scope, the adaptations never provided sufficient opportunity for them to vent and process their frustrations.

Much passive-aggressive behavior has resulted among brother members of clerical congregations. There is a story of a brother loosening the plug on the oil pan of a priest's car so the slow leak would leave him stranded five miles outside town. A novice related a story of being in line behind an older brother to view the body of a deceased confrere. As the brother approached the casket he made a fist and punched the dead priest in the chest! "My gosh, brother, what's the matter?" the novice exclaimed. "That S.O.B. was the first superior to turn me in to the provincial for something I did!" was brother's response. These stories may be unsettling, but both are incredibly sad when one thinks of the years during which those men suppressed their rage over the injustices done to them for fear they would get into deeper trouble.

I have frequently heard this rebuttal from superiors: "It's not like that anymore. Why do so many brothers hold on to those old attitudes? Why can't they just let go, and move beyond those things?" I believe none of us has any idea of how deeply rooted the pain is, or of where and how it may suddenly show up years later. For example, a brother recently made a proposal to enter a new ministry. He was asked to meet with the provincial team, and he confided to me that he was petrified about the meeting. For him it felt like the old days when once a month each brother was called before the local superior, the house bursar, and the prefect of brothers to be reprimanded for infractions of the Rule incurred during the past month. Often, the charges related to distant incidents the brother no longer remembered. While this brother's meeting with the provincial council was of a totally different nature, past memories were so strong that he felt physically ill in anticipation of it. Provincials and others must realize that powerful feelings, bottled up for years, continue to be very real for these men.

Once I met with a group of brothers to help organize an assembly on "the future." Unfortunately, we could not get to our prepared agenda because they kept bringing up issues from past experiences with their province and its leaders. One brother requested a two-week workshop on how to deal with his anger and bitterness. He said *then* we could begin to think about the future.

Obviously many are heavily weighted with baggage from the past. My greatest frustration in working with brothers has been getting them to take the initiative because they have been conditioned not to have new ideas, and to do only what they have been told. Many brothers find that what their congregation is calling them to today is diametrically opposed to years and years of their earlier experience as religious. Communities and provinces have an obligation to help these men work through their fears and aggressive attitudes of hostility; intentionally or not, it was the previous approaches of the church and congregation which instilled these attitudes about religious life. Such brothers need to be helped to unlearn the old ways so they can grow into the new.

Gift of Brothers to Clerical Institutes

A close friend of mine, a priest and a vocation director, once asked me how to explain the vocation of brothers when he spoke to young people. I asked how he explained the vocation of sisters. He replied, "The sisters' vocation is an end in itself." Dear Father, *so is my vocation as a brother!* Brotherhood is the calling of men to religious life simply for its own sake (brothers have not entered religious life as a stepping stone toward ordination). In fact, this is the real gift brothers offer clerical communities: calling them back to the essence of their vocation as religious.

Discernment in the Call to Religious Life

Many priests in religious congregations genuinely have a vocation to religious community living. But many others did not really discern their earlier decision to enter community. A novitiate classmate of mine admits that he entered our congregation because he had three uncles who were members, and because he had grown up in one of our parishes. He never considered any other form of priesthood. Now ordained, he is convinced of his calling to priesthood, but seriously questions his call to religious life. He is facing a very important question. Two older confreres applied for admission to the diocesan minor seminary years ago, but because the quota for that entrance class was filled, they went to the religious minor seminary because it was the next closest to home. They do not seem to have considered the difference in lifestyle. Another priest I know shared his story. While in high school he became interested in priesthood and wrote to two religious vocation directors. He ended up where he did merely because that vocation director "got him" first. Here again, no discernment regarding the distinct charisms of the two congregations took place. Becoming a priest is apparently all that mattered to these men.

Some years ago I lived and worked with a young priest who was involved in many diverse activities beyond his assigned ministry. He was always on the go, seldom with the community. Not understanding why the superior made such a fuss over his missing community prayer, he frequently complained. When a mutual friend asked my impressions of this man, I replied that I believed he would make a wonderful diocesan priest. Today, in fact, he is incardinating into a diocese. Some might lament that we lost him ("but," they would add, "at least we're not losing him all the way," indicating that remaining a priest is more important than remaining a religious). Indeed, this man is extremely talented, hard-working, and energetic; I rejoice because now he is moving to where he may have belonged in the first place. Clearly he is not called to religious community living.

Brothers and Community Living

Brothers entering clerical congregations generally do not have a common ministerial focus drawing them to this life, as do their priest confreres. As apostolic men we are involved in a variety of ministries determined by our personal talents, and appropriate to our congregation's mission. But the ministries in which we brothers engage can be done equally well by women and men who are not vowed religious. For example, since becoming a brother I have done nothing that I had not already done before I entered: catechesis, liturgical development, youth ministry, public relations, and pastoral counseling. If I were to leave, I have no doubt that I would continue doing the same or similar work. I joined my community not as a means to do these ministries, but because I was attracted by my experience of how the Redemptorists I visited lived together and interacted.

I believe the primary focus in a brother's vocation is not directed toward a particular ministry as much as it is toward community. The value of community living calls brothers, and that binds us together as brothers in a religious family. I believe this attitude is in contrast to many priests for whom religious life is often the vehicle providing a platform for them to perform their ministry. Thus, among brothers I often experience a greater sense of fraternal support for one another because such fraternity is the very reason for our presence as religious brothers.

In our Munich (Germany) province a large community of brothers operates a trade school. It is a community where there are significantly more brothers than priests, perhaps two to one.

A former provincial superior of that province considers it the only Redemptorist community he knows where the men live with a true sense of fraternity. He attributes it to the presence of a greater number of brothers than priests, and has remarked that he wishes every community could be like that one. His comment describes very well the gift brothers bring to clerical congregations of men.

Community as Part of the Charism

For congregations like my own, community life is essential to our mission.

> To fulfill their mission in the Church, Redemptorists perform their missionary work as a community. For apostolic life in common paves the way most effectively for the life of pastoral charity. Therefore, an essential law of life for the members is this: that they live in community and carry out their apostolic work through community.[11]

Our founder wanted us to live and work in community because he believed it would make us better missionaries. Without the element of community life there is a danger of altering the very nature of our mission and how we carry it out.

Anyone involved in ministry can easily get over engrossed in work. Yet I believe that brothers, by the very nature of our vocation, have greater concern for community life than do our ordained confreres. In the old days, brothers were considered to be the ones who made "the house a home," perhaps because they performed the domestic chores around the rectory. Today, it is my experience that brothers are the members of the institute more likely to consistently challenge our way of life, continually calling us to and actively pursuing the building up of community.

Indeed, during my work over the last several years with the Permanent Commission for Brothers of my congregation, it has become surprisingly clear that our general government is looking to us brothers to lead the way in the process of community life renewal. Thus, brothers may be the ones best able to promote an essential charism passed on from the founder himself.

Obstacles to Communal Fraternity

Because brothers have this bent toward community their gift could be used most effectively in community government. However, under present structures this cannot happen. Hierarchicalism in our church prevents brothers from taking leadership roles in their communities. Brothers continue to be denied the opportunity and the right to assume responsibility for the congregations to which they have dedicated their lives. Legislative obstacles prevent brothers from sharing their greatest gift most fully.

Many brothers today have a higher education. More and more of them do have the competencies necessary to actively and fully participate in the mission of the institute and in its governance as called for by *Perfectae Caritatis*. Some may be even better qualified in certain ways than many of their priest confreres. Yet nearly 30 years after Vatican II they continue to encounter arbitrary laws which deny them access to full participation in congregational life.

The Second Vatican Council called for an end to discrimination and separation within religious community. But as long as laws remain which prevent brothers from sharing in the governance of their own congregations, community life will never be what it could be because equality and true brotherhood cannot happen. Priests will not be free to be brothers to their lay brothers in community because they are prohibited from sharing full responsibility with them. Brothers who are truly qualified will never be able to exercise their gifts and share them fully with their congregation. That situation is a tremendous loss to each congregation and to the church.

Future of Religious Community Living for Men

Community living can never take the place of a spouse and family, nor can it fulfill all of one's needs for intimacy and companionship. Yet, it does seem reasonable to expect from one's own confreres a certain level of support in one's ministry, and a concern for how one is doing personally. It also seems reasonable to assume that in choosing community life rather than the single life, one is looking for others to be at home with: people who are not only congenial, but who can provide an opportunity for mutual sharing of dreams and struggles, who can help rekindle depleted spirits, people from whom one can find strength and inspiration in communal prayer, and with whom one looks forward to relaxing while watching the 10:00 PM news.

If these are not reasonable expectations, then why would a young man choose to live in religious community if he can do the same ministry on his own as a lay person or as a diocesan priest?

As renewal continues it seems that religious life is growing more sensitive in these areas. From years of working in formation ministry I conclude that young men entering today are in search of such supportive qualities in community. Perhaps a contributing factor to the exodus of so many young persons during periods of initial formation and temporary profession is that they do not find these characteristics in the apostolic communities where they live.

The struggle for community renewal shows a definite trend toward deinstitutionalizing community life. Smaller overall numbers are bringing about smaller local communities. Congregations and provinces seem less concerned about placing personnel to maintain the smooth operation of large institutions because lay persons can be hired for the same positions.

Women religious are far ahead of men in this regard, and especially ahead of clerical congregations. Because of the current need for sacramental ministers, clerical communities are frequently caught in parochial commitments to bishops, and are trapped by the need to assign x number of men to operate the parishes they staff.

Where deinstitutionalization has occurred, intentional or covenant communities have appeared. These have succeeded to greater or lesser degrees depending on the situation and on the criteria used for measuring success. The real advantage of these types of communities is the opportunity for community development along with support for the personal growth of each member while continuing to function in suitable ministries.

What Needs to Happen

Religious authority today is becoming more concerned with discernment: the winds of the Spirit in the personal life of individuals, the best use of their talents, and the needs of the congregation.

The call heard by brothers is not identical to the call heard by priests even within the same religious congregation. Clearly, the gifts and duties of brothers differ from those of priests. Yet, as men, religious brothers maintain a leadership role within the Christian community. Up to now that role has usually been defined in relation to the clergy.

But brothers have a relationship to the laity as well. Thus, brothers in clerical congregations need to explore this relationship apart from the clergy in order to discover their place in the church. Provinces must not merely attempt to fit brothers into positions traditionally held by priests. The church does not need quasi-clerics functioning only where sacramental ministry is unnecessary. Rather, brothers must be allowed to claim for themselves the mission of their congregation through forms of public ministry that belong uniquely to them.

To do this, it may be important to allow some brothers to live independently from their priest confreres for awhile (in a local community consisting only of brothers). This situation will allow them to define their identity as ministers in their own right—not in the shadows of, or dependent upon, the work of their priest confreres.

Because positions of authority in clerical congregations are always filled by priests, any creative possibilities for carrying out the work of the institute tend to be viewed solely through cleric's eyes. The vision may be valid, but priests often have only their own point of view. If allowed to, I believe brothers can demonstrate to their congregations totally new ways of fulfilling, *yet being faithful to,* the mission of their institute. By unleashing the potential of their brothers, provinces and congregations may find the results expanding the outreach of their mission, enriching the whole province, and lifting morale, especially among brothers.

Modern methods of personal discernment place great responsibility on the brother to participate in the mission of the institute to which he belongs. However, if individuals are not allowed to share their unique gifts by branching out into new ventures and developing alternative forms of ministry, I fear that many young brothers will quickly become disillusioned and leave the community.

Signs of the Times

Religious life has always existed as a prophetic response to soci-ety's needs at a particular time. Today's world is full of broken re-lationships; physical, emotional, and sexual abuse; political strife and war. Certainly among the greatest needs in contemporary so-ciety is the witness of people coming together in community, liv-ing a shared faith, supporting one another's personal growth and well-being, working side by side in relative peace and harmony, growing closer to each other as brothers and sisters, and closer to the Lord. Such a lifestyle cannot help but overflow through each person's apostolic endeavors into the surrounding community.

As we move into the future I believe that for religious life to have significance in the world it will have to rely on the quality of its community witness, regardless of ministry. I envision male religious life of the future, even in clerical institutes, as more of a true brotherhood than merely a band of priests. Likewise, I be-lieve that the attraction of candidates to our congregations will depend on how well we live our lives together.

This will probably require a radical shift for most clerical apostolic communities. Until Vatican II religious and secular cler-gy in the United States did not differ much. Those entering reli-gious priesthood in many congregations probably expected to do much the same kind of work as their diocesan counterparts for most of their lives. No doubt a shifting emphasis among religious highlighting lifestyle will have an impact on the way communi-ties live and minister in years to come.

I hope smaller, more person-oriented forms of community living will continue to develop, and become vibrant centers of spirituality and ministry within traditional clerical apostolic in-stitutes. As this occurs, brother members of those institutes will be able to model supportive fraternal living for priest confreres, incoming seminarians and candidates, and all the people of God.

Conclusion

Before the renewal of community life began, brothers in clerical congregations often lived on the margins of their congregations. Today's renewal has still not achieved for brothers what many had hoped for. External adaptation does not automatically renew age-old mentalities and practices. A recent document from my congregation admits this fact. Referring to the attitude toward equal treatment of members not called to the presbyterate, the document states, "When one looks at the history and tradition of our congregation we are convinced that we Redemptorists need a fundamental conversion in this matter."[12]

Part of the reason for this failure in renewal is because of widely held attitudes from prior days among both brothers and clerics that have not been adequately dealt with; part of it is church law prohibiting full participation of some members in the institute; and part of it is due to the fact that brothers constitute a minority among the membership of clerical congregations, tending to get lost or remain hidden.

Yet, ironically, brothers potentially bring one of the greatest gifts to their congregations by connecting them with the original roots of religious life, and by living today most clearly the call to fraternity, the basis of religious community. Unfortunately, this gift and the men who manifest it are not always appreciated. They and their needs are often ignored.

If clerical religious congregations are to adapt and move successfully into the future, can this gift lie hidden any longer? Young people are reluctant to make life commitments because they see broken relationships everywhere around them. Well-lived brotherhood in religious life among clerics, between clerics and lay members, between vowed religious and laity, may be a model that draws people, giving them confidence enough to commit their lives to a community and its mission.

Preaching and sacramental ministry may always be the central focus of the mission of clerical congregations. But in answer to the needs of today's society, *community itself* must become part of the mission of every apostolic congregation. Here is where the gift brothers bring, if it is recognized, can be used most effectively. The example of brothers relating to others can become an inspiration for clerical congregations, serving as the model for true community-building within the broader mission of each institute.

Notes

1. Sandra M. Schneiders, IHM, "Reflections on the History of Religious Life and Contemporary Development," in Carol Quigley, IHM, ed., *Turning Points in Religious Life* (Wilmington, DE: Michael Glazier, 1987) 26–29.

2. Ibid., 34.

3. *Our Lady of the Assumption Trappist-Cistercian Abbey* (Ava, MO: Privately printed, 1960).

4. Ibid.

5. Ibid.

6. *The Constitutions and Rules of the Congregation of Priests under the title of the Most Holy Redeemer,* Constitution 1, "Of the Hours of Recreation" (London: St. Mary's, Clapham, 1939) 270.

7. Ibid., Part 5. "Of the Lay-Brothers," 394.

8. Ibid., Part 5. "Of the Clothing of our Religious," 154.

9. *The Random House Dictionary,* concise ed. (1980), see "coadjutor."

10. Michael Monshau, OP, ed., "The Cooperator Brothers," in *U.S. Dominican* 8:3, 1–12.

11. Constitution 21: "The Apostolic Community," *Constitutions and Statutes* (Rome: Congregation of the Most Holy Redeemer, 1982).

12. Superior General, Communicanda 11, *The Redemptorist Apostolic Community: Itself a Prophetic and Liberating Proclamation of the Gospel* (Rome: Congregation of the Most Holy Redeemer, Dec. 25, 1988) 12.

Obedience, Poverty, and Chastity: A Revitalized View

Brian Henderson, FSC

To many today, the vows of obedience, poverty, and chastity are an enigma. Some wonder whether these vows continue to have relevance for the modern world—particularly for religious brothers and sisters. Some religious conceive the vows as negative and archaic institutions that deaden the experience of life and discourage new vocations. Some outside of religious life wonder whether modern religious actually pay any attention to these vows. A question raised by many in and out of religious communities is whether the three traditional vows contribute to the advancement of the Kingdom of God in our world today. In light of this question, some feel that the vows should either be changed

---

BROTHER BRIAN HENDERSON, FSC, a De La Salle Christian Brother, is a native of Philadelphia, Pennsylvania, and presently lives and works in Baltimore, Maryland. He joined the Christian Brothers in 1979 and made his final profession in 1987. He has a Bachelor of Arts degree in Religion and Psychology and a Master of Arts degree in Pastoral Studies from La Salle University in Philadelphia. He is currently pursuing a Master's degree in Administration as part of a special Catholic School Leadership Program at Loyola College in Baltimore, Maryland. Brother Brian taught high school religion in Philadelphia and Baltimore, and served as a child care worker and summer group home supervisor for court-referred youth. He currently works at St. Frances Academy in Baltimore, conducted by the Oblate Sisters of Providence. St. Frances is an inner-city high school and the oldest African-American Catholic school in the United States. In addition to his work as Dean of Students, Religion Department Chairperson, and religion teacher, Brother Brian also assists in preparing candidates for Confirmation at a local parish and conducts RCIA preparation sessions for adults. Brother Brian may be addressed at 1003 Brentwood Avenue, Baltimore, MD 21202.

and adapted, or replaced in such a way that they better address the experience of modern religious life. Finally, there are also those who maintain that the vows should be eliminated altogether.

For my part, I believe there is both a need and a role for the vows of obedience, poverty, and chastity in today's world. All too often, we lack a sense of obedience that calls for our response to global needs; we lack a sense of poverty that calls for our sacrifice and sharing in such a way that survival is possible for all people at all times while human rights and dignity are respected; and we lack a sense of chastity that calls for our respect and nurturing of human life and all that supports it. To counter this situation, our world needs prophets who will help others become more responsible in caring for this world and its people. As modern religious, we are invited by God, through our vows, to be the prophets that our world so desperately needs today. With this fact in mind, I believe the vows do have relevance for the modern world and for us as modern religious. However, we religious must face both the challenge and the responsibility of revitalizing the meaning of our vows so that they do, in fact, enable us to speak as prophets called by God.

The definitions of the vows have suffered the vicissitudes of time. They have become rigid and even deteriorated into meanings that do not speak prophetically to the world today. Our congregations often fail to provide a more dynamic prophetic voice because we bicker and fight over, as well as hide behind, old definitions and understandings. We indulge in lifeless conversation about lifeless understandings of the vows and thus breathe death instead of fresh life into our religious lives and into our world. As individuals and as communities, we must become a prophetic challenge to our world. But first, we must commit ourselves to examining our own way of perceiving and living out our vows and revitalize them for the future.

In this article I hope simply to pose some of my thoughts about the vows of obedience, poverty, and chastity as I have come to understand them in my life as a brother. I will comment on what I consider to be dated and limiting views of the vows that render them less prophetic than they can and ought to be. Finally, I will offer thoughts on what I consider to be a more vital sense of obedience, poverty, and chastity. My hope is that this article will stimulate reflection upon and discussion about our vows so that we keep their importance and relevance foremost in our minds, and their impact prophetic.

Obedience

What comes to your mind when talking about the vow of obedience? Many conversations among religious revolve principally around questions of what a superior may tell me to do, or about who failed to do what they were told by a superior. Prior to Vatican II, we know, the burden of discernment, decision-making, and responsibility in religious orders was placed squarely on the shoulders of superiors, with little input from the membership. The superior was seen as the channel of God's will on earth. Given the declining number of religious and the increasing complexities of the world's needs, however, this model places too much pressure and too many expectations upon the few who are chosen to lead in our congregations. At the same time, sadly, many competent people are not selected for leadership positions.

Blind obedience was a practice frequently attached to this vow. Other points of view, dialogue, or creative analysis by community members were often seen as violations of obedience. The only point of view to be questioned was my own. Instead of thinking or reflecting, one simply did what one was told—blindly. While these practices may have been appropriate in an earlier age, Vatican II and the present cultural climate call for a new view.

The problem I see with earlier styles of obedience has nothing to do with confidence and trust in leadership, but with how they conveniently provided us with a means of relinquishing responsibility for our own lives and avoiding the contribution each of us needs to make as members of a religious community. We can also hide behind notions of blind obedience as a way of evading the call to be prophetic and truly obedient to God and God's will.

Revitalizing the Approach to Obedience

I believe we should consider obedience in two basic ways. The first consideration involves doing what the word obedience means—to listen; the second consideration directs this ongoing listening specifically to our baptismal call. At baptism, each of us was consecrated to God. We in religious congregations can ordinarily trace how our particular responses to our baptismal consecration have led us to religious community life in a particular congregation.

Since we are consecrated to God at baptism, we are also consecrated to do God's work and will. Clearly, the work of God is to be stewards of creation, not spectators. We are all called to be stewards: of ourselves, our fellow human beings, and the earth (which needs to be sustained since it sustains us). Obedience, as a vow to God, is not a vow to a community but a vow in a community, since it is in a community that we make our own personal obedient response to God.

Thus, obedience means accepting God's gifts to me and accepting the responsibility to use these gifts in coordination with others in stewardship of God's creation. Obedience leads me to prayer where I grapple with and discern, as far as I am able, the will of God for my life. Obedience requires me to be about the work of knowing myself, knowing what I have to contribute, and contributing as best I can. Therefore, I must develop my ability to listen to the realities of the world, to the members of my congregation, to the church, and to the Gospels. While I am listening, however, I am also challenged every day to ready myself to respond and contribute to the world, to my congregation, and to the church. Obedience is not for the blind. I should not be waiting for something to happen, or to be told what to do. Obedience directs me to *make something happen*. We would not revere the apostles if all they did was *listen* to Jesus. Rather, we revere them because they listened to Jesus' teachings, watched his ministry unfold, witnessed his death and resurrection, and eventually chose a course of action for themselves that responded to the world and to their consecration to God. We, like the apostles, must take what we have seen and heard in the Gospels and do something with it in the present world because, "truly obedient people are not submissive, they are powerful."[1] A serious response to obedience leaves no room for me to say, "There is nothing I can do," or "I have nothing to say." True obedience is strongly opposed to passivity. What true obedience demands of every member of a congregation is active and positive participation in the community's mission. This also means that everyone must be involved in the community's prayer, faith-sharing, and dialogue. Apathy is unacceptable!

Mere compliance to directives from superiors without reflection and thought contributes little to the development of my sense of obedience to God's will. I did not enter religious life to be told what to do. Rather, I am called to open myself to be inspired to do what is necessary to follow God's will. My vow of obedience as a brother enables me to discern the will of God in my life through the support of, and working with, men of similar values and faith. My brothers enable me to discover and take responsibility for what I can contribute. Make no mistake, I have no problem with following through on a decision made by my superiors. But at the same time I cannot let my gift and my ability to think and contribute deteriorate through disuse! When I abdicate my responsibility to consider and reflect upon the will of God for me and my religious congregation, I let the gift of myself atrophy, and in turn I let my congregation atrophy. This, in my opinion, is the ultimate violation of the vow of obedience. Rather, obedience must always be seen as a call for me to listen and respond with creativity and vitality to God's will in my life.

Superiors should not be left to make decisions alone while the rest of the membership critique the superior's decision as spectators. Obedience means that everyone in a congregation must take responsibility for considering the position of others, making their own positions known, and being accountable for decisions made. In addition, even after decisions have been made, we must further realize that the vow of obedience directs us to listen unceasingly for the continual movement of God's spirit in our lives. No decision we make can really be final; it can only direct us, God willing, to listen more attentively and understand more deeply the will of God.

Thus obedience requires me to be responsible as a consecrated person to God and to those with whom I commit my life to God. Through their support of me and my support of them we mutually strengthen our vow of obedience to God. Obedience is a constant search for God's will both in my life as an individual and in our lives together as a community. No one can tell me God's will: I must experience it for myself. However, I am directed toward God's will through the mediation of others, just as I myself am a mediator of that same will to others. In the end, we must all strive to listen, not to each other, but to God through each other. In short,

> obedience . . . has nothing to do with the selfishness and passivity of people who submit to everyone in order to avoid having to think or make decisions of their own. Obedience is the greatest free decision one makes for God.[2]

Poverty

What comes to your mind when talking about the vow of poverty? Much of the time, our focus seems to settle on comparing the material possessions of one over another. True, we must be careful not to accumulate possessions just to have them, especially since our culture often seems to equate goodness and success with the amount one possesses. But there is more to be considered when talking about poverty.

On the one hand, sharing and giving of self on a consistent basis is often considered impractical and foolish in our society. When natural disasters occur, people's response in sending relief funds and volunteering themselves to aid the victims is initially very generous. However, this attitude usually lasts for a short period of time. When it comes to the long-term sacrifice necessary for transforming our social structures and our way of life so that all people are guaranteed their human rights and dignity and access to what they need for survival, the generosity is not so great. Granted, volunteerism may be on the rise and response to short-term need greater than ever, but so too are the number of people who are victimized by systemic greed. One has only to look at the rising number of homeless and families below the poverty level as examples of how our long-term sacrifice and sharing fall short of what is needed.

On the other hand, we can become obsessed with the concept of giving away by renouncing everything, including the very world we are called to change through our involvement in it. Some religious seem to give up their very selves as human beings, which prevents them from using their gifts for the service of others. If not careful, we can spend more time renouncing the world and ourselves instead of transforming the world and ourselves for God. Some religious even abandon their individuality and responsibility in the name of community.

A consideration of the vow of poverty raises several hard questions: How often do we spend time being suspicious of those who think, look, act, and pray differently from the way we do rather than coming to know, understand, and celebrate the vitality that individual differences can bring to our community? How many of us become arrogant and pretentious about our own individuality and, in the process, become impossible to live with? How many of us give of ourselves in the apostolate or community in order to compete for the "prize" of working in the most politically correct apostolate or being the most perfect religious? How many of us become sanctimonious hoarders of self-righteousness while condemning others? We violate the spirit of poverty when we become possessed by our own individual views of what it means to be religious or part of an apostolic work while we miss opportunities to consider the contributions and views of others.

The principal breach of the spirit and vow of poverty is the abuse of power through our desire to seize and hoard it. People, corporations, and governments use possessions to gain prestige, notoriety, and self-gratification as well as to intimidate and control others. People cling to certain ideologies and resist considering other people's thoughts and opinions in order to make themselves more powerful and influential. Poverty is not so much a matter of what we have, but what we are prepared to do with what we have for the sake of others. This is the everyday struggle in which we must engage as religious.

Consider the gospel story of Jesus and the rich young man. The man asked Jesus questions for which he already knew the answers, attempting to justify his righteousness in the eyes of the audience. In this way, he probably felt he could prove his greatness, his righteousness, his agenda, and his self-assurance. But when Jesus challenged him to act by giving up his possessions for the poor, exposing the shallowness of his self-righteous rhetoric, the man could not do it. Why? Perhaps he was protecting himself with his material and intellectual possessions. He could not deal with being less powerful, less esteemed, and thus in God's eyes, on equal footing with those who had no possessions with which to protect themselves. He could not deal with being vulnerable to God's will because to do so meant he could no longer be self-assured and self-justified by his own agenda. The man was not prepared to be individually less powerful, and so he could not offer what he had for the good of others. He could not join Jesus and his followers to struggle with them as one of them. Rather, he wanted Jesus to give him answers that would serve his own ends. He could not deal with the question, "What does God require of me today?"

Yet this is the most critical question to be considered relative to the true spirit of poverty: "What do you, Lord, require of me today?" This question takes us far beyond self-denial or comparisons of each other's possessions. It challenges us to answer the question that the rich man could not: "How will I give away everything I have today?"

Revitalizing the Approach to Poverty

The vow of poverty embodies a paradoxical reality. Poverty is not in and of itself a good. Yet, unless I empty myself for the sake of God's will, I can accomplish nothing. True poverty is not what I do or do not have. Poverty is a way of life. As I suggested earlier, we are not obedient simply by doing what a superior tells us to do, but in discovering what God requires of us. It is the same with poverty. We are not called to give away for the sake of giving. We are called to give away in order to listen better to the movement of God's spirit directing us when, where, and how to give of ourselves openly and generously. In this way our poverty becomes a way of life. Contributing money or material possessions to charities or episodic disasters is good, but it is not a way of life. It is not enough. What we have must be the means through which we give ourselves away for God's sake. By living poverty, we come in contact with God more intimately, and so we become identified not with what we give away, but by our way of life, our openness, our generosity, and our humanness to others.

Poverty is not an end in itself, but a way for us to respond to our baptismal consecration to God, which is our true end. God has given each of us different gifts, not to keep them for ourselves but to use them to transform the world according to God's will. Therefore, I need not cling to what I have, whether it be material possessions or accomplishments or prestige or ideologies. I must open myself to the possibilities of God's will. In the end, poverty requires me to be available and vulnerable to others, and this is the difficult part of the vow.

Often we use what we have as a way of holding others off. If my education, my health care benefits, or my opportunities to travel lead to self-gratification, I violate the principle of poverty because I use these gifts to separate myself from others. However, if what I have serves as a means for me to offer more of myself to others and to connect with them more intimately, then I direct myself toward fulfilling my consecration to God. In my experience, people do not begrudge me what I have so long as I make a genuine effort to give of myself for their sake. When I do not give of myself, my possessions, my attitudes, my intellect, and all I do become ways of separating me from the people with whom I live, work, and serve, and through whom I am called to meet God.

I do not believe that those who are poor in any way want more poor people. Rather, they need people who will give perhaps money and possessions, but what is more important, time, energy, love—humanness. So we look upon our humanness, abilities, and talents as gifts to be cared for, and we search daily for opportunities to share them with others, to enable everyone in the struggle to discover and follow God's will. Thus, the question is not a matter of whether we put ourselves at the disposal of other people. Rather, have we put ourselves at the disposal of our baptismal consecration to God through sharing ourselves with others? One of the most challenging aspects of the vow of poverty is that it continually urges me to abandon my agenda in favor of God's agenda, and to give of my total self every day.

Poverty also brings me to see that what I possess is really not much and of little value on its own. I come to understand that I do not have that much power by myself, and so I must connect with others in order to be effective. I become powerful when I recognize my powerlessness and my need for others to share what little they have with my little bit. The poor, for example, can teach us a great deal if we relinquish our know-it-all attitudes, if we open ourselves to the beauty of each person we meet, if we empower others out of respect for their humanness, if we see them as co-stewards of God's creation. True poverty abolishes the question: "What am I going to get out of this when I give of myself?" Rather, it asks: "Is this the right thing to do to affirm the life of my brother or sister in God's world?" So, I seek to offer what I have as something that will become a beautiful gift when connected with others.

The point of poverty, then, is that it directs me to empty myself of the importance of my own humanly-constructed values, such as my material possessions and my life agendas, in order to be directed toward and by the will of God as experienced in the world around me. Poverty offers me a chance to be freed from blindness by my agenda of being perfect in community or perfect in my renunciation of myself and the world. Rather, true poverty opens my eyes to the beauty of God in each individual, in each community, and in the world in which all communities live and share.

If we seek to live in true poverty, we should experience a measure of tension or discomfort within us over whether we have really put ourselves at the disposal of our baptismal consecration to God; whether we are using our possessions to hold people off or below ourselves; or whether we are hiding from God's will behind our material and intellectual possessions and personal agendas. Poverty is the struggle to make our best selves available to others, both in our religious communities and to those outside our communities who are in need.

We should look upon our possessions as farmers look upon their equipment. In order to grow a rich harvest, farmers do not use their tools haphazardly. Rather, they take care of their equipment and use it to enhance their skill as farmers and to increase the yield of their crops. Farmers also understand that their harvest is not only for their benefit, but for the benefit of others as well. Therefore, the care of their tools and equipment affects not only themselves, but others who depend on their harvest.

We need to look upon our possessions and abilities as tools and equipment that God has given us. Like the farmer, we must take care of our possessions and abilities. We must also know and understand how to utilize what we have to enhance our skill as caretakers of God's creation. Poverty reminds us that our possessions and abilities are not just for our own benefit, but the benefit of others as well. Therefore, we must use our possessions and abilities in doing God's work rather than our own.

Since poverty is not only a giving of our possessions but includes the giving of our very selves, it also challenges us to take risks. The vow of poverty is challenging because living it can truly cost me my life. Like Jesus, I am not interested in losing my life, yet the price of poverty could end up costing me that much. The true spirit of poverty urges me to be so dispossessed as to allow God's spirit to control my life, to bring me to give it away every day as far as I am able and as God requires of me, even if my very existence must be given up for another's sake. What greater love is there? In short,

> Our poverty calls us to a radical sharing of all that we are and all that we have, so that we may produce a quality of community life that makes people stop and wonder. When the world sees that all our efforts are directed, not to personal aggrandizement, but to the support and strengthening of our life in Christ, then we may be seen as "world stoppers," questioning the futile values that the world creates when it makes a god of personal success and material values.[3]

Chastity

What comes to your mind when talking about the vow of chastity? For many the answer is no sex. Chastity is often reduced to a simple-minded, narrow, and anemic view of sexuality that is concerned with whether or not an individual is abstaining from physical sexual activity. In numerous ways, our culture spoils the true beauty and power of chastity. Virginity is perceived as a social disorder rather than a responsible decision, and abstinence becomes unthinkable for any red-blooded human being. Commitment to a person or people is deemed foolish. Respect for men and women, heterosexuals and homosexuals, adults and children, the unborn and people of differing races and creeds are after-thoughts, if thought of at all. The scope and thoughtlessness of individual physical and psychological violence, the brutal efficiency of one group of people feeling justified in oppressing, starving, raping, and murdering another group of people are all examples of chastity being ignored in our world. For many today, other humans are merely objects for pleasure and control. At times, our culture seems to behave as if it simply does not know what sanctity of life means.

In religious life, the vow of chastity has suffered from both narrow definitions and poor understanding, thus keeping its powerful message from our culture. Many men and women in religious life seem to lose their humanness in the name of chastity. They understand the vow to mean doing without sex and not giving in to the ways of the flesh. Hence, chastity involves a series of taboos that includes keeping modesty of the eyes, avoiding particular friendships, suppressing emotions, and rarely speaking about or pursuing healthy relationships. Intimacy is never discussed, as if the mere mention of it might lead to uncontrolled sexual desires. Both in and out of religious life, people assume that as a consequence of the vow of chastity, religious brothers and sisters know little, if anything, about sexuality and relationships, as if they have somehow ceased to be human beings. What ends up being renounced through the vow of chastity is the manhood and womanhood of the religious who, in the process, lose their ability to appreciate and value their humanity as an instrument of God's love.

Worsening the problem are religious who live as if they are no longer human, but different or better than others. I speak of religious who strive for self-righteous piety and holiness to the point of forgetting who they are as human beings. Along with the loss of their humanity, these religious also lose their ability to critique the world because they no longer see themselves as part of it. Some male religious are so consumed by loneliness, they have become unhappy bachelors, contributing little vitality to the community. If we are not careful, we religious can lose our sense of consecration to God and behave more like robots devoid of emotion, insensitive and incapable of experiencing God's love, let alone sharing it with others. Instead of becoming homes of fraternal charity and concern, communities become battle zones of "back-biting conversations, deep divisions among confreres, carelessness about prayer, and a lazy living off the hard work of the rest of the community."[4] This leaves us with embittered religious in community houses chilled by selfishness and hurt rather than warmed by fraternal concern and charity.

Much work has to be done to create a truer and fuller sense of chastity. It is necessary for our future as religious that we rediscover what it means to be a human being and to celebrate this reality. We will never contribute to the creation of God's kingdom if we forget and forsake who we are—human beings who, though broken and imperfect, are yet lovable and capable.

Revitalizing the Approach to Chastity

Chastity is a way of life I choose that both directs and binds me to my consecration to God. Living the vow of chastity is not merely a matter of doing without sexual intimacy or without a family. Nor is it, as some suggest, a way of escaping from an inability to perform sexually, dealing with one's sexual identity, or uncomfortable relationships. I am chaste in my life as a brother because through chastity I experience God's love and will in my regard more clearly.

For me, chastity is about faithfulness and fidelity to being life-affirming. It is "a universal vocation to a wholeness of life and love."[5] This is why it is important that we do not allow people or ourselves to pigeonhole this vow into narrow and limited views. For example, I think it is important that a clear distinction is made between celibacy and chastity, which are often used synonymously. I think this is incorrect. Celibacy, in my opinion, is an outgrowth of chastity. Chastity encompasses much more than celibacy. I define celibacy as refraining from physical sexual involvement with others. Chastity is the reason for this abstinence, because chastity

> refers to the manner in which one lives one's sexuality. A chaste person is one who has a healthy, holy, loving, and God-directed attitude to the gift of his own and others' sexuality.[6]

The fact that all human beings are called to be chaste is often overlooked nowadays. Everyone is called to have an appropriate respect for one's own sexuality as well as that of others, whether married, single, or religious. We need to recognize the immense power that God has entrusted to each one of us as human beings: the ability to participate in creating and nurturing life. In their shortsightedness, some fail to recognize the creative and nurturing roles of men and women religious. Though we do not engage in the physical intercourse that initiates the conception of human beings, we do participate in the creation and nurturing of the human mind and soul. Our chastity, lived through the practice of celibacy, is our way of life that directs its focus on and to the love of God. Therefore chastity needs to be freed from the perception of being a vow that sacrifices physical sexual contact to human companionship and procreation.

In a world given to the pursuit of pleasure, and with so much emphasis on the negative value of chastity, it is not surprising that people often think religious life is designed to be miserable. Chastity needs to be seen as a yes to certain types of healthy relationships and yes to God's love that breaks into human experience in new and unexpected ways. I believe religious do have much to say about sexuality, relationships, emotions, intimacy, and love. We present important aspects of and viewpoints to these human experiences that are currently and frequently ignored or debased in our society. Our challenge is to stop ignoring these aspects in our individual and communal religious lives so that we can provide society with a more dynamic prophetic voice.

For this reason, we must examine seriously and carefully the quality of our lives together. How can we expect to transform our world into the harmony that God intends unless we establish that harmony within our religious communities and congregations? Chastity calls us to accept and love all of God's works, yet we easily slip into being hateful or uncharitable to members of our own communities. That God loves us with unconditional love is a basic tenet of our faith. If we are truly consecrated to God, then we must love others with the same love that God extends to us. This is not an easy thing to do when we live with people who frustrate or infuriate us, yet this is the substance of our vow. Chastity draws us to community despite our many differences; it disallows bachelor lives that disconnect individuals physically, emotionally, and spiritually from the community.

We do not choose each other as religious or community members, rather God chooses us to be together. Chastity demands that I relinquish my personal agendas, wants, and desires enough to be able to love the person in front of me even though, and especially when, that other person has a different view or style from mine. Chastity is a powerful "Yes!" to life that enables me to engage in the struggle against sin's lifelessness in ways different from those who live chastity through married or single life. Chastity directs me to trust in the providence of God, not myself. So radical is chastity in religious life that it directs me to be particularly attentive to those I deem strangers, those who are different from me, whether I meet them in or outside of community.

The difficulties that I experience as a result of chastity are not occasions to focus on what is wrong with my life, but opportunities to see where God is leading me. God has led me to many unique relationships as a brother and the key to them is the faithful belief that God is working through these relationships. Not only is it difficult, it is nearly impossible to explain logically why I am a brother. But because of my faith in my relationship with God, I have no other choice to make. I am more intimately in touch with God through the relationships that I am responsible to as a brother, both inside and outside of my community. Chastity leads me to be happy and content in living obedience and poverty, never seeing these as problems of being a male religious, but opportunities that override the difficulties in living a fuller and deeper life in God's love.

Final Words

In my opinion, the vows of obedience, poverty, and chastity have the potential to speak loudly and clearly to our world. They are relevant to us as religious and to our world because they offer important critiques of the cultures and societies that form our world today. But these vows have to be freed from perceptions that fossilize and corrode their meaning and impact.

As advocates for our church and for our world, we religious are challenged to live a more positive, life-giving, fruitful, wholesome, and powerful sense of what it means to live in God's world. As brothers today, our vows of obedience, poverty, and chastity are important tools in prophetically educating our global society to the value of listening for God's movement in the world, of giving ourselves totally for the world's sake, and of honoring the sacredness of life and all that supports it. We need to move from nostalgically ruminating about the vows to rethinking and reflecting upon their relevance for our lives as religious today.

We must also stop settling for perceptions that permit the vows to be viewed as ancient and foolish practices adhered to by religious fanatics. Rather, we must live the vows as responsible life-affirming choices that can help us to re-create our world into one of true justice and peace. By our vows of obedience, poverty, and chastity we can make the face of God tangible and real in the lives of those with whom we share community, those we meet in the world, and our own.

We need to pay close attention to our vows because they contribute a great deal to advancing the reign of God in a world that cries out in need for the affirmation of life they reveal. Thus, I feel strongly that we need to discuss these vows and retool them within ourselves and in our communities so that we can enter the future as the powerful prophets God calls us to be.

Notes

1. Juliana Casey, IHM, "Toward a Theology of Vows," in *Turning Points in Religious Life,* Carol Quigley, ed. (Westminster, MD: Christian Classics, 1988) 114.

2. Francis Moloney, SDB, *A Life of Promise: Poverty, Chastity, Obedience* (Wilmington, DE: Michael Glazier, 1984) 152.

3. Ibid., 69.

4. Ibid., 113.

5. Ibid., 77.

6. Ibid., 76.

Being a Brother
Is What Brotherhood Is All About

Sean D. Sammon, FMS

"What is a brother?" That frequently asked question has neither a simple nor easy answer. Brothers are often defined by *what they are not* or compared to groups with whom they bear some faint resemblance: no, they do not preside at eucharist nor minister the sacraments; or, yes, while they face unique challenges in their current process of renewal, brothers and women religious do share some common concerns.

These few facts about brothers, however, are certain. They total far fewer in number world wide than either ordained ministers or women religious; since Vatican II they have also suffered greater losses in membership than either of these two groups. Next, brothers number among the church's "invisible people." You still hear some laity, clergy, and other religious talk about the need for more priests and sisters; brothers, if included at all, are often added as an afterthought. Finally, the suspicion continues to exist among some that brothers are men who simply weren't good enough to be something else!

———————

BROTHER SEAN D. SAMMON, FMS, a native of New York City, has been a Marist Brother of the Schools since 1966. He received his BA from Marist College, an MA from the Graduate Faculty of the New School for Social Research, and an MA and PhD in clinical psychology from Fordham University. Brother Sean currently serves his congregation as Provincial of its Poughkeepsie Province; he is also past President of the Conference of Major Superiors of Men (1989–1991). Prior to his current work, he served for several years as International Clinical Director of the House of Affirmation. The author of a number of articles and four books, the most recent of which is entitled *An Undivided Heart: Making Sense of Celibate Chastity* (Alba House), he resides at the Marist Brothers Provincial House in Pelham, New York. Brother Sean may be addressed at 26 First Avenue, Pelham, NY 10803.

All these details, though, still haven't answered the question with which I started. As religious, of course, brothers are called to live fully and radically the gospel plan as the object of their life. Apostolically, they teach and counsel, minister to the sick and dying, administer large and necessary institutions, and serve in a variety of church and secular settings.

Perhaps a proper answer to our query eludes us because we are asking the wrong question. This article will attempt to shed some light on the brother's identity—the *who* rather than the *what*. It will also take a look at how this identity changes over the course of one's life. Early in life, for example, many brothers over-identify with what they *do*. Be they teachers or administrators, doctors or nurses, or parish ministers, the work they carry out appears to mean much more to them than who they are. In contrast, at midlife many of these same men become aware of this fact: I don't have to be a brother to do what I am doing. This realization gives rise to crises of identity and meaning.

To accomplish our task, we will need to understand something about the nature of personal identity and life transitions. We will also want to measure what is written below against our own life experience. As the article concludes, I hope you will agree that brotherhood, more than anything else, is a particular way of being in the world, that it has much more to do with *who* brothers are—men of prayer, mission, and communion—than with *what* they do. Let's begin by taking a look at the issue of identity.

Personal Identity

Personal identity answers the question: "Who am I?" During the adolescent years, for example, everyone is called upon to form some sort of initial adult identity: that feeling of knowing who you are and where you are going. Identity, however, is never purchased cheaply. To achieve one, we must do a few things: explore our options for living; experience confusion and any crises that may follow; and eventually make some choices and commitments.[1]

What are the experiences of exploration, confusion and crisis, choice and commitment like? Consider this simple example. With 25 dollars in your pocket and no more, you set out to buy a shirt. Entering a department store, you spy one that you like;

after examining it, you look at its price tag: 25 dollars. You move on and another attractive shirt catches your eye. Its price? Also 25 dollars. You find still another one, equally attractive; its price: the same as the other two. Since you have only 25 dollars to spend, the more you explore in this store, the greater will be your confusion or crisis of choice. Eventually, though, you will have to choose one shirt from among a number of attractive options. While this choice, and the commitment it entails, will be difficult, you must make it to complete the task you set out to accomplish.

Forming an identity is much the same. We spend time looking at our options for living and exploring various paths in life to follow. Many adolescents find themselves in this dilemma; they experiment, in fantasy, with a variety of careers and relationships. On Monday, for example, a 15-year-old boy plans to be a chemist; by the following week, the field of medicine is more attractive to him.

Confusion and crises follow naturally after exploration. These words refer to those periods of struggle and questioning, throughout the course of life, during which we rethink old roles and life plans. Finally, in forming an identity, a time comes when we must make some choices about the meaning and direction of our life; the word commitment describes our investment in what we have chosen.

The formation of a brother's identity is a complicated matter. Many religious brothers, however, can identify quickly with the process of initial identity formation outlined above. A number of them, for example, came to the brotherhood originally "to try it out," encouraged in this process of exploration by a brother who had taught them in high school or one who served in their parish.

For a few, a magazine article or advertisement about this way of life sparked their interest and moved them to ask for more information. Most of these men, though, were doing little more than exploring; brotherhood was one option among many others.

When a young man announces that he may have a religious vocation, others start to ask questions. Men several years into formation, for example, report that parents and some friends still ask, "Are you happy?" or "Is this really the life for you?" Similar inquiries are rarely directed at their married brothers and sisters.

Today there are also fewer social supports for a vocation to religious life. Much of our society suffers from a plague of individualism; to toy with the idea of surrendering possessions and some freedoms, and to live out one's sexuality in a celibate chaste manner frequently elicits skepticism from others. Even in the absence of these external questions and doubts, most people in religious formation experience considerable confusion as they struggle to become aware of what is in the heart of God for them. Candidates for the brotherhood have never been exempt from this turmoil.

Eventually, an aspirant to religious brotherhood must make some choices about the direction of his life and arrive at a commitment. A failure to choose, to put down roots, interferes with the process of spiritual and psychological growth. There comes a time in the life of every young brother in formation, then, when he must take a chance and move toward initial and final commitments or point his life in another direction.

The early commitments of many young brothers, however, are based on limited information and a shallow understanding about the nature of consecrated life. These men are not alone in this developmental dilemma. Yale psychologist Daniel Levinson points out that most people make major choices about their life before they have enough information to make the best possible decision. If they wait until all the data is in, though, they'll be dead before they do anything![2]

Foreclosing Identity

What about people who skip the exploration and crisis stage of identity formation: those who jump into a life commitment, hoping that it will tell them who they are. These men and women foreclose their identity; the results of this decision are disappointing.

Some people, for example, unsure of their life's purpose or frightened by their sexual impulses, look to marriage, priesthood, or religious life for an answer. They hope that one of these life choices will answer their concerns and allay their fears. It just doesn't work that way. Foreclosing personal identity is like ordering a suit of clothes through the mail; it never fits right! The jacket is a bit too tight, the pants too short. Not tailor-made for the person, the suit looks as though it belongs to someone else. Foreclosed identities appear much the same.

What do foreclosed identities look like? Usually stable, sober, and responsible; they are also somewhat passive, lacking curiosity and a sense of independence. Their relationships with others are often stereotyped: they are more at home relating through a role than person to person.

People who foreclose their identity commit themselves too early. Failing to explore their options for living, they refuse to question their values and goals. Instead, they commit themselves because of external circumstances or to please an authority like parents, or a pastor, or former teacher. They make a dangerous decision; later in life it exacts a cost.

Suppose a religious brother forecloses his identity early in life; does that decision condemn him to years of walking around with hunched shoulders bemoaning the fact that he is a fore-closed identity? Not really. Although it appears, first of all, during the adolescent years, an identity "crisis" can reoccur during any period of life transition.

In the midst of change and transition, we re-evaluate our commitments, explore alterative ways to live out our life, and move toward building a new identity, one that will serve us well during the years ahead. Novelist John Updike's fictional character, Tom Marshfield, for example, began one of his life transitions with this question: Who am I? Searching his face in the mirror, he said, "I do not recognize it as mine. It no more fits my inner light than the shade of a bridge lamp fits its bulb."[3] Many midlife religious brothers identify easily with Marshfield's bewilderment.

During early adulthood, we wonder who we are becoming; later in life we question who we have become. This second task is more difficult for those who foreclosed identity early in life; during times of transition, they are more vulnerable to a crisis of identity. A quick look at life transitions will help us to better understand this notion.

Life Transitions

Transitions are times of disorientation and reorientation that mark the turning points on the path of human and spiritual growth.[4] These special times of change begin with an ending; we sense that a chapter of our life is coming to a close. Although we hope earnestly that a new chapter will get underway immediately, the second stage of any life transition usually finds us feeling a bit lost, up-in-the-air, confused, lonely, and alienated. At times like this, we can be sure of only these facts: we cannot go back to where we came from, and we are not really sure where we are headed. Psychoanalyst Erik Erikson, quoting a text he once saw hanging over a western bar, summarizes our dilemma this way: "I ain't what I ought to be, and I ain't what I'm going to be. But I ain't what I was!"[5]

During the middle phase of any life transition, people often report one or all of four unsettling feelings: disengagement, disenchantment, disorientation, loss of identity. To begin with, they find themselves cut off from familiar people, places, and events. Like the character in Eugene O'Neill's play, *The Iceman Cometh,* they are sitting in life's grandstand, observing more than living. While painful, this separation helps us to better confront ourselves and see our relationships with others and God in a new light. Jesus, after all, went into the desert; there he was tempted by power, wealth, and prestige. After 40 days, he emerged more deeply aware of his future mission.

Next, a number of people complain about disenchantment during a transition's middle phase. This experience begins with the discovery that to change, we must realize a significant part of our old world is not real; it is in our head. Author William Bridges, for example, points out that the noble leader, flawless parent, perfect wife, husband, or community, and utterly trustworthy friend are an inner cast of characters that we need to surrender.[6] One final point: most significant life transitions not only include disenchantment in their middle phase, they begin with it. Does disenchantment have a positive side? Certainly; it helps us mourn those illusions we have about ourselves, our world, and the way it should work. Disenchantment, then, is an important first step in the process of personal and spiritual transformation; it is also a key factor in identity reformulation.

People also lose their familiar roles and self-understandings during the middle phase of any transition. Those healthy roles we lived out in life, the ones that always made sense, no longer do so. We are just not sure who we are anymore.

Finally, during these times of life change, most men and women generally feel disoriented, confused, lost in an unfamiliar world; things that once seemed so important, now no longer matter much. While far from enjoyable, disorientation can be meaningful. Despite its discomfort, this experience helps us become lost enough to find ourselves anew.

Identity Reformulation Over the Course of Life

Have you ever found yourself asking any of the following questions: What am I doing with my life? Is it possible for me to live in a way that best combines my talents, current desires, values, and aspirations? What do I truly get from and give to others? Does anyone really care about me; do I really care about anyone else? Another blunt question summarizes those listed above: If I were to die today, what in my life would be left unlived?

We often ask questions like these when in the midst of life change. During any transition we run through this rather sobering inventory: Where am I going; who am I aside from what I do; do I love anyone; does anyone love me?

What lies at the heart of all these concerns about identity and intimacy? A spiritual question: On whom or what do I set my heart? While it comes to the fore during each period of life change and transition, my age, time in life, and life commitments influence the shape it will take.

Central Elements in Forming a Brother's Identity

As mentioned earlier, young brothers struggle with the same developmental issues as their age mates. After all, most are living through the years of *early adulthood;* these get underway during the late teens and continue until the mid-40s. This period includes some of the most stressful years of life.

The period from the late teens until the mid-thirties makes up a substage of early adulthood often referred to as *novice adulthood*—that time in life when we learn what it means to be an adult.[7] Many of us, however, feel more as if we are impersonating an adult. We know very well that even though we are functioning like an adult, it is only a matter of time before we are found to be impostors!

What is the challenge of these years of novice adulthood? To address four tasks of maturity: developing a dream, mentoring relationships, a ministry or life work, and relationships of intimacy. Let's take a brief look at the dream and mentoring relationships, elements clearly related to our topic.

The Dream

Forming and living out one's dream is an important challenge of novice adulthood. Often vague at first, the dream answers this question: What am I going to do with my life?[8] For those who give it a place in their life, the dream becomes an important motivating influence; those who betray it face later consequences.

A young man, for example, struggles with two possible life directions: one that expresses his dream, another that does not. He can move in the first direction or allow himself to be pushed away from his dream by parents, or external factors such as money or a personality trait or special talent. In betraying his dream, this young man may succeed in life; having lost touch with it, however, his motivation and sense of purpose will die eventually. At midlife, he will have to revisit his early dream and try, once again, to bring his life into line with its spirit.[9]

In his attempt to build a life around his dream, a young man takes advantage of a psychosocial moratorium: he delays his adult commitments. This postponement allows him to experiment with various roles and ways of being in the world and, thus, give greater definition to his dream and ways to live it out.

Some men, however, prematurely terminate their psychosocial moratorium. They commit themselves too early, maintain great continuity with their pre-adult world, and fail to explore new options for living, or to question their values and goals. These men define themselves, their identity, and aspects of their dream too early; they commit themselves because of external circumstances or because authorities commit them.

Evelyn and James Whitehead, a developmental psychologist and theologian respectively, point to another aspect of the dream: our vocation or, put another way, God's dream for us.[10] During novice adulthood we are all called upon to imagine, both psychologically and spiritually, what our life is to be about; discovering what God has in mind for us is an important part of that process.

Vocations, however, are not "once and for all" calls; no, they are lifelong conversations. Fidelity has to entail more than recalling an early invitation; at midlife, for example, I must still be able to believe that God is up to something in my life.[11]

Mentoring Relationships

Mentoring relationships are another important part of novice adulthood. Serving as both parents and peers, mentors provide young people with support and counsel; they are often models by their own achievements and way of life. Who are important mentors? Some spiritual directors, colleagues and friends, teachers, religious superiors, and those people who initiate us into religious life by their example.[12]

How do these developmental tasks of forming a dream and mentoring relationships get lived out in the lives of young religious brothers? For many, their dream is intuitively connected to some of the deeper elements found in a fraternal way of life. Consciously, though, it may be little more than a vague vision; the full realization that brothers are men for whom prayer, mission, and communion are central life elements lies well in the future.

In the absence of good mentoring, many young brothers look for their identity in the work they do. Fresh, energetic, and somewhat self-involved, these young men often throw themselves into their ministry with abandon. In many congregations of teaching brothers, for example, those in temporary profession take on a full load of classes and a number of extracurriculars. Popular with students and encouraged by the community to be involved fully in the institute's work, they quickly overextend themselves. Prayer, time with the community, and a deeper sense of mission take a back seat for the time being; at midlife this picture changes dramatically.

Changes at Midlife

By midlife, most of us can appreciate the wisdom of Oscar Wilde's observation: "The gods have two ways of dealing harshly with us: the first is to deny us our dreams, and the second is to grant them." Midlife is a time for taking stock, for removing rose-colored glasses and calling things by their right names. Dante said it well in *The Divine Comedy*.

> In the middle of the journey of my life, I came to myself within a dark wood where the straight way was lost. Ah, how hard it is to tell of that wood, savage and harsh and dense. The thought of it renews my fears. So bitter is it that death is hardly more.[13]

The challenges of midlife, those years between the early forties and mid-sixties, are many: facing personal mortality; bridg-
ing the gap between early and middle adulthood; trying to pull
together all those disparate parts that make up each of us. Midlife
also brings new roles and is a time for life re-evaluation. Saul Bel-
low's fictional character, Moses Herzog, puts it this way: "Maybe
I am going through a change in outlook." In crossing the line between early and middle adulthood, this midlife man lost his easy
sense of immortality; he knew more clearly than ever before that
he had probably lived more years already than the number that
lay ahead for him. This knowledge made a difference. Moses Herzog realized that he couldn't live someone else's life; the values
and standards that would guide him henceforth had to be his
own.[14]

Many midlife brothers go through a similar change in outlook. Their ministry, once so captivating and a chief source of
their identity, has lost some of its luster. If a man is a teacher, for
example, he is now old enough to be the father of his students;
no longer a contemporary, he finds they relate to him differently
from the way they did just a few years earlier. Another brother,
serving as a member of a parish team, is bored by the routine of
work; living in a difficult community, he longs for some genuine
companionship.

During midlife, religious brothers re-evaluate their early life
dream. They examine the disparity between the person they once
dreamt of becoming and the person they are in fact. Those failing to realize their cherished dreams must come to terms with
their disappointment and settle on new choices around which to
build their lives. Others who realized some of their early hopes
and dreams now need to consider the meaning and value of their
success. With what result? To discover the ways in which they
have neglected or fulfilled the dream in their life.

For those who spent the years of early adulthood becoming
somebody rather than doing something they loved, their victory
now seems hollow and gives rise to these questions: What is the
fate of my youthful dreams? What possibilities exist for change
in the future? During midlife, religious brothers must come to
terms with the past and prepare for the future. In doing so, they
will question virtually every aspect of their life. As in every transition, termination and initiation are essential to this process.

At midlife we also begin to shed some of the illusions we have
about ourselves, others, and the way the world should function,

and put our energies into working on the developmental tasks of the period. About this time, many religious brothers come to realize that without roots in the spiritual life, their life has little meaning.

Consider one who spent most of his early apostolic life involved in a number of distracting activities. Burning the candle at both ends, he forced certain aspects of his life—friends and community, spirituality, leisure time, a deeper understanding of the nature of his brotherhood—into second place. While quite effective in his ministry, his religious life has become little more than functional. Although successful, around midlife this man begins to wonder what he is doing with his life. Questioning the significance of his life and his very self, he finds that both are strangers to him. Solitude, if embraced, will introduce him to these fellow travellers.

The Whiteheads point out that early in life all of us look for ways to "prove ourselves," to have someone or something testify to our identity and worth.[15] Midlife is a time for "finding ourselves." Once we have done so, we discover that there is much less need to prove ourselves. Self-intimacy is the real gift of midlife.

Midlife Elements of a Brother's Identity

Self-knowledge is a key ingredient in the mix we need to grow close to others and to our God. It is also tied up intimately with our sense of identity; the years between the early forties and mid-sixties offer one of life's best opportunities to rediscover ourselves and, in so doing, the meaning and purpose of our life.

At midlife, we all face this question: Can I, will I, take responsibility for nurturing life? In attempting to answer it, religious brothers need a broader self-definition than the work they do. Let us spend a moment examining three key elements—prayer, mission, and community—that start to emerge as brothers in the middle years reformulate their answer to this question: On whom or what do I set my heart?

Men of Prayer

Around age 40 a number of religious brothers feel an increased need to foster their interior life. Even though their way of life should provide them with the structure and time to develop a spiritual life during all the years of adulthood, it is not until midlife that many of them leave the often compulsive, unreflective busyness of their ministries and once more become explorers of the world within.

Their journey homeward to themselves usually begins in their middle years and continues throughout the remainder of life. What sets it in motion? For some, a spiritual awakening; for others, a growing awareness of personal mortality, or a profound experience of change. Regardless of what initiates this passage, making it is essential for every brother who longs to be at home with his chosen way of life.

What is at the heart of mature religious living? Something quite simple: the spiritual life. To be at home with his choice to live out his life as a brother, a man must face what it means to be a spiritual person.

What does it mean to be a spiritual person? A number of things.[16] First of all, recognizing that spiritual awakenings take place during the course of life. When they occur intense spiritual desire emerges, gradually or dramatically, as in a conversion.

Not everyone welcomes a spiritual awakening. Many people are uncomfortable with them and experience fear and anxiety. Everyone's spiritual life has a long history: it begins in childhood, passes through the adolescent and early adult years, and often comes to maturity in midlife and the later years.

At whatever time in life a spiritual awakening comes, however, all of us are faced with this challenge: integrating this new capacity for God into our self-understanding. If we fail to carry out that task, we run the risk of spiritual stagnation.

Second, a spiritual person accepts the fact that God loves each man and woman in a unique and special way. Consequently, everyone's spiritual life is singular. Throughout life many of us are presented with formulas and plans of action that carry with them some guarantee of success in the spiritual life; rather than enhancing our relationship with God, though, many just get in its way. There are as many ways of being a spiritual person as there are people. At midlife, a religious brother's task is to find out just what that means for him. Various spiritualities are only assists; they should not get in the way of his unique relationship with God.

Third, spiritual people know they don't have to do anything to earn God's love. It is given freely. God's love is extravagant: it brought us into being, it sustains us in life, it will bring us home. We can accept or reject God's love, but we do not have to do anything to earn it.

Finally, being a spiritual person means coming to let God love us on God's terms not ours. Jesuit Thomas Green wrote a book several years ago entitled *When the Well Runs Dry*. In it, he talks about the life of prayer; he also suggests that God's way of loving us may be different from human love. If we mistakenly insist that God love us in a human way, we may miss the extraordinary relationship into which God invites each of us.

Let us stretch the image in Green's title to make our point. The water in the well is God's consoling grace. Early in the spiritual life, we are young, energetic, strong; the well also brims with water. It is relatively easy for us to take a bucket and satisfy our spiritual thirst with the cool refreshing water of God's grace.

As we grow older in the spiritual life, however, the water level drops and our earlier strength has diminished some; it is harder to get water from the well. With human effort we can still satisfy ourselves with the water of God's grace, but that task is not so easy as it was years earlier.

The day will come, however, when we have grown to maturity in the spiritual life—we will have prayed long and hard—and the well will run dry. What can we do then to share in God's comforting grace? Nothing. About all we are able to do is to sit and wait for the rain! When any of us reaches this point in the spiritual life, we are ready to allow God to love us as God chooses to love us.

How do most of us respond to this situation? By declaring that we are barren, empty, and living in a wilderness! What a remarkable conclusion; just when God has cleared away the distractions and led us into the desert to speak to our heart, we insist that God has abandoned us.

By midlife, religious brothers come to understand, perhaps better than ever before, how to be men of prayer. Less self-reliant, many report a growing sense of their need to be redeemed. With a growing dependence on God, they are invited to new forms of prayer. For some, it is one that is deeper and free of thoughts and images. What must they do to enter this new form of prayer? Surrender.

Several signs indicate that such an invitation is being extended. Some brothers find that they can no longer actively meditate. For others, prayer is uneventful and arid: consolation is lacking and old forms of prayer are found wanting. Many people describe their experience in these words: "I long for a simple presence before God; I want to be with God, not think about God."

Teresa of Avila apparently faced the same dilemma as many modern-day midlife religious brothers. Her solution was simple. She often said that when she was unable to find words for her prayer, she would go into the chapel and sit before the Blessed Sacrament so that the Lord could look on her with love.

Mature religious living, then, must be rooted in the spiritual life. If a loving relationship with God is not at its heart, it gives trivial witness. Eventually most people wonder just what the lives of those living religious life are all about.

Stop for a moment and consider what has just been said above about the attributes of the religious brother's midlife spirituality. Do you find yourself asking: Doesn't everyone need to become a spiritual person? Absolutely. At midlife, religious brothers bear witness to the fact that a growing spirituality is an essential element in any life lived well. Keep that fact in mind as we consider our next two elements.

Men on Mission

Apostolic religious life brings men and women together for the sake of mission.[17] Brothers are no exception to that rule; they are consecrated and set apart for this new purpose: to continue the mission of the Lord Jesus. Intellect, personal gifts, or superior virtues have little to do with this blessing; only the grace of the Spirit, freely given, can justify it.

Marist Brother Charles Howard points out that consecration implies much more than being available for service.[18] God uses our lives, freely surrendered, to continue the Lord's work. We are called to be brothers to people in the same way that Jesus was; that entails a commitment to all those forms of collaboration, dialogue, and reconciliation that help bring about communion among all men and women.

Midlife brothers, however, face a common challenge in this area: many must struggle to discern God's will for them as they attempt to continue the Lord's mission. Authentic discernment and the vow of obedience are closely related. Mature obedience has little to do with "following orders." Rather, it invites us to develop a listening heart, one that is open to God's will. At midlife, this solicitation takes on new meaning.

Some people talk about a "God of surprises"; many of us, however, are a bit afraid of such a God. We prefer to keep God at arm's length and are more at home with a predictable God, one who will not disturb our well-made plans.

In recent years, for example, the meaning of the word discernment has often been misunderstood. Discernment entails a process of coming to know what is in God's heart for me. If I pray regularly and enjoy intimacy with God, often enough God's desire ends up being my own.

Some of us, however, approach discernment in another way: we make up God's mind to serve our own purpose. For example, asked by our community to take on a new assignment, we promise to pray over the request. In reality, though, we refuse to talk with God about our mixed feelings, our fears, and God's and our heart's desire. Authentic discernment demands that I risk intimacy with God, a closeness that could, in the long run, change my self-definition and my life. For a number of midlife religious brothers it does just that.

Men of Communion

James and Evelyn Whitehead frame their definition of intimacy as a question: Am I sure enough of myself and confident enough of my ability that I can risk being influenced through closeness with someone else?[19] Think about that notion for a moment. The connection between identity and intimacy is clear: unless I am at home with myself, closeness with another will frighten or overwhelm me.

As religious brothers grow into a new sense of midlife identity, they are better able to risk closeness with others. Mentoring relationships are one of the ways in which this gamble takes place. This type of love relationship is egalitarian: mentors are neither parents nor peers; they are both.

Caught between two generations, most midlife brothers find themselves responsible for both older and younger people. However, they usually have little opportunity to choose those for whom they will be responsible or how this task is to be carried out!

Mentoring offers many of them a unique opportunity to expand their care for others. Exercising this role with a younger generation is fairly straightforward: help facilitate the answer to this question: "What am I going to do with my adult life?" Mentors provide encouragement for young people and, at times, a life worthy of emulation.

The task of mentoring an older generation is not so clearly defined. Some guidelines, however, do exist. To begin with, mentors can help older people rediscover parts of themselves lost when they made earlier life decisions. In making those choices, many, by necessity, had to neglect aspects of their personality. During life's second half, they can rediscover these forgotten gifts.

In addition to mentoring, religious brothers foster communion through their life together. By learning to be brothers in community, they develop an ability to be brothers to all whose lives they touch.

Living with others in simplicity and equality, and with patience, sensitivity, and encouragement, brothers also bear witness to the fact that our church today can have an ecclesiology of communion.[20] All too often our past actions have betrayed a power-controlled ecclesiology. Brothers, through their life together, and their relationships of mentoring and intimacy, bear witness to the fact that it can and must be otherwise.[21]

Without doubt, then, a religious brother's identity is transformed over the course of his life. Every time he tries to answer anew the question, "On whom or what do I set my heart?" the process of identity reformulation begins anew. To embrace that question in midlife can be frightening; failure to do so, however, can bring stagnation.

As religious brothers take on this challenge in their middle years, they come to discover something that has been there from the very beginning: at the heart of their life together are prayer, mission, and communion. What a blessing that find is for the church; what a gift to religious life!

Notes

1. The notion of personal identity as well as a number of other areas addressed in this article are discussed more fully in Sean D. Sammon, FMS, *An Undivided Heart: Making Sense of Celibate Chastity* (Staten Island, NY: Alba House, 1993).

2. Daniel J. Levinson, *Seasons of a Man's Life* (New York: Alfred Knopf, 1978).

3. John Updike, *A Month of Sundays* (New York: Fawcett, 1975).

4. William Bridges, *Transitions* (Reading, MA: Addison-Wesley, 1980).

5. Ibid.

6. Ibid.

7. Levinson, *Seasons;* and Sean D. Sammon, "Relationship between Life Stress, Level of Ego Identity, and Age of Commitment to Central Life Structure Components in Age Thirty Transition Catholic Religious Professional Men" (PhD dissertation, Fordham University, 1982).

8. Levinson, *Seasons.*

9. Sammon, "Age Thirty Catholic Religious Professional Men."

10. Evelyn E. and James D. Whitehead, *Seasons of Strength* (New York: Doubleday, 1984).

11. Ibid.

12. Sean D. Sammon, FMS, *Growing Pains in Ministry* (Mystic, CT: Twenty-third Publications, 1983).

13. Dante Alighieri, *The Divine Comedy,* John Aitken Carlyle, trans. (New York: Random House, Vintage Books, 1950) 11.

14. Saul Bellows, *Herzog* (New York: Viking Press, 1964) 233.

15. Evelyn E. and James D. Whitehead, Christian Life Patterns (New York: Doubleday, 1979).

16. The material in this and the two sections that follow also appears in Sammon's *An Undivided Heart: Making Sense of Celibate Chastity.*

17. Charles Howard, FMS, *Conference Given at the African Congress of the Marist Brothers,* August 1992.

18. Ibid.

19. Whitehead, *Christian Life Patterns.*

20. Howard, *Conference Given at the African Congress of the Marist Brothers,* August 1992.

21. Ibid.

Blessed Ambiguity

Exploring Futures

Religious Brothers: Blessed Ambiguity, Future Possibility

F. Edward Coughlin, OFM

The 1994 Synod of Bishops is devoted to the theme of "Consecrated Life and Its Role in the Church and in the World." Like previous synods on the vocation of the laity and the priesthood, this upcoming Synod proposes to focus on the vocation of those who profess the evangelical counsels and to consider their identity and mission in the church today.[1] The preparatory document, or *Lineamenta*, which is intended to introduce this topic and foster study of it, envisions the Synod as

> a propitious occasion to undertake an objective discernment of the present situation, so that consecrated life might receive from the pastors of the church, united in assembly, the necessary help to maintain the vibrancy of its life and works and to look confidently to the future.[2]

Christifideles Laici (1989) was issued following the Synod on the lay vocation. It emphasizes the laity's role and mission in transforming the world and temporal affairs according to God's plan. The bishops' reflections on the vocation of those called to Orders can be found in *Pastores Dabo Vobis*. Both these documents proposed rather positive, clear, and practical definitions of these two vocations, even though problematic areas of ambiguity and dichotomy persist.

BROTHER F. EDWARD COUGHLIN, OFM, a native of Buffalo, New York, is a member of the Order of Friars Minor, Holy Name Province (New York). He is currently the Director/Dean of The Franciscan Institute at Saint Bonaventure University. He previously served in various capacities within the province's Program of Initial Formation and as a Provincial Councillor. Brother Edward may be addressed at Saint Bonaventure University, Saint Bonaventure, NY 14778.

If the 1994 Synod is going to realize a similar goal, however, it will have to grapple with two fundamental challenges. First, it will have to address many of the areas of ambiguity and dichotomy embedded in definitions of the lay and priestly vocations which have been proposed. In contrast with those two vocations, religious have served in a variety of roles in both the church and society. Second, the bishops' task is fundamentally complicated by the charismatic nature of religious life.[3] Historically, the Spirit has gifted the church with a rich variety of forms of religious life that have invariably played important but diverse roles in its life and ministry.[4] For example, the Mendicant Orders emerged as a creative response to the pastoral realities of the medieval church while the Fourth Lateran Council was decreeing that no new forms of religious life would be approved. The Council of Trent and subsequent papal legislation mandated enclosure for apostolicly-minded religious women in the sixteenth century, only to witness the Spirit calling forth great numbers of women desiring to be actively engaged in a ministry of service to the emerging and unmet needs of their societies. Therefore, the charismatic nature of the religious vocation demands attentive listening to the Spirit in this time of change and transformation. It requires of religious, in particular, hearts tuned to the Spirit in the midst of their experience of life today, hearts ready to take risks on behalf of God's Reign, and hearts compassionately open to the deepest needs of the church and society.

In addition, the proposed discernment of this Synod must include three considerations. First, it must be rooted in the seminal vision of contemporary religious life as found in the documents of Vatican II. There, the Council situated religious life within the rich variety of ways women and men are called and choose to live out their basic Christian vocation. More specifically, in *Lumen Gentium,* the Council challenged religious "to give an increasingly clearer revelation of Christ" (LG, 46), and to let "their purpose be a more vigorous flowering of the Church's holiness" (LG, 47). *Perfectae Caritatis* described religious life as "a very clear symbol of the heavenly kingdom," as enabling the church to "be prepared for the work of ministry unto the building up of the Body of Christ," and as a way in which the church is able "to manifest in herself the multiform wisdom of God" (PC, 1).

Expressing its desire to "benefit more fully from lives consecrated by profession of the evangelical counsels and the vital function which they perform" (PC, 1), the Council also provided norms for the updated renewal of religious life. The 30 years since Vatican II give ample testimony to the serious and diligent efforts of those who profess the evangelical counsels to undertake this challenge of renewal and adaptation. Not every effort has been successful and the process is far from complete. I believe, however, that the desire of professed religious to better understand the inspirations of their founders and foundresses has renewed their dreams, visions, and hopes. While the experience of renewal has been difficult, confusing, and at times filled with conflict, it has also been marked by graced moments and has released new energies for living the Gospel in our contemporary world which have inspired many in religious life, the church, and society.

Second, the discernment of this Synod must be attentive to the complex and interacting levels of change in the contemporary church and society. For example, as the vocation of lay men and women becomes increasingly normative in the church, how does it impact the prevailing sense of identity and mission of contemporary religious?[5] Viewed from another perspective, how able and prepared are contemporary religious (now older and fewer in number) to address the unprecedented costs, for-profit competition, and performance expectations that now undergird their traditional areas of ministry and service (health care and education)? These and other changes which are spiritual, personal, psychological, communal, social, and ecclesial constitute a serious challenge to the traditional sources of identity and self-understanding in the lives of contemporary men and women religious. Long recognized and generally understood in terms of what they did rather than who they were, modern religious are searching for a renewed vision of who they are and how they might serve the church and world in radically changed circumstances. These changes, despite their confusing and painful dimensions, must be acknowledged and addressed in practical but faith-filled ways. Ideally, religious will see in them a graced invitation to discover deeper and renewed visions of religious life in today's church and society.

Third, a clear understanding of the vocation of men and women religious can only be discerned in the context of the manner in which lay and ordained vocations are understood in the contemporary church. For example, *Lumen Gentium* clearly states that the profession of the evangelical counsels "does not belong to the hierarchical structure of the church" (LG, 44). Subsequently, Canon 588.1 of the 1983 Code of Canon Law declares that "by its very nature the state of consecrated life is neither clerical nor lay." These statements by negation, in conjunction with the rather idealistic and vague descriptions of religious life in various church documents since Vatican II,[6] have left religious life today in what I consider to be a state of "blessed ambiguity." It is blessed because it invites laity, pastors, and religious in particular to ask: How are religious called to contribute to the holiness, life, and ministry of the church in this age?

Within the context of these broader issues, this article will concern itself with three core challenges: 1, spiritual life and leadership, 2, adult relationships in partnership and mutuality, and 3, a vibrant witness of service. While these challenges dwell at the heart of every Christian vocation, I will consider them in the context of the vocation most people refer to as "the religious life," particularly the life of religious brothers. I believe that religious might discern in these challenges a way to come to a deeper understanding of their identity and mission. They might also discern in them the invitation to make a significant contribution to building up the contemporary church, making it a better symbol of God's reign. In addition to indicating the demands for personal and communal renewal embedded in these challenges, I will also suggest how religious brothers in particular might discern in them a graced opportunity to become a prophetic paradigm of Christian commitment, "a sign which can and ought to attract all members of the Church to an effective and prompt fulfillment of the duties of their Christian vocation" (LG, 44).

To What Are Religious Brothers Called?

Spiritual Life and Leadership

Contemporary people express great hunger for a life that is whole and permeated with meaning. While they often seek it in diverse things, places, or activities, many discover, as Augustine did long ago, that this desire is only satisfied in and through a relationship with the "One Who is All Holy." Unfortunately, much of what has been written or taught with respect to this relationship fails to connect in a meaningful way with the human-religious experience of contemporary men and women in the ordinary circumstances of their lives.

Lumen Gentium declared that "in the Church, everyone . . . is called to holiness" (LG, 39). The church's understanding of holiness is then developed in terms of a personal relationship which is 1, initiated by God, 2, ratified through baptism sought in faith, and 3, given concrete expression in an individual's "striving for the perfection of charity" (LG, 39) and the fullness of Christian life (LG, 40). Thus, as *Lumen Gentium* says, "in the various types and duties of life, one and the same holiness is cultivated by all who are moved by the Spirit of God" (LG, 41).

This conciliar presentation is important because it emphasizes that the call to holiness is addressed to all Christians, whatever their rank or status, can be cultivated in a variety of ways in the ordinary circumstances of life, and promotes a more human way of life "even in this earthly society" (LG, 40). Perhaps even more important, growth in holiness is to be measured in terms of the manifestation of charity in the everyday circumstances of one's life, the "fullness of the Christian life," and the showing of "the love with which God has loved the world" (LG, 41). This understanding of holiness calls into question many commonly held assumptions about the meaning of holiness and the criteria by which holiness is to be judged. Some of the commonly-held assumptions of the pre–Vatican II Church, lingering today, quickly illustrate this point. For example, clergy and religious were typically assumed to be more holy than lay persons because of their state in life. Personal qualities such as being quiet or uninvolved in everyday matters were (often mistakenly) interpreted as signs of holiness. People involved in extraordinary activities, such as the work of Father Damian, Mother Maryanne, and Dunstan with the lepers, would be more readily acknowledged as indications of holiness than parents caring for their children, or teachers in inner-city schools who inspires students to perform beyond anyone's expectations.

As the laity, in particular, have grown in their understanding of and personal response to the call to holiness, the whole People of God are being invited to ask hard questions about the quality of their relationship with God, the depth and breadth of their response, and the concrete ways in which God's love is mirrored in their lives. Thus a more adequate understanding of holiness—life in the Spirit of God as revealed in Jesus—presents every Christian in the contemporary church with the call to a clearer sense of identity and mission. Men and women religious must not only hear the call to holiness, but hear it in the context of their vowed commitment within the unique charism of their community.

In this context, religious are challenged to "let their purpose be a more vigorous flowering of the Church's holiness" (LG, 47). This implies a twofold commitment. First, in virtue of their profession, religious publicly declare their intention to conscientiously cultivate their relationship with God. The transforming impact of this dynamic, if authentically embraced, should become increasingly evident in their "more human way of life" and their showing "the love by which God has loved the world." Second, in view of their public commitment, religious must take seriously the church's desire that they be, in fact, a "shining witness and model of holiness" (LG, 39) and that they "help others grow" in holiness, a call to spiritual leadership.

Spiritual leadership was recently described by Richard McBrien as a search for those persons who, in whatever state of life, could

> speak to us out of the depths of their own personal faith, ratified by compelling witness of a life lived in accord with that faith, and permeated with an understanding and empathy for the problems and experiences of ordinary human beings.[7]

These three elements of spiritual leadership embrace the challenges of transforming faith, embodied faith, and faith that does justice after the example of Jesus. They are the qualities of faith typically and readily recognized in the lives of the founders and foundresses of various religious institutes, and in many of those men and women who walk in their footsteps.

Spiritual leadership assumes a rich and continually unfolding spiritual life, a life of faith in response to God's loving presence: holiness. Invited in faith to give their whole selves freely to God, individuals enter this relationship as creatures who are loved, blessed, and good, as well as limited, needy, and dependent.[8] Regrettably, the experience of the self as limited, needy, and dependent is often denied or carefully avoided. Perceived to be signs of weakness, these qualities of human nature are seen as obstacles to be overcome. The sense of vulnerability they arouse in a person frequently blocks rather than facilitates a relationship with God, self, and others. Paradoxically, human encounters with limits, needs, and dependency are doors through which persons are invited to experience God's abiding presence, unearned action, and purpose in their lives. This ongoing and dynamic faith-encounter, as Regis Duffy, OFM, aptly summarizes it,

> reveals our profound need in such a way that it does not destroy us. It continually heals our wounds so that we might serve others. . . . It is the source of the ongoing conversion we are called to and the root of all faith . . . worship, and sacrament.[9]

Growth in faith and holiness therefore requires a humble and listening heart which creates the possibility of encountering God's revealing presence in the midst of our human experiences of prayer, life, and service. This process includes an encounter with limits, need, and dependency even as it empowers us to know, love, and serve God in new ways. Indeed this human experience of the transforming and dynamic process is at the core of the spiritual life. These are the concrete moments when individuals are invited to deepen their faith and to see the specific demands of living their faith in the present. In their honest, open, and increasingly faith-filled encounter with these moments of grace, individuals come to true self-knowledge in Christ Jesus. Ideally, individuals who are working with and growing through these experiences are prepared to accept, struggle with, and compassionately understand the limits, needs, and demands of interdependence in human relationships. These can also be graced moments wherein individuals are enabled to see their inclination to avoid learning what it means for them to grow in holiness.

The courage to accept one's goodness, face limits, experience healthy dependency, and acknowledge one's need for grace are critical components of a personal relationship with God. They can guide the believer to a faith which includes a personal, concrete, and practical understanding of what it might mean for them to live according to God's plan today. In this way, life with God becomes the foundation for understanding the meaning of life in community and ministry. It constitutes the formative and continually transforming experience which is the basis for offering the kind of spiritual leadership so needed in our time.

The call to a vibrant spiritual life and the demands of spiritual leadership ought to speak forcefully to all Christians and to religious in particular. However, the call can be easily muffled by issues related to: 1. function (state in life); 2. office (lay-clerical); 3. place (sacred-secular, church-world); 4. traditional form and enculturated adaptation (for example, prayer, manner of celebration); 5. over-reliance on role expectations and the tendency to overlook or deny an individual's gifts, and 6. an emphasis on traditional needs (health care, education) over the emerging demands for pastoral care and service (spiritual direction, adult education, and formation). These and other related issues are very real in the life of the contemporary church. They have generated conflicts which have absorbed enormous amounts of attention and energy in the 30 years since Vatican II. While religious are not exempt from being caught up in or perpetrating these issues, their vocation demands a responsible and conscious attentiveness to them, not only for themselves but the sake of the whole church in virtue of their vocation.

Those called to religious life, in the context of their vowed commitment and community charism, ought to be very familiar with the demands of the spiritual life. The critical question, of course, is the degree to which they are striving to become holy and open to the Spirit's transforming action in their lives. This question may be especially pertinent, since many of the religious practices and institutional settings which, at least theoretically, promoted and supported the spiritual life prior to Vatican II have disappeared or are in transition. It is an area where religious openly speak about the discrepancy between the values they espouse and their personal and communal practice.

Challenge for Brothers

The call for spiritual leadership, and the willingness to become actively involved in helping others to grow in holiness may, however, constitute the more radical and greater challenge, especially to the majority of nonordained religious in the post–Vatican II church. For many it may require a different self-image and self-understanding as it focuses attention on the embodiment and articulation of gospel values and faith.

Religious brothers ought to be especially open to this challenge in these times of change and transition. Called to a vocation which many in the church (and world) find difficult to understand, brothers may be in a unique position to give fruitful witness to holiness of life as men of faith. They might then be more ready, personally, to consciously exercise the kind of spiritual leadership for which the church and the world hunger. Showing forth "a more vigorous flowering of the holiness" (LG, 47), brothers could be increasingly perceived as men who are good role models and potential mentors, persons of faith who live the Gospel in contemporary society.

Brothers must therefore be conscious of the wider implications and impact of their public profession. Precisely because they have no official function, status, or place, brothers are freed in the midst of this blessed ambiguity. This situation invites them to see renewed or new possibilities for embodying their faith, to become more responsible to give witness to their faith in their words and deeds. In this way, brothers might discern a new vision of who they are called to be and how they might make a much needed and significant contribution to building up the church today. For brothers, and those who think of them more in terms of their service (such as teacher) or their "lack" of ordination, this call may constitute a substantive departure from the more familiar and expected. However, spiritual life and leadership are urgent needs of the present. A more attentive and fruitful response to these challenges could enlighten the brothers' discernment of their identity and mission in the church and society today. The vibrant response of brothers could also constitute a prophetic witness to the deepest reality of what it means to be a religious in today's Church and world.

Relationships of Mutuality and Partnership

Lumen Gentium proclaims that everyone is called to the "fullness of the Christian Life" (LG. 40), a life which the US bishops have declared is best understood through a variety of experiences as the People of God (church) respond to the calls to adulthood, holiness, community, and ministry.[10] While an authentic spiritual life (holiness) plays a central role in the "fullness of life" to which all are summoned, the challenges of an embodied adult spirituality have too often been taken for granted, or given only minimal consideration.

As the US bishops indicated, "adulthood implies knowledge, experience and awareness, freedom and responsibility, and mutuality in relationships."[11] The experience of being and becoming an adult therefore raises two important and related questions. First, what is the breadth, depth, and quality of a person's relationship with the whole self? Second, is the person's capacity for relationship being developed and expressed through authentic relationships with God, self, and others?

The Christian tradition has consistently celebrated the wondrous ways in which God has made us (Ps 8:6–7), even if in practice it has not always understood and encouraged us to embrace the diverse gifts of our human nature: our sensual and sexed natures (biological sex, sexual identity, physiological capacity for pleasure, procreation, and tension release); our capacities to think, imagine, and desire; our freedom with respect to choice; and, in particular, our emotions and sexuality (orientation to relationship, gender identity, and sexual orientation). These diverse ways and means of knowing, loving, and serving are pathways to a full and rich knowledge of God, self, and others. They are doorways through which the Divine Presence can be disclosed in our lives and through which we are invited to respond to God, self, and others in faith, hope, and love. However, important dimensions of human nature—such as desire, emotions, and sexuality—are often feared, misunderstood, avoided, denied, or elaborately controlled. Thus, the goodness of these freely given gifts has often remained unknown, unloved, and underutilized in the life of many Christians.

Seeing the tragic and limiting implications of these realities, Evelyn and James Whitehead, among others, challenge us to befriend our passions and emotions so that "we learn to transform the ambiguous energy of our emotions into illuminating and encouraging guides on the journey of faith."[12] This challenge of befriending will no doubt evoke a broad range of responses. It may disclose our ignorance or fear, dislodge a mechanism of denial, or invite a new distancing of what is vaguely known, yet carefully avoided. Some will rush to contextualize the challenge, while it will delight others. Many will simply say, "Who will teach me and guide me on this part of the journey?"

Reflecting on the affective revolution in society in the context of celibate commitment, Sandra M. Schneiders expresses the belief that religious life can, and in many cases has, created opportunities to discover new patterns of living, relating, and working that challenge the normative and dominant patterns of relationship found in the church and society. Schneiders believes, however, that

> although religious are playing a genuinely prophetic role in the affective transformation of society, many men and women celibates find it much more difficult to tackle their own personal affective transformation.[13]

The challenge of an affective development which is rooted in the Gospel and "radically healed, purified, and liberated in the intimacy of a profound personal and communal prayer life"[14] is Schneiders' vision of a meaningful celibacy in the contemporary church and society.

In a similar vein, the sexed nature of humans and human sexuality pose enormous formative and life challenges for all men and women in the contemporary church and society. Narrow anthropological, psychological, theological, and moral perspectives have limited or prohibited and many times distorted an adequate understanding of human sexuality. Awareness and sensitivity to these realities, or the lack thereof, have generated conflict and confusion which cry out for understanding, justice, and compassion.

Personal maturity—realizing the various degrees of fullness of which one is capable—is a primary characteristic of adulthood; it is also a challenge which spans the whole of life. Desire, emotions, and sexuality play a more critical role in the maturing process than has often been realized or appreciated. However, in conjunction with the other dimensions of the individual, all these gifts of humanity are "the stuff" that enables a man or woman to embrace fullness of life. At the same time they inform the person's freedom and challenge the imagination to choose in the present circumstances of life, a pattern of life centered in Christ Jesus.

Maturing persons are therefore continually invited in a variety of ways to know and celebrate their goodness and strength, even as the process confronts them with their limitations, needs, and unfinished business. The humble, loving, and compassionate embrace of their truth and reality has powerful implications for the self, and the self in relationship. Fully alive and humble persons are likely to approach relationships with a healthy self-consciousness, the capacity for appropriate levels of self-disclosure, readiness both to give and receive, and openness to the demands of growth and transformation which are an integral part of the spiritual life and ongoing relationships. Persons who are fully alive and humble are, in all likelihood, able to acknowledge joyfully a healthy sense of dependence on the Creator and others. These individuals should also be able to enter into relationships of true mutuality in the process of working within their limits and brokenness. Finally, humble persons should also actively participate as partners in creating, shaping, and animating community life. Collaboration in the fulfillment of their shared mission, as unique individuals with distinct but mutually enriching vocations, then becomes a genuine possibility. As persons of faith, they strive to love with their whole self while ready to be loved and to participate in the life and ministry of the community. In this way they may indeed "help others to grow."

These rich possibilities for quality and depth of relationship with God, self, and others presume that a person truly welcomes a fullness of life and relationship, and has experienced the formative challenges and guidance of others in nurturing and supporting this kind of development. The whole process of personal development and growth in faith is, of course, greatly enhanced by the presence of a variety of persons who can model and give witness to the meaning of fullness of life in Christ Jesus.

Brothers as Models

Unfortunately, the call to adulthood is often only quietly heard in the lives of many Christians. Guides for the journey into adulthood are frequently not available. Numerous obstacles to mutuality and partnership are encountered as gifts are denied, the sacramental power of Orders and Baptism are frequently set over and against one another, and hierarchical roles are given greater emphasis than personal abilities for leading prayer, building community, or serving those in need. Lacking the necessary personal experience, formation, and commitment to adulthood, the People of God encounter numerous difficulties in hearing and answering their invitations to holiness, community, and ministry—the fullness of life in Christ to which they have been called. Given these realities, all Christians—lay, religious, and clerical—are summoned to an honest and careful consideration of where they are on the journey into adulthood. Religious brothers might see in this process not only an invitation to grow, but a unique opportunity to provide leadership in an area of critical need. Being male, belonging neither to the hierarchy nor the laity, religious brothers, as individuals and as a group, might discern a unique opportunity to work for the transformation of the present moment if they are prepared to provide the witness of life and guidance so urgently needed. Their much needed gift could, in different ways, cut through contemporary issues related to status, gender, and vocational identity. Brothers might also find a clearer vision of their distinctive religious vocation and a renewed sense of identity for the future.

If brothers, as vowed men, have a deep and continuously unfolding sense of their human and religious identity, they might well be expected to discover within themselves the readiness and resources to risk being open, trusting, compassionate, respectful, and inclusive beyond normative expectations in their personal, social, communal, and ministerial relationships. In sponsored institutions, they could attend to the broader issues of spiritual leadership, witnessing to and calling forth a fullness of life, and being responsive to the needs for mentoring beyond career development. Brothers in positions of leadership, in particular, could take increasingly prophetic stances with respect to justice issues as well as in making deliberate choices about how individuals are valued, power is shared, decisions are made, and ministry demands are met. In this way, brothers might find themselves genuinely disposed to engage the emerging issues and assume various forms of leadership for the future among the People of God. These actions might, indeed, prompt others to a greater actualization of their own Christian commitment.

Vibrant Witness of Service

The obligation to give witness—to make known one's beliefs through one's actions—is an integral dimension of every Christian vocation. It has, however, been subject to a variety of interpretations. Historically, the witness of prophets, saints, and martyrs has been often more admired than understood as a concrete challenge to all Christians to witness to their faith. Typically, religious and clerical persons were expected to give greater witness than lay persons. Thus, the emphasis on mission in such contemporary church documents as *Gaudium et Spes, Ad Gentes,* and the encyclical letter *Evangelii Nuntiandi,* has created a new consciousness in the Christian community. It is perhaps most evident in the many ways lay Christians have become more visibly involved in building up the church and more active in bringing gospel values into the marketplace. The theological vision emerging from these documents has encouraged lay persons to collaborate more closely with men and women religious as well as clergy in a variety of ministerial settings and to assume positions of influence and leadership unimaginable 30 years ago. These positive developments have not always been universally welcomed, and they have raised some questions for religious and clerics about their own identity and mission.

Religious orders have classically arisen in the church to serve emerging and unmet human needs.[15] Or, as Patricia Ranft has noted in the case of medieval canons regular and military orders, they "both desired to communicate basic truths of Christianity to a changing society by a living witness" and "both retained traditional aspects of religious life while adopting new external forms of service." Neither type of religious community enjoyed a permanent position in the church because, in Ranft's judgment,

> instead of adhering to the concept which motivated them to create new forms of religious life, in time they focused on the specific activity chosen to render their witness. This inevitably led to the forms being outdated and ineffectual.[16]

Christian Brother Louis DeThomasis sees parallel issues confronting contemporary apostolic (and, I think, all other) forms of religious life in the midst of the momentous social, economic, and political turbulence of our times. Analyzing the situation, DeThomasis says:

> This is not to say our founders were wrong. . . . The apostolates they passed down to [their followers] are wrong only when [they] fail to adapt them to the conditions and needs of those who are disadvantaged by contemporary society.[17]

Though the arguments of these authors are nuanced and set in different contexts, their observations may assist religious men and women in discerning how they are called today to make known and to build up the Body of Christ into the next century. Religious, regardless of their monastic, contemplative, mendicant, or apostolic traditions, are being asked to more clearly and explicitly discern:

    a. how they are, in reality, making known the wisdom of God today;

    b. how they are remaining faithful to their founders' spirit and responding to critical and unmet human needs;

    c. how the personal and communal gifts of religious individuals and communities are building up church and society through their gospel witness of life.

Admittedly these complex and demanding issues may well make uncomfortable those with fixed and familiar visions of their identity and mission. The questions they raise will certainly not generate any common set of responses, given the variety of charisms and traditions which must struggle with them. However, men and women religious can no longer avoid these issues, especially if their congregations fail to attract and hold new members and lose their capacity to influence, direct, or sustain the ministries they have carefully nurtured. Religious are also increasingly encouraged to develop individual gifts for service, but opportunities for using those gifts are often limited, or take religious into nontraditional areas of ministry, many times outside church structures. In addition, the emerging needs of contemporary society cry out for new forms and styles of ministry.

The tension inherent in these questions can be sensed in a careful reading of the *Lineamenta's* section on brothers. There, the consecrated life of brothers is seen as representing "consecration in its utter simplicity" (CLCW, 21). The document then summarizes the various kinds of traditional apostolic service which brothers have contributed to the pastoral work of the church; the contribution of brothers in monastic and mendicant communities seems to be overlooked. Little encouragement is expressed for brothers to discern future, perhaps alternative, forms of pastoral apostolic service. The focus raises substantive questions about the potential role and contribution of religious brothers in response to new and emerging needs of the church (adult formation and education, nonclerical forms of pastoral ministry performed by men). The vision found in the document also fails to anticipate some emerging trends among brothers. A recent study of teaching brothers in the Unites States, for example, indicated that 46 percent of those surveyed believe that young men are not attracted to a teaching career and that 41 percent of those surveyed support diversifying their apostolates.[18] The study also quotes one brother who said:

> I believe we must have a clear focus on education, but it must be expressed in creative and radical ways, not just teaching in a conventional Catholic school. It means new types of service for adults, homeless children, incarcerated youth, and so forth.[19]

Given the charismatic nature of religious life, the call to spiritual leadership, the growing need for models and mentors for mutual adult relationships, as well as the emerging needs in the church and society, religious, and brothers in particular, must commit themselves to discerning in faith what the Spirit is inviting them to in this age. They must resist any temptation to bring the process to a premature close, for surely this would have long-term negative consequences. The church, therefore, ought to encourage them and patiently support them in waiting on the Spirit as they explore the diverse ways they might build up the church and proclaim the Gospel.

Brothers: Witnesses to a New Paradigm

The prophet Ezekiel fell on his face when he saw the vision of the likeness of the glory of God. Although his face was buried in the dirt, Ezekiel heard a voice say to him: "Stand up . . . I wish to speak with you . . . I am sending you" (Ez 1:28–2:5). Ezekiel was then sent by God to those who were described as "hard of face and obstinate of heart." The description might apply variously to the present reality of the church. I suspect it applied, with various nuances, in previous times when religious brothers such as the Capuchin Franciscan, Felix of Cantalice, heard the Lord's call. While Felix and other brothers might have been more comfortable with the label *faithful* than prophetic, they were both.

These holy men were true prophets who showed the people of their time how the Gospel could be effectively and fruitfully lived in new ways. The witness of their lives enabled others to

> assume responsibility for a broader vision of themselves as people gifted for new as well as old tasks in their lives. Their challenge was not negative but therapeutic: the blind [did] see again and the deaf [heard]; young people [saw] visions and the old [dreamed] dreams.[20]

They were "paradigm breakers"[21] in that they established new patterns of gospel living and service as they responded to different personal, spiritual, and pastoral needs. Following their example, brothers who live their profession in this way might constitute a new "crowd of witnesses" who give others the strength and encouragement they need to seek more vibrant, effective, and fruitful ways of living their lives in Christ Jesus.

Freed by their profession to pursue life in the spirit, establish new patterns of relationship with others and within the church, and embody a life of witness and service, brothers can and do make a unique and important contribution to the life and ministry of the church. The simplicity of the brothers' consecration creates a powerful paradox, making of their lives a prophet paradigm: "a sign which can and ought to attract all members of the

Church to an effective and prompt fulfillment of the duties of their Christian vocation" (LG, 44).

Brothers, stand up! Consider the life and example of those who have gone before you. Look at the brothers within and outside your community who are making a difference in traditional or nontraditional situations. Listen to the Spirit. See if there is hardness in your face or obstinance in your heart. Look at your gifts and service from different vantage points. Stand ready to take risks both familiar and new on behalf of God's reign as you extend compassionate and understanding hearts to your brothers and sisters in Christ Jesus.

Notes

1. "The Consecrated Life and Its Role in the Church and in the World," *Lineamenta* for the 1994 Synod of Bishops, *Origins* 22:1 (Dec. 10, 1992).

2. Ibid.

3. Zachary Hayes, "The Charism of Religious Life," *Proceedings: Super Conference IV*, St. Bonaventure University, July 12–17, 1987; Theme: Our Franciscan Charism in the World Today, Alcuin Coyle, ed., (Clifton, NJ: FAME, 1988).

4. Philip Sheldrake, "A Question of Development: Religious Life," chapter 5 in *Spirituality and History: Questions of Interpretation and Method* (New York: Crossroads, 1992) 107–132. See also Patricia Ranft, "The Concept of Witness in the Christian Tradition," Revue Bénédictine (1992) 9–23.

5. Sheldrake, "A Question of Development," 107.

6. See Sharon Euart, "Responsible Leadership," *Church* (Spring 1993) 28-30. This brief article begins to articulate some of the more specific issues to which I am alluding.

7. Richard McBrien, "In Search of Spiritual Leadership," *National Catholic Reporter,* 29:16 (Feb. 19, 1993) 2.

8. Regis Duffy, OFM, "Unnamed Gifts and Their Symbols," *Real Presence* (San Francisco: Harper and Row, 1982) 43.

9. Ibid., 34.

10. National Conference of Catholic Bishops, *Called and Gifted: Reflections of the American Bishops Commemorating the Fifteenth Anniversary of the Issuance of the Decree on the Apostolate of the Laity* (Nov. 13, 1980).

11. NCCB, *Called and Gifted,* "The Call to Adulthood."

12. James and Evelyn Whitehead, "Christians and Their Passions," *Warren Lecture Series in Catholic Studies,* No. 21, University of Tulsa, public lecture (Sep. 2, 1992).

13. Sandra Schneiders, IHM, *New Wineskins: Reimaging Religious Life Today* (New York: Paulist Press, 1986) 105.

14. Ibid.

15. David Nygren, CM, and Miriam Ukeritis, CSJ, "Future of Religious Orders in the United States," *Origins,* 22:15 (Sept. 24, 1992).

16. Patricia Ranft, "The Concept of Witness in the Christian Tradition," *Revue Bénédictine* (1992) 21.

17. Louis DeThomasis, FSC, *Imagination: A Future for Religious Life* (Winona, MN: Metanoia Group, 1992) 52.

18. Eleace King, "Vocations among Teaching Brothers," *Review for Religious* (Jan.–Feb. 1993) 106.

19. Ibid., 103.

20. Duffy, "Unnamed Gifts," 93–94.

21. DeThomasis, *Imagination,* 28.

Impossible Thoughts, Improbable Dreams

Francis J. Presto, SCJ

This article is about a dream that has been accompanied by a good deal of pain and confusion. Many readers will resonate with this dream as brothers in clerical orders, others may find it eye-opening, and still others just a dream. But in dreams, a new arrangement is often given to our experiences which can then only be made sense of through re-definitions or re-interpretations of those experiences. Like Joseph in the Book of Genesis, I risk the possible resentment of my brothers as I explain my dreams. But like him also I trust that I will not be abandoned, and that behind the dreams is a reality worth risking everything for. "Look! Here comes that dreamer!" (37:19)

There is a tale about a moth who had a dream the other moths considered improbable. While the other moths were content to circle local street lights and house lamps achieving pleasure, albeit with singed wings, this moth dreamed about reaching a great, bright light caught in the branches of the old oak tree down the block. This light was so bright that it was irresistible,

---

BROTHER FRANCIS J. PRESTO, SCJ, is a member of the United States Province of the Priests of the Sacred Heart. He is a native of Pittsburgh, Pennsylvania and presently resides in Eagle Butte, South Dakota. He joined the Priests of the Sacred Heart in 1976 and professed final vows in 1981. He earned a BA from Northeastern Illinois University and an MDiv from Catholic Theological Union in Chicago. He currently serves with the Catholic Pastoral Team of the Cheyenne River Sioux Tribe Reservation in South Dakota as the parish minister for Saint Joseph Church of Ridgeview. He also serves as President on the Board of Directors for the Sacred Heart Center Corporation. Previous ministry has included parish ministry among Hispanics and African-Americans as well as teaching at the undergraduate level. Brother Francis may be addressed at P.O. Box 110, Eagle Butte, SD 57625-0110.

despite the fact that the moth found it unreachable. The moth continued to exhaust itself, but always short of the mark. Each morning, though it limped home to the ridicule of others, at night it persisted in its vain yet valiant attempt to reach the light in the oak tree, the moon.

Despite the taunts and jeers of others who not-so-politely insisted that the moth was crazy, despite its continual frustration in not being able to reach the bright light, the moth believed in its quest. The moth believed in its improbable dream.

Personal Story and Observations

In my own life as a Christian, as a brother, and as a church minister, I have on occasions identified with this tale. Not only have I found myself pursuing "unreachable" goals, but situations arose which caused others to suggest to me that I might find an easier way to live. Some of these situations are unique to me; some have been experienced by many others involved in ministry. In the midst of these "taunts and jeers," in the midst of the sorrow and grief of apparent failure, our improbable dreams survive by perseverance and the grace of God.

I have responded to God's call to live as a religious brother in a clerical order, but I sometimes find myself in a world where I am neither fish nor fowl. Canon law defines me as a lay person because I am a male religious who believes God is not calling me to receive the Sacrament of Orders.

However, in responding to God this way I have chosen to identify myself as a member of a religious congregation, abiding by its Constitutions, traditions, and charisms. This choice has provided me with the opportunity for education, personal growth, employment in ministry, and a sense of security. This choice also sets me apart from the "rank and file" of the church who comprise the bulk of God's people. Compared with their lives and situations, I am not a lay person but part of the church's vast leadership organization. Some lay people consider me holier than they because of the sacrifices they presume I make. Others consider me odd and impractical for the same reasons. Still others scornfully list all the sacrifices I do not make. Regardless of these views, the common thread is that I am not a lay person as they are.

I exist, therefore, neither fish nor fowl but both. Here I give witness to God, and here I minister to the best of my abilities despite views (and misconceptions) not of my own making. It is here that my improbable dream grows.

Dreams and Bedrock

The dream began at my baptism. Though I did not grasp the infusion of grace or potential direction in life that it offered (I was only a month old), later years would spell out how this event transformed me while providing foundation and meaning.

Much later, I began to decipher the various road signs which led me to life in a religious community and profession of the evangelical counsels. In the vast array of choices comprising my life narrative, I chose to join the Priests of the Sacred Heart as a brother. Unlike the apostle Paul, I was not knocked from a horse on the road to Damascus. My steps in responding to God were often small, hesitant, and slow, but my dream persisted.

In recent years I have begun to confront the reality of what I earlier called being neither fish nor fowl, discovering that I am somehow both. This realization began to shape the dream into what may be seen as the "impossible thoughts" I present in this article.

Two foundational elements are the bedrock of my life as Christian and as brother. First, I believe in the words of Paul to the Galatians where he urges them to realize that their baptism has changed them. He writes: "There does not exist among you Jew or Greek, slave or free person, male or female. All are one in Christ Jesus" (3:27–29).[1] This statement implies a condition without status or rank which provides a base for my dream that all in the family of God are equal. What I am does not matter, only who I am. This bedrock conviction prompts me to examine who I am in a brilliant light. Reflecting on my being and my commitments, I experience others as equal in the search for truth and holiness. Part of this bedrock is my belief (and dream) that all share equally in grace, inspiration, and vocation as we testify to God's intervention in human history. It goes without saying that this view has led to frustration, but also to conversion.

The second foundational element is my life as a brother in the order of Priests of the Sacred Heart. *Priest* here does not denote presbyter, though the congregation is comprised of brothers and presbyters (and a few bishops). Our founding spiritual charism has evolved out of nineteenth-century France; our spiritual focus involves love and dedication to the Sacred Heart and the offering of our lives in reparation—acknowledging the love and fidelity of God in spite of our human limitations.

Like so many other orders of women and men religious, we experienced the exhilaration of the Second Vatican Council. In the wake of that Council, we re-examined and further defined our charism. The Constitutions of our order state that "all its members are equal in the same profession of religious life, without any distinction except that of ministries."[2] Savoring this statement and considering my first foundational element above, one would think I had discovered the Promised Land! But wait. Within that same section we read: "The Congregation of the Priests of the Sacred Heart of Jesus is a clerical apostolic religious institute of pontifical right . . . ,"[3] and here begins another part of my tale of improbable dreams.

Problem with the Bedrock

The word "clerical" in our Constitutions has become a source of confusion and disorientation. In the first paragraph of Canon 588 in the *Code of Canon Law*,[4] the claim is made that the consecrated life is neither clerical nor lay. However, the second paragraph adds parameters to the first which cause our Constitutions to be cast in a different light. This paragraph defines my community in a manner not intended. Earlier on, we struggled with our identity in a number of ways. One choice was to state that we are all equal except for ministries. Another way is to see ourselves in light of our common title. In the United States, since 1976, my congregation has had three different names. Our current title is Priests of the Sacred Heart, a title with deeper distinctions than first meets the eye. Aside from occasionally being confused with other orders who use "Sacred Heart," this phrase is fairly self-explanatory. The discussion changes, however, with the word "priests."

In ordinary civil usage as well as that of the institutional church, the term "priest" has come to designate those who are ordained and preside at sacramental rituals. In the church, it has replaced the term "presbyter," and this is where my concern lies, because there is more to the word "priest" than is often considered.

I define "priest" in a substantially broader sense as that person who offers his or her life in prayer and in action as a gift to God. A priest is a person who proclaims the goodness and love of God by word and deed. Priests are not just those who have received the Sacrament of Orders. I believe one is called to be a priest through Baptism. As such, all presbyters are priests but not all priests are presbyters. As a brother I am a priest. This is not merely a case of semantics. Rather it is an attempt to reclaim a lost definition which describes Christian women and men. Through God's grace at Baptism and at religious profession I am called to be a priest. This role involves celebrating my relationship with God. It expresses the need for sacrifice and service to God and others; it flows from the love of God. This definition of priest is implied in the great teaching section of Matthew's Gospel,[5] and it is in this light that Paul's exhortation to the Galatians makes sense. It is also in this light that I define myself as a Priest of the Sacred Heart.

Unwelcome Intrusion

The inclusion of the word (and attitude) "clerical" into our Constitutions distinguishes us from one another, a distinction which intrudes unsettlingly upon my dream as it seeps into our collective thoughts and actions.

There was a time in the not so distant past when formation was different and distinct for brother candidates and presbyter candidates. Different arrangements for dining and recreation existed. Job availabilities were distinct, with brothers assigned "silent ministries," often unseen and blue collar. Higher education was out of the question because the prevailing attitude suggested that a brother did not need it. A story circulates among us of a man who wished to be a brother but was refused because he was intellectually gifted; it was judged that his calling was to the presbyterate.

Recent years have seen this earlier reality altered considerably. Brothers have freedom to pursue educational and ministerial opportunities. A common formation emphasizes community life and tradition. We have moved from the days of menial tasks for brothers to an incorporation and utilization of our gifts and talents for the good of everyone in the community. Vocabulary shifts from the "problem" of brothers to "issues" regarding brothers.

Still, the obstacle of the word "clerical" in our documents creates pain, suffering, and discrimination. The arena of government is a mine field. Let me illustrate this point. In my congregation a brother cannot be named as provincial or general superior even if he is elected unanimously. We are a "clerical institute," and therefore no brother (who is a lay person and not a presbyter) will be approved by the Holy See for these offices. At the local level, brothers named as local superiors must jump through hoops to be approved. When a number of local communities were recently involved with leadership changes, persons thought to best fit the leadership roles were proposed to the provincial administration. This list (containing both presbyters and brothers) was approved by a deliberative vote of the provincial and his council and sent to the generalate.

The presbyters on the list were approved without delay. However, brothers were engaged in a process akin to defending a doctoral thesis, except they were defending themselves. They were required to present detailed descriptions of their lives, ministry, formation, and education, and were asked to explain why they should be approved and how they would treat the presbyters in their communities. None of this was required of the presbyters. When all was said and done, two brothers received a rescript allowing for their leadership.

Why the distinctions? We are a clerical community. Further legal opinions hold brothers have no jurisdiction over presbyters because brothers cannot be pastors of souls. Other opinions suggest that brothers as local superiors might try to restrict a presbyter from offering the Sacrament of Reconciliation in his local community, thus denying a right granted by ordination and law. One bewildering assumption is that the brother in leadership would treat the presbyter in an unchristian or unprofessional manner. No such assumptions were made about the nominated presbyters.

The situation was and continues to be frustrating, though there are signs of hope as the Union of Major Superiors works to remove this injustice. Still, a brother proposed for leadership by his local community must decide whether to jump through these hoops, and then how far. Women and men find a similar reality as they seek further involvement in the broad expanse of the church. It causes me to wonder what happened to Paul's admonition to the Galatians that there is neither slave nor free; rather, all are one in Christ. This situation creates tremors in my bedrock.

Joys and Pains of Parish Ministry

These sources of conflict work their way into church ministry. I am involved in parish ministry which could be called a "ministry of presence" as I visit with, listen to, and relate to others. I also deal with the financial and spiritual administration of the parish. My ministry calls forth a great deal of energy, time, and effort, yet it is greatly rewarding. But some factors create situations where I become unseen. Assisting in the preparation for the sacraments of Baptism, Eucharist, Reconciliation, Confirmation, Anointing, and Marriage, I can share my faith with parishioners, and God is powerfully present with us in these moments of dialogue. But at the end of this period of preparation, I must step aside for another to celebrate the sacrament's ritual. Though I rejoice in heart and soul at my parishioners' encounter with Christ in these sacraments, I feel a pain of absence because I am present only as a witness at the time of public celebration. I struggle deeply over why it is permissible for me (and other lay women and men) to be so integral to the process of these sacraments, but so limited when it comes to the ritual celebration. Why must the status of lay or cleric determine how the grace of God is presumed to work? Here I am, the dreamer, and I realize Paul speaks very eloquently to me in 1 Cor 3:3–10.[6] But I feel that the constraints of law and interpreted tradition have brought frustration and ill will. Like so many others, I wonder how long this situation will remain. Is this all that God is calling me/us to be as a brother, a "priest," a church?

Questions, Questions, Questions

If all Christians are called to witness to the kingdom by baptizing in the name of Jesus Christ, why is the ordained cleric the only one permitted to preside at the celebration? How strange it seems, for example, that in cases where one is baptized in danger of death, the full ritual must be performed if recovery of health occurs. Or, if the sacramental ministers of marriage are actually the two persons professing their vows to each other, why must the official witness of the church be only an ordained person? Could not the local ordinary delegate the faculty of witnessing a marriage to others? A similar case might be made for the sacrament of Anointing. Women and men who are ministers of the eucharist bring the Body of Christ to those confined by illness. These people represent the assembly's activity at the eucharist by their presence to the sick with that same eucharist in the pyx. Why must we restrain the power of the Spirit by not allowing them to bring the consolation of the anointing with oil as part of this eucharistic presence?

My questions come from a firm and hope-filled belief. In my ministry I experience a reality which demonstrates that God's people strengthen their faith by the sacraments and the rituals. I see this when parishioners assemble for communion services when a presbyter does not preside. They are not concerned about the canonical status of the presider; their only desire is for someone to bring Christ to them. I find it deeply painful to be told as a parish minister that I can share my faith only so far in the ritual celebration.

Dreaming New Answers

Yes, I chose to respond to God's call to service as a brother. I do not yearn to be a member of the clerical structure of the church, and I am not asking to be considered a "mini-sacramental machine" in the absence of a presbyter. I am asking that attitudes and unnecessary restrictions be seen for what they are and removed. I am one of many who are willing, ready, and able to respond to the needs of God's people. I dream of the day when I and others will not be confronted by the legal complications of status in the church. I dream of the day when some of the sacraments need not be celebrated only by Father X. I dream of the opportunity to celebrate my life and my ministry as a brother without having to answer the sincere question: "Weren't you good enough to become a priest?"

Improbable dreams? Am I another moth trying to reach the moon in the branches of an oak tree? I think not. As Christians, and in our response to God as brothers, we have the ability to challenge and change the status quo. We know the injustice of a legal system preoccupied with status and the maintenance of order to the exclusion of change. We in clerical Institutes have experienced this pain in our silent service all too often. We justify it to varying degrees with theological and spiritual mandates that we be like Saint Joseph who was meek and humble of heart, who worked without being seen or heard.

But Saint Joseph was also a dreamer and a provider. As a brother, I, too, must dream of the improbable with the grace of my baptism and profession. It is from dreams like those I share here that challenge and change find expression. Like Saint Joseph we need to have faith in ourselves and in our God in the face of those who would kill the dream.

Old Terms, New Definitions

With these dreams as part of the bedrock of my being, I face the twenty-first century with an eye to our roots as Christians because I believe that in those roots is the raw material for needed changes. In our vast Christian heritage and vocabulary we have three concepts which we must recover for the future. In theology, we are accustomed to speak of the triad "priest, prophet, and king." I suggest here that we think in terms of "priest, prophet, and procreator."

Reclaiming the Definition of Priest

Earlier in this article, I offered my definition of "priest," and I repeat here that it does not correspond with the popular interpretation and understanding that "priest equals presbyter." The terms are not the same. For me, the term "priest" involves three major phases of relationship with God: keeper of tradition, person of prayer, and one who sacrifices. These Hebrew Scripture models are exemplified in the life of Jesus Christ.

Priesthood and Tradition

All persons are called to relationship with God, with each other, and with the cosmos. Created in the image and likeness of God, we are infused with the grace and dignity of the Divine Mystery. As Christians, our heritage of experience with God in faith and revelation is a vast treasure. Through baptism we inherit this tradition and live within it. One of the functions of "priest," as I see it, is to know, reflect, and understand this treasured heritage as a guide to our beliefs and activities as Christians. We must continue to study what has been proclaimed to us so that we can understand and live this proclamation in the world. The Vatican II document, *Gaudium et Spes,* challenges us in these words:

> At all times the Church carries the responsibility of reading the signs of the times and interpreting them in the light of the Gospel if it is to carry out its tasks. In language intelligible to every generation it should be able to answer the ever recurring questions which men [and women] ask about the meaning of this present life and of the life to come, and how one is related to the other.[7]

As brothers and ministers of the Gospel, we know God is present in our life story. Salvation history has changed human history, our history. Sharing the priesthood of the faithful[8] in a unique way through our ministry, we strive to make this salvation event a part of the lives we touch.

Priesthood and Prayer

The priest is also a person of prayer, as Jesus himself demonstrated by word and deed. In Leviticus 19:2, we read "Be holy, for I, the Lord your God, am holy." But to be a person of prayer takes time for growth, and maturity. This prayer of the priest is both private and public. In the experience of the Divine the energy to live and dream is realized. It is in prayer that the loving commitment to God and others is found.

Priesthood and Sacrifice

I think of priestly sacrifice in terms of service that stems from prayer. This sacrifice can be viewed in two interrelated ways. The first is by witness. Priests who know God's power in history and feel that power in prayer are bound (almost forced) to speak of it. They cannot hold it in. This speaking is the witness; here the priest's relationship with God becomes visible. The powerful presence of God shines forth in this person who gives authentic witness to God as a visible sign of the kingdom.

The second aspect of this sacrifice is service. Priests put themselves on the line for others. This involves a deep appreciation of our calling as children of God, and it can be seen in a caring for all forms of life and creation. This kind of service also calls others to share the heritage and prayer by our priestly example. In this way, as the Gospel suggests, we become lights on lampstands.

Can a Brother Be a Priest?

How do these views affect my identity as a brother? I believe that my baptism and my religious profession as a brother call me to be a priest of God in the three ways I have outlined. When I made my vows, I chose Christ as the focus for my life, a focus framed by the charism of my religious congregation. But this focus is also a living choice. As a brother I become immersed in the historical legacy both of my community and of Christianity by ongoing instruction, study, and reflection on what it means to be a Christian and a member of my community. Immersed as we are in our history and traditions, we interpret this religious heritage as we live in the midst of creation. We examine the signs of the times and we respond. We fulfill that first part of the definition of priest.

Brothers are men of prayer. The hours spent over a lifetime in the presence of God bring growth in one's relationship with the Holy. Our times of silence and solitude, of reflection and sharing, of reading and probing are spent that we might hear the voice of God in the whisper of the wind, as Elijah did. This growth in prayer has graced my ministry when I have led a parish in formal public prayer. More than this, though, we lead prayer when we live the Scriptures in the midst of those we serve. This is an integral part of our identity as priests. How and where God chooses to make this evident is often miraculous in its simplicity.

The element of sacrifice—in witness and service—is all too often silent and hidden. Yet there is great power in our priestly sacrifice. A presbyter in my order recently stated:

> The ministry of the brother is often more effective and convincing than that of the instruction of the [presbyter], it goes to the heart and touches people. It is the same in community. The cook shows a more practical charity—which members gratefully perceive—than that of even the superior. His absence is felt more personally.[9]

The sacrificial witness and service of brothers' lives is unmistakably priestly, even in the pain and hurt of their unfulfilled dreams for the sake of the kingdom. This sacrifice is our response to God who calls us; out of this sacrifice we have much to say to others in spite of the frustrations we experience as a result of attitudes and laws that restrict our witness. Those same laws declare that the brother makes a contribution to the salvific mission of the church;[10] that the brother is an outstanding sign of the church[11] attempting to follow Christ, announcing the Kingdom and doing the will of God.[12] All Christian women and men who would serve the People of God are challenged both by their need to serve and the laws that restrict it. In all this we must strive to hear the clarion call of the prophet's voice in the wilderness.

What is a Prophet?

I believe that our very baptism is a call to be prophetic. Out of this call, we witness to the experience of God in life and call forth appropriate responses from those we serve. As a prophet, Jesus demonstrated the priestliness of this call. He interpreted the tradition, he showed the power of prayer in his service of reconciliation and healing. His words and works were a witness to a new, personal understanding of God open to each one of us. In his message of conversion the reign of God is evident now and in time to come.

Being prophetic demands the witness and prayer of the priest, and more. It demands a great love and a positive response to God who calls us. It requires time, energy, and growth in the relationship between myself, God, and others. It extends my frame of reference far beyond myself without denying personal dignity. It requires the ability to give and take, to speak and listen, to do and to be simultaneously.

As with the term "priest," "prophet" is also often misunderstood. Prophets are misinterpreted as being bizarre and foolish, haters of humanity bent on destruction. Without love, however, the prophet's words are merely wind and the message is shallow. A prophet without love is false. The prophet's message of conversion is not so much a call for destruction as it is a call for transformation, a belief in a better, deeper relationship with God and creation.

To be prophetic is to call the community of faith to stand in opposition to injustice, racial hatred, and economic exploitation of life. It requires a stance against the consumerism of Madison Avenue advertising and the vague value definitions from Capitol Hill. Being a prophet is to cast a critical eye on prevailing attitudes of the institutional church. Prophetic witness means putting yourself on the line and allowing the Spirit of God to work within you to proclaim God's powerful, encompassing love.

Being a prophet of the kingdom of God means demonstrating gospel values within your life, often in opposition to prevailing views, even within the church.

Brothers as Prophets

Being a prophet acquires new meaning with the choice for brotherhood. In a society which emphasizes material possessions and instant gratification, commitment to the gospel ideal of loving one's neighbor is an ultimate challenge. But the brother, among others, bears witness that this challenge can be met. Our life within the world and yet separate from it can challenge the world's attitudes, behavioral patterns, and directions. Prophetic living continually proclaims in thought, word, and deed that one can live in relationship with God and with others. By living in the world and reading the signs of the times, the brother as prophet has the ability to evaluate without the need to buy, as it were. By his prophetic witness in the midst of the institutional church, he can serve without being ensnared in the false trappings of pretension and grandeur. Most important, the brother as prophet is a living bridge between the church and the world. By the example and quality of their lives and ministry, brothers offer an alternative to both worlds. The lay person might claim an inability to pray because of the demands on time and energy at home and work. Yet there stands the legion of brothers living similar types of struggles and attempting to integrate prayer into their busy lives. The cleric engaged in the details of administration, meetings, and spiritual development might claim to be too harried and exhausted from ministry to appreciate life outside the institutional edifice. Yet there stands the legion of brothers engaged in similar ministries finding the time to love and be loved by others. These often nameless brothers witness the genuine power of holy love in quiet and unassuming ways. Here are prophets of God walking with their sisters and brothers. Here the heart of God may be felt reaching out with love and compassion.

So the brother/prophet stands between two powerful forces (the church and the world) in service of another force: God. We do not desire clerical rank, nor do we need worldly recognition. But we have the training, dedication, and graced strength to minister affectively and effectively to both church and world.

No One Said It Would Be Easy

Like the prophets of old, brothers run the risk of being misunderstood. People often question our qualifications and our motives, judging us to be part of the hierarchical structure of the church and failing to see us as their kin. Perhaps in their anger at both the church and the world, they fail to recognize us for who we are. At the same time, the institutional church has difficulty with us. We are not "priests." We belong to religious congregations, but canonically we are lay people. We are graced by baptism to serve the people of God but not without institutional restrictions. Within our communities severe limitations exist if the word "clerical" appears in a constitution. So both the church and the world might rightfully ask: "Why do brothers exist?"

However, like the Hebrew Scripture prophets, we do exist. We continue to proclaim and interpret the Word of God in a vast array of services and situations. A powerful and stirring grace is in this vocation, a perseverance which flows from the waters of our baptism. As prophets, brothers today share the pained anguish of those who yearn to serve God but are turned away. As prophets, brothers engage in the struggle to be holy in the context of the world. Living often in pain and frustration, we nevertheless proclaim the kingdom of God yet to come. By our lives the prophetic voice of God is heard in human history. We live in the hope that our dedication to a lifestyle and message of love will enable us to address the injustice of the status quo. We recall that in the quiet dignity of life God speaks like the gentle breeze experienced by the prophet Elijah.

Lest the reader think this view is romanticized and sanitized, listen to the young and old who walk as brothers. They experience pain and anguish, frustration, despair, and sorrow. Yet in this desert the love of God is ever blooming. Prophetic witness is never easy, romantic, or sanitary. It is wrought with the pain and suffering Jeremiah discovered to his horror. It involves decrying the unjust acts of the complacent powerful on ivory beds of the status quo, as Amos realized. But the force of God's spirit working within us as prophets inspires us to new visions, as Isaiah and Ezekiel proclaimed. The task of the prophet complements that of the priest. This, too, is the task of the brother: to bring the experience of God and the promise of the kingdom to persons everywhere by the witness of our lives lived in faith, hope, and especially love.

Old Word, New Meaning

I now come to the term "procreator" as the last in my triad. Accustomed to controversy, I do not shy away from using this word in a rather different context as I have already done for the words priest and prophet. The concept of procreator has a great deal to offer.

I have stated that the prophet needs to be stirred by powerful love, of both God and of one's neighbors. As I see it, however, it is also in prophetic proclamation that one becomes a procreator. The people of God are not static entities. We are living beings relating to each other and to creation. We are involved in salvation history to varying degrees. As brothers (priests, prophets, and now procreators) our mission is to go forth and direct our energies to the service of others. We are challenged to bridge human boundaries bringing God's word and love with us. In short, as "pro-creators" we become missionaries and ministers of God's ongoing work of creation.

The focus of the procreator is mission. I do not create out of nothing. Rather, as procreator, the brother uses the vast heritage of priesthood and the searing vision of prophet to bring the creative message of God to others. This mission involves both leadership and nurturing, assisting others to discover and grow in knowledge of God while maintaining one's own dignified differences. In this "pro-creative" (and pro-active) effort the church grows as a visible sign of the kingdom in the midst of the world. I think Paul realized this when he appealed to the generosity of early Christian communities on behalf of the Jerusalem Church. The money itself was not the issue. Rather, its collection was a witness of solidarity, recognition of a common salvation history in the context of an expanding church. It reminded everyone not to forget the foundation as the "building" of the church was going up.

To be procreator is to be aware of the needs of others. It means recognizing the dignity and worth of people. It calls for a deeper understanding of God's creation and humanity's place in it. As brothers, we share God's love and recognize our activity as procreators by becoming involved in the reality of others. In the outward movement from one context to another God's love and grace are shared. If that love flows from the priestly and prophetic facets of our baptismal call, then our mission as procreators will be ever mindful that all life, human and otherwise, is part of God's goodness and also to be respected.

Brothers as Procreators

As a brother I am involved in the life-giving action of God as salvation history unfolds. The prophets realized that they could not keep silent the word of God. So too must the love of God I experience be proclaimed. My task is to share my gifts and talents in the world and in the church. I bring the good news of salvation with me as I discover and live the role of procreator. It is intertwined in my commitment to God and community. It is found in the use of time, talent, and treasure, even if these are not in the public eye. It is demonstrated whenever and wherever lives touch and God is included. It is seen in the service that goes unrecognized while the voice of God thunders mightily. It is felt in the pain brothers experience as they face a society and institutional church bewildered by them. It is where brothers confront (and even fall in the face of) attitudes and laws that seem to disintegrate humans instead of re-creating them.

So our priesthood requires of us knowledge, prayer, and sacrifice. Our prophecy, infused with and tempered by a genuine love promotes God's word. Our pro-creation is an actual sharing in the mission of God. These dimensions added to our brotherhood, if we claim them as our own, are characteristics which I firmly believe will bring us to the twenty-first century as a renewed and ever more viable force for good in both the church and the world.

What Does All This Mean?

Brothers stand on the cusp of a new vision of the church and the world as we embrace, rather than shun, the fact that we occupy an awkward place in both. Neither standing within the clerical structure of the church nor swayed by the passing whims of the world, we have much to offer both by embracing our real strength as bridges between the two. As we recover and lay claim to the other dimensions of our calling—as priests, prophets, and procreators—we become living witnesses to the dynamic presence of God in our midst, we point with our very lives to those things that divide us as church and as world, and we work with the power of God to bring together in a new creation what has grown apart.

We brothers see ourselves as part of God's activity. We involve ourselves in a profusion of ministries, and we stand in solidarity with the people of God whom we serve. We can be priestly while part of the world, struggling to demonstrate the power of God's love. We can show that the halls of government and the forces of advertising are not the sole guardians of truth and value. In the institutional church we find ourselves allied with those who feel the burdens of legal impositions. We, too, stand willing and able, striving for fuller participation. We often work in areas of the world where presbyters are seldom seen, here coming to understand with compassion those lives that touch our own.

Finally, as dreamers but also as critical observers, we need to persevere with our questions as we strive to recover and uncover definitions which will open up more church ministries to those called by God, trained and educated to serve regardless of gender and marital or clerical status. In doing this, we point clearly to the fact that responsibility for the kingdom lies ultimately with all baptized persons, united with one another and with God.

Impossible thoughts? Improbable dreams? Or is the Spirit at work prodding an ever-developing church? Part of the answer is to be found in the conversations and dialogues in which we brothers are, and must continue to be, involved. Jesus did tell Peter that he was the rock upon which the church was to be built (Mt 16:18). But is that rock merely a piece of granite, never moving, and slowly eroded from without by the forces of nature? Or is it rather a foundation above which a pilgrim (and dream-filled) people venture forth in a spirit of discovery of self, others, and God? Priests, prophets, and procreators: mortar by which we brothers contribute to building up the kingdom of God.

Impossible Thoughts?

The queen remarked "Now I'll give *you* something to believe. I'm just one hundred and one, five months and a day."

"I can't believe *that!*" said Alice.

"Can't you?" the queen said in a pitying tone. "Try again: draw a long breath and shut your eyes."

Alice laughed. "There is no use in trying," she said. "One *can't* believe impossible things."

"I daresay you haven't had much practice," said the queen. "Why, when I was your age I always did it for half an hour before breakfast. Why sometimes I believed as many as six impossible things before breakfast."[13]

Notes

1. All Scripture references are from *The New American Bible* (Nashville, TN: Thomas Nelson, 1971).

2. *Constitutions of the Congregation of the Priests of the Sacred Heart* (1982) 8, par. 3.

3. *Constitutions*, 8, par. 1.

4. Canon Law Society of America, *Code of Canon Law: Latin-English Edition* (Washington, DC, 1983) canon 588, 223.

5. See Matthew 5–6.

6. "For you are still of the flesh. While there is jealousy and rivalry among you, are you not of the flesh and behaving in an ordinary human way? Whenever someone says, 'I belong to Paul,' and another, 'I belong to Apollos,' are you not merely human? What is Apollos, after all, and what is Paul? Ministers through whom you became believers, just as the Lord assigned each one. I planted, Apollos watered, but God caused the growth. Therefore, neither the one who plants nor the one who waters is anything, but only God, who causes the growth. The one who plants and the one who waters are equal, and each will receive wages in proportion to his labor. For we are God's co-workers; you are God's field, God's building."

7. Austin Flannery, OP, gen. ed., *Vatican Council II: The Conciliar and Post-Conciliar Documents* (Northport, NY: Costello Publishing, 1975) GS 4.

8. Ibid., *Apostolicam Actuositatem*, 2. "The laity, too, share in the priestly, prophetic, and royal office of Christ and therefore have their own role to play in the mission of the whole People of God in the Church and in the world."

9. From a discussion regarding the vocation of brothers within the United States Province of the Priests of the Sacred Heart.

10. Canon Law Society, *Code*, canon 574, 221.

11. Canon Law Society, *Code*, canon 573, 219.

12. Canon Law Society, *Code*, canon 577, 221.

13. Lewis Carroll, "Through the Looking Glass," *The Complete Illustrated Works of Lewis Carroll* (London: Chancellor Press, 1982) 173.

Creating Right Relationships in Clerical Institutes

Bernard P. Spitzley, SVD

Imagine a mixed community in which all participate as equals in rituals, rotating leadership, and receiving equal pay regardless of education, skills, or years of service. The word "brother" implies such an egalitarian relationship. Yet when one examines the internal relations in clerical institutes today, a hierarchial order with a clerical-lay division still exists.

In this article I will present some of the challenges involved in moving toward equal or right relationships in clerical institutes. I review the deliberations at the Generalate level and the effects of clericalism, and I also explore the prophetic, dynamic role of religious life, and the call to live on the threshold, open to creating new realities of being in ministry and community. I will conclude by describing an alternative model for clerical institutes to consider.

BROTHER BERNARD SPITZLEY, SVD, is a member of the Society of the Divine Word. He is a native of Westphalia, Michigan, and is presently the Director of Formation of Brother Candidates for the Society and an Associate at NETWORK. He joined the Society of the Divine Word in 1975 and professed perpetual vows in 1981. He has a BA from Divine Word College and an MA from Loyola University of Chicago. Brother Bernard's previous ministries have included junior high and college teaching, formation work, and college administration. He also serves as a spiritual director in the Washington DC area. Brother Bernard may be addressed at 1009 Bunker Hill Road, Washington, DC 20017.

Deliberations in Rome

As a brother in a clerical institute, I applaud the work done by the Union of Superiors General (USG) to encourage the Vatican Congregation for Institutes of Consecrated Life and Societies of Apostolic Life (CICLSAL) to allow election to the office of superior in clerical institutes for *all* members. Canon law states clearly that in clerical institutes, though the clerics and brothers live as one religious community, the competence of authority is placed on the clerics only. This regulation eliminates the possibility of a brother in a clerical religious institute becoming a rector or provincial or taking any leadership role.

The result of the constant requests and challenges by the USG of CICLSAL in recent years (May 1986 Plenary Session of CICLSAL, papers by Father General Kolvenbach, SJ, and Father General Michael Boyle, CP), plus the request by the Camilliani, Capauchins, Paolini, and Divine Word Missionaries,[1] has led to obtaining an indult for some brothers to be appointed local superior of their community. Nevertheless, it seems evident that the overall change in canon law desired by many clerical institutes—opening the office of superior to lay *and* cleric members—is far from becoming a reality.

Some would say we need the patience and perseverance of the widow in soliciting the unscrupulous judge (Lk 18:1–5), for as she eventually received her just rights, so will brothers in clerical institutes. While it is necessary for the arduous task of these negotiations to take place in Rome, I believe much work can and needs to be done on the local level in creating right relationships. We need to reread and reclaim the Vatican II documents that have led to lively discussion of the lay person's place in the church.

> The laity, too, share in the priestly, prophetic, and royal office of Christ and therefore have their own role to play in the mission of the whole People of God in the Church and in the world.[2]

The laity are becoming more aware of how real the general priesthood of the faithful is. For example, various lay ministries are being taken seriously as elements for building Christian communities, and gifts of grace are being experienced in deeper reality by all.

Within clerical institutes the clear-cut distinction between clerical and lay states still needs to be overhauled by a more complex and subtle notion of the diversification of ministries and the discovery of their complementary roles. The research of Cada et al., *Shaping the Coming Age of Religious Life*,[3] illustrates that the relationship between clerics and lay in religious institutes has changed over the centuries. The authors' insights free us from any illusion that the present practice of a hierarchial order is the norm. The terminology "clerical-lay" and "priesthood-laity," although ancient, corresponds neither to the intent of the Scriptures (the term "hierarchy" is not even found in Scripture) nor to the present demands of the church's active presence in the world.

Clericalism: A Definition

Yet we still are bound to the constraints of the institutional church, which Mary Ann Donovan, SC, describes as "hardened by clericalism and by the accompanying patriarchalism which is destructive of healthy relationships among adults."[4] The Conference of Major Superiors Of Men's 1983 study defines clericalism as

> the conscious or unconscious concern to promote the particular interests of the clergy and to protect the privileges and power that have traditionally been conceded to those in the clerical state. . . . Among its chief manifestations are an authoritarian style of ministerial leadership, a rigidly hierarchial world view, and virtual identification of the holiness and grace of the church with the clerical state and, thereby, with the cleric himself.[5]

This definition of clericalism is not characteristic of all priests, nor are brothers themselves immune from clericalism. Thus it is imperative that *all* in mixed communities, especially those in leadership, reflect on whether they are in right relationships with members of their community and those whom they serve.

Dynamic Dimension of Religious Life

A mixed religious institute offers the opportunity to counter an excessive attachment to the distinction "clerical-lay" and the destructive relationships that result from a hierarchial institution. We need to view religious life as a social movement, a dynamic, value-oriented movement in the church and society arising from a gospel vision of what ought to be. The Gospel, when lived with integrity, always leads to right relationships. We need to believe that religious congregations are vehicles for social movement and, as such, are shaped by, and in turn shape, social and ecclesial realities. If we are true to this concept of religious life, we are challenged to be dynamic rather than static entities. Thus, as religious in clerical institutes we need to live in what Diarmuid O'Murchu calls a stance of "prophetic liminality,"[6] an indefinable, ambiguous space thrust upon a person or group. O'Murchu describes liminality as being at the threshold between "what is" and "what ought to be," a position of privilege and of pain, both inviting and frightening.

This stance calls for re-examining how we make decisions, and in particular, what model of management we employ in our ministries and communities. We are all familiar with the hierarchial and impersonal administrative model of management found in most secular and male religious organizations. Such a model often leads to a two-tiered approach to management—a leader and followers—creating a class of "starry-eyed disciples," who depend on a superior for leadership. In time, these disciples refuse to view the world, their community, and their ministry for themselves; they see only through their superior's eyes. Such a model leads to passive, lethargic organizations, far from the countercultural communities we are called to be: communities that are on the frontier, open to new horizons, and able to dream new possibilities.

We have to be liminal or threshold people who can read the signs of the times and articulate alternative futures individually and corporately. This position requires the kind of faith that knows God is alive and operative in our history rather than set aside from it, a faith that believes we are co-creators with God in developing other ways of being in right relationship. It means accepting the difficult and onerous task of examining our ministries, our institutions, the structures and systems which sustain or impede our movement with focus and flexibility.

As a result of this scrutiny we will be able to create anew, to envision a different reality, and to take steps to create that new way of being. This process of re-creating right relationships needs the gifts and talents of all. For religious life to respond to the demands of the world, it is necessary to have cooperation and not control, consensus instead of competition, collaboration rather than coercion.

Yet many men's religious communities subscribe to the hierarchical model of administration—an experience that leaves one tired, weary of meetings, de-energized, and "tied down." Gerald Arbuckle, SM, speaks of "rituals of control,"[7] where in corporate cultures, subtle and not-so-subtle methods are used to tie down or neutralize innovative people much as the people of Lilliput did to Gulliver in Jonathan Swift's classic, *Gulliver's Travels*. Such a model runs counter to what we as dynamic religious are called to be. The hierarchical model is confining, controlling, and leads to coercion. Creativity is crushed, and as Arbuckle concludes, reforming one's community becomes almost impossible. Arbuckle believes we need re-founders, men who can create new, vibrant communities. Yet so often these religious are over burdened by the institutional demands placed on them by their communities or orders.

Some brothers in clerical institutes have given up hope and are filled instead with cynicism and anger. Their experience is that brothers are kept in a subservient role and not recognized as competent for the role of leadership. Instead of giving up hope and falling into a lethargic state, we need to seize the stirrings of change we experience and name injustice where it exists. Then we must work for change.

Naming the Injustice

Saying that clericalism exists, that hierarchical structures are repressive, and being concrete in naming the injustice is necessary to begin the work of creating right relationships. Through honest dialogue, communities need to ask what can be done to bring about change, to make a difference. We need to see that a number of people are willing to be brought into the change into action. For most groups who are exploited or who are not in right relationships, Dorothy Soelle identifies three stages in their response to injustice.[8] First, they are unaware of or mute to their status. Second, once they begin to reflect on and assess their plight, consciousness-raising takes place; this includes naming the injustice and leads to lamenting or lifting up one's voice to cry for justice. The third and critical stage is bonding together to work for change.

Our communities need to reflect on and evaluate every aspect of our lives as religious. For example, is the sacrament of the Eucharist a celebration of unity, or a daily reminder of our differences as some members stand at the altar while others remain in the pews? What role does concelebration have in our communities? Do we correct homilists who mention only priests and sisters, and so perpetuate the "hidden Joseph" myth of brotherhood? Do we question seminarians in temporary vows who use the title "Brother," thus confusing our identity for those with whom we work and live? Do our community celebrations of anniversaries for our ordained confreres tend to discount the place of religious vows in their lives? These and similar questions need to be raised and discussed by all in mixed communities.

Peter Henriot, SJ, defines social justice as "loving people so much that I work to change the structures that violate their dignity."[9] To be people of justice, we need to have this kind of love whereby we can change institutions, the way we live, the way we view life. We need to review our interrelationships and change the way we relate to each other. We need to deal with problems across and beneath the divisions among us, examining which parts of our history, ideology, and training keep us apart. We need to learn again to think together, to discuss together—not in competition but in collaboration.

Need for Local Community Involvement

An example of how change can take place on the local level rather than be imposed from on high can be seen in the realm of federal politics. Conventional wisdom suggests that Americans do not care about, and no longer want to participate in, political life. A study released after the Persian Gulf War by the Kettering Foundation, found that people

> are not apathetic, but do feel impotent when it comes to politics . . . "pushed out" of virtually every area of the political

process . . . cut off from the political debate . . . do not see their concerns reflected as current issues are discussed . . . [and] do not find issues framed in terms they understand. . . . [They] have lost faith in available means for expressing their views . . . [and] even question the usefulness of voting.[10]

Thus many feel alienated on the national level when they do not perceive government as addressing their needs. The study concludes, however, that Americans will participate in specific areas of public life, most often in their local communities and neighborhoods, but only when they believe they can make a difference. Therefore, the challenge is to reconnect citizens and politics, to find a place for citizens in the political process.

So it is with brothers in clerical institutes. We must do our work with hope and realism, maintaining the vision of what a just community looks like. We need to develop concrete alternative models of decision-making, prayer, and the spirit in which we do our ministries. Our purpose is to be pro-active, shaping the change into creating right relationships within our communities and work places.

Fritjof Capra describes one model of change in his book, *Turning Point.*[11] Drawing on the insights of quantum physics, he believes social change will take place when there are enough pockets of energy in enough places; the buildup will be a catalyst for the quantum leap to a different level. The linking together of small communities can be a powerful force of related purpose and mutual encouragement enabling us to work together to create change. Using Capra's model we need to focus on the local level where change ultimately has to happen. In time, this change will create a momentum and influence policy within our institutes.

All of us need to change our existing institutions from within. All of us need to approach our ministry, be it in schools, hospitals, soup kitchens, or parishes, with new concepts of the relationships between people, alternative methods of expressing status, creative ways of resolving conflict.

Integrating Spirituality and Justice

In recent years numerous small Christian communities have been addressing social problems through systemic and structural analysis and by applying Christian values to those problems. Through their lived experience these small communities are also bringing spirituality and justice together. Spirituality is a process of personal transformation. Through spiritual practices (meditation, prayer, ritual) and through the living out of the fruits of these practices in our lives, we become better persons, more loving, more congruent with the values we profess. We grow and mature as persons and become psychologically and spiritually integrated. Justice is the process of bringing social groups into right relationships with each other. It involves eradicating the legal enforcement of one group's domination over another (men over women, rich over poor, clerics over laity). Justice transforms dominant/submissive relationships into partnerships. Experience has shown that spirituality and social justice are a graced dynamic, but when separated from each other both are rendered ineffective, destructive, and irrelevant. When these two are integrated, the world and the Christian community are graced with life-giving energies.

NETWORK'S Alternative Model of Management

There are many examples of communities such as the Catholic Worker community, Sojourners, and Pax Christi, who combine the elements of spirituality and activism. The organization where I work, NETWORK, is a national Catholic social justice lobby which attempts to influence the formation of public policy in the interest of the poor and powerless.[12] It lobbies members of Congress to enact laws providing access to economic resources, fairness in national funding, and justice in global relationships.

NETWORK's advocacy to bring about systemic change is rooted in the tradition of Catholic social teaching and gospel values. We incorporate into our workplace the values we advocate in the public arena, creating new models of management in which the values of participation, integration, and mutuality are woven into the lifeblood of NETWORK. As an alternative to hierarchical power, relationships where the decisions-makers are at the top and the workers are at the bottom, NETWORK staff members are encouraged to contribute to the life of the organization; all have access to influence organizational decisions. We share rotating leadership at meetings and create work plans for our respective areas of responsibility. We are all accountable to each other for the quality of our work and work relationships. All staff members engage in annual peer evaluation of job performance, thus engendering mutuality, honesty, openness, support, and challenge among the staff.

A sense of collaboration is further enhanced by the equal pay policy. All full-time staff receive the same salary regardless of tenure, experience, or education. This policy rests on the underlying principles of the worker's dignity and mutuality in work relationships. As an alternative to hierarchical pay scales, it virtually eliminates competition for scarce organizational resources and promotes a sense of equality for all.

Several days a year are set aside to reflect on our "political ministry"—our choice to live out our response to the Gospel in the public arena. We develop and participate in rituals and liturgical events which strengthen our sense of solidarity as persons of faith committed to justice.

Conclusion

As dynamic and creative agents of change, we religious can adapt and implement such alternatives in our communities and in our ministries. We need to visualize the result if we adopted NETWORK's management structure for clerical institutes, for example, in which all participated in rituals as equals, with rotating leadership within communities and equal pay for all, regardless of education, skills, or years of service.

For the past few years my local community of brother candidates and members in temporal and perpetual vows has adopted this model. We all create, review, and regulate our budget in which we pool together monies received from summer employment, ministries, and the province subsidy. Everyone receives the same allowance, shares one phone line and one vehicle. All have equal voice in developing community decisions. Rituals such as bible sharing, creative liturgies, and rotating leadership at meetings give a sense of collaboration and help us create right relationships.

We can create right relationships within our clerical institutes if we are open to adopting alternative models of leadership. Then the words of Saint James can find a home in us and the biblical value of inclusivity can become a reality: "Do not try to combine faith in Jesus Christ, our glorified Lord, with the making of distinctions between classes of people" (Jas 2:1).

Notes

1. *Nuntius Societatis Verbi Divini,* "Canonical Status of Our Society and the Resulting Limitations placed by Canon Law on the Offices open in the Society to Our Brothers," 13:5, 1988.

2. *Apostolicam Actuositatem,* 2.

3. Lawrence Cada et al., *Shaping the Coming Age of Religious Life* (New York: Seabury Press, 1979).

4. Mary Ann Donovan, "A More Limited Witness" in Felknor, ed., *The Crisis in Religious Vocations* (Mahwah, NJ: Paulist Press, 1989) 88.

5. CMSM Documentation, 37 (April 8, 1983) 2.

6. Diarmuid O'Murchu, *Religious Life: A Prophetic Vision* (Notre Dame, IN: Ave Maria Press, 1991) 41.

7. Gerald Arbuckle, *Out of Chaos* (Mahwah, NJ: Paulist Press, 1988) 43.

8. Dorothy Soelle, *Political Theology* (Philadelphia: Fortress Press, 1974).

9. As quoted in R. Hofbauer, D. Kinsella, and A. Miller, *Making Social Analysis Useful* (Leadership Conference Women Religious Document, 1983) 5.

10. Kettering Foundation, "Citizens and Politics: A View from Main Street America" (1991).

11. Fritjof Capra, *Turning Point* (New York: Simon and Schuster. 1982).

12. "Celebrating 20 Years of Creating Alternatives," *NETWORK Connection,* 20:3 (May–June 1992).

Created and Consecrated:
A Cosmology of Brotherhood

Thomas Grady, OSF

The geocentric representation of the world was commonly admitted in the culture of [Galileo's] time as fully agreeing with the teaching of the Bible, of which certain expressions, taken literally, seemed to affirm geocentrism. The problem posed by theologians of that age was, therefore, that of the compatibility between heliocentrism and Scripture.

Thus the new science, with its methods and the freedom of research it implied, obliged theologians to examine their own criteria of scriptural interpretation. Most of them did not know how to do so.[1]

Pope John Paul II recounted this story on October 31, 1992 as he closed the nearly 400-year-old Galileo case. In his address to the Pontifical Academy of Sciences he cited several lessons to be learned from this case, one being that "in order to account for the rich variety of complexity, we must have recourse to a number of different models."[2]

BROTHER THOMAS GRADY, OSF, is a Brother of the Third Order Regular of St. Francis in Brooklyn, New York. A native of Massachusetts, he entered the Franciscan Brothers in 1963 and professed life vows in 1971. His ministries have included elementary and secondary education, inner-city parish ministries, and prison ministry, all in Brooklyn. In his congregation he has served as General Councillor and Formation Director, and since 1985 as Superior General. His many services on diverse boards include the editorial board of *Haversack: A Franciscan Review*, the co-chairmanship of Franciscans International, a nongovernmental organization at the United Nations, being a past president of the Franciscan Federation of the Brothers and Sisters of the United States, and currently serving on the General Council of the International Franciscan Conference. Brother Thomas may be addressed at 135 Remsen Street, Brooklyn, NY 11201-8217.

In recalling the debate about whether Earth or the sun is the center of the universe, the pope noted that both sides of the argument accepted the cosmos as contained within our solar system. "Lacking an absolute physical reference point was inconceivable." The lesson here, he continued, is that "often beyond two partial and contrasting perceptions there exists a wider perception that includes them and goes beyond both of them."[3]

On the eve of a new millennium we face contrasting perceptions of reality as tumultuous as those of Galileo's time. The tumult for us lies not in accepting the fact that the universe is not centered on our planet, but in accepting the possibility that it is not centered on ourselves and, indeed, may not have a single center. It is in the context of this shifting perception that I will explore the question of who we are as brothers.

In preparation for the 1994 synod on consecrated life, the Vatican Synod Secretariat issued the *Lineamenta,* a paper designed to elicit input for developing a final working document for the synod. The *Lineamenta,* issued on November 20, 1992, contains a short section on brothers. It quotes *Perfectae Caritatis,* saying that "the lay religious life constitutes a state which of itself is one of total dedication to the profession of the evangelical counsels." It adds that "the lay consecrated life for men . . . represents consecration in its utter simplicity,"[4] meaning, I assume, free from the complexities of ordination. Be that as it may, I take "simplicity" as a compliment and a grace. The section concludes by saying that

> lay religious . . . open themselves to everyone in the universal love of Christ . . . in a universal brotherhood of communion, a fellowship which is inspired by the title they bear, that is, "brother."[5]

These two descriptions of brothers—consecration and communion—are the basic notions I will try to expand in the light of the new perceptions of our place in the universe.

Primary Revelation

The photograph of Earth from space has become a religious symbol to some, an icon of the unfathomable mystery of creation manifesting only beauty and harmony. We have seen what humans have never seen before, and have come to know that we are floating in space, imperceptible beings on a planet that has a life of its own: a fragile, interdependent, developing life. We know that the boundaries over which wars are fought are invisible and, ultimately, artificial. We know that Earth can die and that what happens to her happens to *us*. We know in a profound way which we cannot un-know that we are creatures. And with this knowledge, everything else we know changes.

For the first time in history, the human family has one common creation story, says Passionist priest Thomas Berry, an historian of cultures and self-described "geologian."

> The universe, the solar system, and the planet earth in themselves and in their evolutionary emergence constitute for the human community the primary revelation of that ultimate mystery whence all things emerge into being.[6]

This is the first of Berry's "Twelve Principles" for understanding the universe and the role of the human in the universe process. Forty years earlier Paul Tillich wrote:

> One thing is made very clear in the visions of the prophet, that salvation means salvation of the world, and not of human beings alone. Lions and sheep, little children and snakes, will lie together in peace, says Isaiah. Angels and stars, people and animals, adore the Child of the Christmas legend. The earth shakes when the Christ dies, and it shakes again when He is resurrected. The sun loses its light when He closes His eyes, and it rises when He rises from the tomb. The resurrection of the body—not an immortal soul—is the symbol of the victory over death.
>
> Let me ask you a question: are we still able to understand what a sacrament means? The more we are estranged from nature, the less we can answer affirmatively. For in the sacraments nature participates in the process of salvation. The sacrament, if its meaning is alive, grasps our unconscious as well as our conscious being. It grasps the creative ground of our being. It is the symbol of nature and spirit, united in salvation.[7]

This unity of nature and spirit, necessary if the meaning of a sacrament is to be alive, according to Tillich, is also necessary, I believe, if the meaning of vowed life is to be alive. I propose that we can understand the evangelical counsels more profoundly and vibrantly in the context of our new cosmology and in the specific gift of brotherhood we receive from and return to creation.

The new cosmology, articulated in *The Universe Story* by Thomas Berry and physicist Brian Swimme, sees creation as grounded in three characteristics manifested from the beginning of the universe: differentiation, subjectivity (or autopoiesis), and communion.[8] These, according to Berry, "constitute the ultimate basis of a functional spirituality for the human community just as they constitute the functional cosmology of the human community."[9] In my view, each of these three characteristics corresponds to the three evangelical counsels of poverty, obedience, and chastity. In the following pages I will draw out some of the connections I see between differentiation and poverty, subjectivity and obedience, and communion and celibate chastity. Each of these connections is presented from the perspective of brotherhood, or fraternal relationships with God, creation, and people. Although all of these cosmological characteristics are interrelated, as are the three evangelical counsels, the pairing I propose is not arbitrary. Each of the three characteristics and each of the three corresponding counsels attempts to express deeply-rooted beliefs that have their source in the wisdom of the universe.

As a Franciscan I have learned that the manifestation of virtues and values which Saint Francis saw in the elements of creation, and proclaimed in his mystical "Canticle of Creatures" is real. Yes, we can learn about obedience by contemplating an oxygen-producing tree, and about poverty from a dying star, or about chastity from sparkling streams of water.

I offer the connections I see between Berry's principles and the evangelical counsels as a preliminary reflection on new insights which call for further exploration. For me, an examination of each characteristic in relation to a counsel heightens the dynamism of our consecration by vow to universal brotherhood.

Differentiation and Poverty

The immediate expression of primordial reality is what Berry calls differentiation. We find the articulated reality of created existence in each being, unique in its ultimate reality, historically irreplaceable, fulfilling its proper role while constantly being transformed. This is not a new idea. Aquinas puts it this way:

> [God's] goodness could not be adequately represented by one creature alone. God produced many and diverse creatures, that what was wanting to one in the representation of the divine goodness might be supplied by another. For goodness, which in God is simple and uniform, in creatures is manifold and divided; and hence the whole universe together participates in the divine goodness more perfectly, and represents it better than any single creature whatever.[10]

The compatibility between these two Thomases is obvious. The difference lies in their cosmologies, which for Berry is emergent, for Aquinas more fixed. Of course we have new data since Aquinas, who wrote before Galileo had his problems about a geocentric universe and long before geologist John McPhee told us that "the summit of Mt. Everest is marine limestone,"[11] that is, the highest point on earth is from the ocean floor!

With our consciousness of an emergent creation I address the counsels not as fixed disciplines, though discipline is essential to integrity, but as developmental, dynamic commitments which shape our life's journey toward the fullness of brotherhood.

Poverty has always included the dual commitment of becoming poor in spirit and in fact. In recent years, poverty has emphasized service to the poor over being poor. Whether manifested in direct service, advocacy, or entering into solidarity with the poor, these good works have emerged from the urgent call to an option for the poor in our time. But the de-emphasis on being poor in fact makes poverty in spirit illusive. Consequently, beyond our ministries to the poor and our occasional acknowledgement of personal brokenness and need for healing, we give no corporate witness to an evangelical poverty that is exciting or inviting.

The principle of differentiation offers some paths out of this impasse. One is to take joy in our utter dependence on the rest of creation. This is true humility (*humus*, earth), knowing our place in the schema which Aquinas described: "The whole universe together participates in the divine goodness more perfectly."[12] Such an attitude rekindles a poverty in spirit which transforms our greed to gratitude and, in turn, changes behaviors.

Accepting our unique creaturehood joyfully and gratefully enables us to face some of the decisions demanded by what I called earlier the tumultuous question of our era: that we are not the one center. David Tracy has explored the implications of this question on Western thought. He writes:

> A fact seldom admitted by the moderns, the anti-moderns, and the post-moderns alike, even with all the talk of otherness and difference, is that there is no longer a center with margins. There are many centers. . . . The others must become genuine others for us—not projections of our own fears and desires. The others are not marginal to our centers but centers of their own.[13]

Tracy is not writing about the human's place in creation, but about pluralism in the human community. The center which he says "cannot hold" is that "which was once construed as the center of history—Western, including Western Christian theological culture."[14] Among his several suggestions for getting unstuck in this "age that cannot name itself" is one which I find extremely relevant here: "We need, above all, the ability of post-modern thought to allow the marginalized ones—especially the mystics—to speak once again."[15] Here we have a key to unlock the dynamism of a poverty which enables us to move from an artificial center to a celebration of differentiation in spirit and in fact.

The mystic sees in the diversity of creation what Aquinas called "the representation of the divine goodness."[16] From that vision actions are shaped. Indigenous peoples, for example, have among themselves some of the marginalized mystics from whom we are only beginning to learn about our place in nature. The famous words ascribed to Chief Seattle are startlingly clear 140 years after being spoken yet not understood.

> How can you buy or sell the sky, the warmth of the land? The idea is strange to us. If we do not own the freshness of the air and the sparkle of the water, how can you buy them? This we know. The earth does not belong to us; we belong to the earth. This we know. All things are connected. Whatever befalls the earth befalls the children of the earth. We did not weave the web of life; we are merely a strand in it. Whatever we do to the web, we do to ourselves.[17]

Chief Seattle's vision of interdependent differentiation among all elements of creation led inexorably to a nonproprietary relationship to the earth's resources. The vision has an economic consequence. The economic systems within which we function today are far from the notion that Earth's resources are a community rather than a commodity. But from within those systems people committed to evangelical poverty must become what Tracy calls "historical subjects with memory, hope and resistance."[18]

Our industrial economic system has done irreparable damage to the earth. This is well known, yet it continues. We must factor an earth equation into our economic decisions. What is the cost, not in terms of our gross national product, but in terms of the life of Earth, the life of differentiated creatures and resources, and indeed the life of future generations?

All these factors must be seen as connected. Even in our services to the poor we must broaden our vision. Feeding the hungry is a manifestation of our commitment to poverty. So too should be a commitment to resist economic policies that cause the United States to lose over four billion tons of topsoil each year, soil created over millennia, without which feeding the poor or anyone else becomes impossible. Unless we see and accept the connections we may be destroying life while we think we are enhancing it. "If the water is polluted it can neither be drunk nor used for baptism, for it no longer symbolizes life."[19] As we kill our physical world, our spiritual world dies inseparably.

Daniel Martin writes:

> Our dust is star dust, our family tree has intergalactic branches. This is a new story of the oneness and interconnectedness of all life, where everything we do affects everything else. We are part of an unfolding mystery that has been going on for 15 billion years. Our species is the most recent child of this process: in the clock of the universe, we appear on the scene only seconds before the midnight hour. This miracle of Creation is clearly not staged simply for our benefit.[20]

Our view of poverty moves us to enter into a differentiated creation as brothers to its elements. This movement is away from anthropocentrism and toward an expanded fraternity where interdependence is liberation and humility produces justice and joy. We can choose again to be poor in spirit and in fact. We can finally live simply grateful for "the divine goodness."

Subjectivity and Obedience

Subjectivity, the second aspect of Berry's cosmology, indicates the inner form, the radiant intelligibility, the ultimate mystery of the universe, all of which can be experienced in the energy of the nuclear structure as profoundly as anywhere in the world, and which shines forth in every articulated mode of being. This subjectivity, which is both matter and intelligible form, increases as complexity increases through the stages of life and consciousness. The spirituality, or numinous presence we experience, was there in the beginning. Its articulation is increased as subjectivity increases. We humans, then, are at our core the entire universe mystery that is at the core of everything that exists, and we are also the flowering of creation's divine consciousness.

Obedience has traditionally engaged us in discerning and following God's will and has included limiting our personal freedom in favor of the common good. Again I refer to the evangelical counsel of obedience as part of a dynamic and developmental spirituality, not as a political discipline reduced to juridical questions of authority.

Subjectivity, which characterizes the process of the inner articulation of each mode of being, can revitalize an obedience which calls us to become the holy human being God not only created but also became. In *The Incarnation of God,* Hans Kung wrote that

> Jesus is really the Christ precisely as our brother and the one for others: in ultimate underivability and ongoing significance he is the Word and Son of God and the Lord . . . and in him precisely as the *Word* of God, *God truly became flesh so that we might become human.*[21]

God's way of being in the world was indeed human; surprisingly so as theologian John Dunne wrote:

> God, according to Hinduism and Christianity, instead of eliminating the ills of human existence, becomes a human and shares in them. When God becomes human he must act as a human being, and a participant in the human drama rather than as its author. He can attempt to persuade the other human beings, to dissuade them from seeking to destroy one another, from seeking the fruits of action, but cannot compel them. . . . This is a surprise. We would dearly love to have the kind of power we imagine God to wield.

The prospect of doing without such power altogether is hard to contemplate. That God should do without it is amazing. [22]

The concept of becoming human is profoundly more expansive than it appears at first glance. Obedience within this context is a fiat to an unfolding mystery. Previous notions and practices of obedience derived from world views based upon an assumption that the universe was governed by unchanging laws. Twentieth-century discoveries of quantum indeterminacy in physics and genetic mutation in biology have taught us that the laws of the universe are not unchanging but are developing. The physicist Brian Swimme has written that these discoveries call us to "learn a new depth of obedience."

We can enter this work by learning to listen ever more deeply to the center of things . . . the great mineral cycles, the water cycle, the wind cycle. And we must discover at last that these are not somewhere outside our skin. All the achievements of the wilds are layered everywhere throughout our bodies and minds. A great energy has given birth to fifteen billion years of magnificence. Obedience begins there.[23]

I am neither a scientist nor a theologian, but I believe Berry, Martin, and Swimme because their discoveries and insights are true to my experience. We must listen to the universe to discover God and ourselves. This is the root of obedience.

My earliest recollection of a profoundly religious experience is standing beneath the aurora borealis as a boy. I felt overwhelmed, elated, and assimilated into something of infinite beauty. Traces of those feelings returned last year when I discovered geology, plate tectonics specifically. I was fascinated, and devoured what new information I could find. I learned then what I quoted earlier from John McPhee, that Mt. Everest came from the ocean. I learned about plates and faults. I learned that Japan, once attached to Asia, is moving toward Alaska one centimeter a year, that Boston came from Africa and northern Ireland from America. I learned that after India separated from Africa some 70 million years ago and moved northeast as rapidly as any drifting continent in the calculable history of plate tectonics—126 miles per million years—it collided with Asia, thereby creating the Himalayas (including Mt. Everest from the ocean floor), and that the movement continues, compressing at the rate of two inches per year.

I was amazed and excited. As McPhee noted, "The eye seldom sees what the mind does not anticipate."[24] My mind and eyes opened to something new. But the excitement was accompanied by dismay. I had learned that *terra firma* is an illusion. My world view was challenged. Then my reflection last summer turned to obedience, because in my psyche I had somehow connected it to solid ground (Peter, The Rock, perhaps). I concluded that I, like the moving mountain, am a human work in progress, and obedience is fidelity to that work. If our vision of such a venture is foggy, let us join the aged and blind Cherokee Chief in the 1970 film Little Big Man who faced death praying, "Thank you for my vision and for my blindness in which I saw further."

Brothers are in a unique position among those in consecrated life to revitalize obedience. We do not have the juridical and hierarchical confusions attached to clerics and we have generally been spared the authoritarian heavy-handedness visited upon our sisters by patriarchal ecclesiastics. In this reality Pope John Paul II's application of "simplicity" to the brother's vocation finds its truth. We are less bureaucratically oppressed and freer to emancipate the counsel of obedience from its institutional chains and to release its potential for shaping a common good for all of creation.

For brothers dynamic obedience arises from fidelity to fraternity, which lies at the core of the mystery of our being and bonds us at that core to everything that exists. Obedience requires a degree of asceticism, an ability to be transformed, to let go and create anew. The paschal mystery began with the death of a previous generation of stars and the birth of our galaxy. The universe obeys the cycle of death and rebirth, and teaches us to obey our call to consciously create more fully human reflections of the divine within creation. Obedience as subjectivity is a radical affirmation of brotherhood.

Communion and Chastity

Communion as a characteristic of the cosmos is based upon the gravitational attraction which holds every being in its identity and its relatedness. It establishes the unity of the entire creation in its every manifestation, enabling it to be a universe. According to this principle, every atomic particle is present to every other atomic particle in an inseparable unity, a unity that says that the volume of each atom is the volume of the universe. Communion unfolds the universe in the full complexity of its living and non-living forms, and fulfills its expression in conscious human affection and in the revelation of the divine.

Consecrated chastity, which includes celibacy, is probably the most stark of the three counsels in witnessing to something mysterious. It is also the least adequately described counsel. A treatment of the vows as dynamic and developmental is more easily understood in relation to poverty and obedience than it is to celibacy, which has usually been described as something one lives (or endures) rather than something one becomes.[25] But, in a fuller sense we grow in chastity, as we do in poverty and obedience, as we grow in love. Communion as a principle of cosmic spirituality adds to our understanding of chastity the attraction and allurement into affective relationship with God, people, and all creation.

Swimme's challenge to listen to the wild applies here as well as to obedience. The longing for fulfillment and completion is a divine yearning for unity. Consecrated chastity listens to the wild movement of sexual energy and directs it toward fulfillment in a sacred communion with all that is. It unites body and soul, will and heart, reflection and action with faith and hope and drives them all toward love. Celibacy only makes sense as a choice to fall in love with all of life in our perpetual desire for God.

To do otherwise, to resist, or reverse the drive toward communion is destructive. After fleeing the violence in Boznia and Herzegovina, a refugee friend of Croatian novelist Slavenka Drukalic asked her if she knew what war is. Drukalic wrote:

> I don't know what war is, but I can see that it is everywhere. It is in a street flooded with blood after twenty people are shot in a bread line in Sarajevo. But it is also in your not understanding it, and in my unconscious cruelty toward you. It is in the fact that you have that yellow (refugee) certificate and I don't. I can see the way that it is growing within us and changing us. We are the war. I am afraid there is no one else to blame. We all make it possible. We allow it to happen. There is no them and us. There are no numbers, masses, categories. There is only one us and, yes, we are responsible for each other.[26]

The call to communion recognizes the oneness at the core of the differentiated us. Lived in consecrated chastity, communion not only recognizes that oneness, but calls us to intimate union, intimate enough for us to be changed by the other. This is no easy task. Drukalic's story from Croatia is but one example of the deeply rooted tendency in the human psyche to order relations in superior-inferior categories, to label, dismiss, and even destroy the "other." We do not have to look beyond our borders for examples: in Los Angeles the riots, in Brooklyn the murders in Crown Heights and Bensonhurst remind us that one does not have to scratch the surface deeply to uncover fear of what is "other."

When I encourage an attitude of fraternal union with all of creation I am well aware of the fact that we are far from such union within human societies. Our own religious communities manifest our preference for homogeneity over pluralism. We have yet to unleash the power of fraternity, to create communion in a world which has fostered isolation, self-interest, and classes of people considered to be less than human. Fraternity in a radically gospel sense would demonstrate concretely that brotherhood-sisterhood is a viable alternative to the dominant superior-inferior model of relationships. The perfect curve of the universe holds everything in relationship. This gravitational attraction is the cosmic source of human affection. It reaches fulfillment in our gracing the principle of communion, or bonding, with the spiritual activity of compassion.

A friend to whom I was describing this article asked, "What does any of this mean in relation to dealing with broken people?" A good question, which I pondered inconclusively that evening. The next morning's Office offered an answer in Psalm 147.

> The Lord lifts up the lowly,
> heals the brokenhearted,
> counts the number of the stars
> and calls each by name.

God gave us the capacity and the call to relate to both broken stars and broken people as brothers and sisters. Either relationship is diminished by the absence of the other. Our consecration to fraternity is a commitment to unite those two apparently disparate dimensions in what Thomas Berry calls "mutually enhancing" relationship.

The cosmological principles tell us that the potential and energy for such compassionate communion has been there from the beginning. Part of our call is to release and demonstrate it in the human community. Only then will we be able to look out upon the stars together, gratefully recognizing that we all share the same source and destiny.

Admittedly, this may all seem a bit too cosmic to help a celibate brother on a lusty spring day, or during a midlife transition wherein he grieves the lack of intimate companion and progeny. But consecrated chastity, to be life-enhancing, must embrace both intimacy and generativity. It can no longer be defined in terms of eschatological witness alone; the doctrine of the resurrection of the body, as Tillich says, demands that we forego such facile explanations. Chastity is a call to communion, to attraction, to loving what unfolds before us here in the creation "God so loved as to send his only Son."[27]

The witness of celibacy, I believe, is manifested in our ability to demonstrate a life that lovingly generates not more of ourselves, but more love. We begin that process by loving our poor, obedient selves. Marie McCarthy describes the starting point.

> The emerging self is always a sexual, relational self. It is always, fundamentally and unalterably, an embodied self. Without a body there can be no self. Throughout one's developmental life a person faces the task of coming to be at home in his or her body, coming to know, claim, and live comfortably with one's own embodiedness. Since it is only in, with, and through one's body that a person learns to communicate and to relate, each of us must take the risk of coming to know, appreciate, and befriend our bodies.[28]

Chastity as communion is a call to love all creation, beginning with our embodied selves and growing into intimate, transforming, compassionate relationships with God, other people, and the universe. Celibate chastity as communion is the fullest expression of a brother's call to fraternal love.

Beginning and End

In 1989 a group of brothers gathered at Maryknoll to do a theological reflection on brotherhood. The following year the National Assembly of Religious Brothers invited a number of us to continue the dialogue by writing reflections on the group's definition of brothers. At that time I wrote about Dorothy, an elderly Jamaican immigrant in our inner-city parish who had suddenly died. Dorothy's nontheological notion of brothers had moved me much more than the NARB definition. I am reminded of Dorothy again. She knew we were her brothers because we shared dirty work, food, jokes, Eucharist, neighborhood service, because we could be trusted to be there smuggling cigarettes into her hospital room or opening our house as a safe haven for celebrating New Year's Eve and birthday parties. I knew she was right; we were her brothers.

Unlike Thomas Berry, Dorothy could never have created a new cosmology; Berry, unlike Dorothy, could not have opened a soup kitchen each day by peeling vegetables to a reggae beat. I've learned about brotherhood from both of them. Differentiation, poverty, subjectivity, obedience, communion, chastity—all these concepts can be reduced to a one-word definition of brothers: relationship. Berry teaches me its cosmic source; Dorothy taught me the lived reality of its earthy expression.

So the end point is the beginning. Brothers: who are we among the people of God, and God's creation? We are neither pseudo-priestly mediators of the divine, nor parenting generators of the species; we are not primarily apostolic ministers or eschatological witnesses. We are brothers, called to free ourselves from accepting definitions imposed by world views built upon artificial "centers" in order to embrace the radical call of our own vocation: to become the grateful, humble, loving, and true friends of God, the people of God, and all the marvelous wonders of creation. Friends who, as T.S. Eliot writes:

> Shall not cease from exploration
> And the end of all our exploring
> Will be to arrive where we started
> And to know the place for the first time.
> Through the unknown, remembered gate
> When the last of earth to discover
> Is that which was the beginning.[29]

Notes

1. Pope John Paul II, "Lessons of the Galileo Case," *Origins* 22 (1992) 371—372.

2. Ibid., 371.

3. Ibid., 373.

4. "Consecrated Life in the Church and the World," *Origins* 22 (1992) 441.

5. Ibid.

6. Anne Lonergan and Caroline Richards, eds., *Thomas Berry and the New Cosmology* (Mystic, CT: Twenty-Third Publications, 1988) 107.

7. Paul Tillich, *The Shaking of the Foundations* (New York: Charles Scribners Sons, 1948) 85–86.

8. Brian Swimme and Thomas Berry, *The Universe Story* (San Francisco: Harpers, 1992).

9. Thomas Berry, "Classical Western Spirituality and the American Experience," *Cross Currents: An Anthology* (New York: Crossroads, 1990) 189.

10. Thomas Aquinas, *Summa Theologica* I,47.1. Quoted in Lonergan, *Thomas Berry,* 30.

11. John McPhee, from "Basin and Range," *Exploring our Living Planet* (Washington, DC: National Geographic Society, 1983) 320.

12. Thomas Aquinas, *Summa,* 30.

13. David Tracy, "On Naming the Present," *Concilium 1* (1990) 67.

14. Ibid., 66.

15. Ibid., 79.

16. Thomas Aquinas, *Summa,* 30.

17. "Chief Seattle's Statement," *Haversack: A Franciscan Review* (April 15, 1992) 3, 5. In the same month *The New York Times* reported a debate among historians about the authenticity of ascribing these words to Chief Seattle.

18. David Tracy, "On Naming the Present" 73.

19. Ibid.

20. Daniel Martin, "The Earth Charter: A Religious Voice," *Creation Spirituality* 8 (March/April 1992) 37.

21. Hans Kung, *The Incarnation of God* (New York: Crossroads, 1987) 507–508.

22. John S. Dunne, *The Way of All the Earth* (New York: McMillan, 1972) 193–194.

23. Brian Swimme, "Is the Universe Obedient?" *Creation* 4 (Nov./Dec. 1988) 22.

24. John McPhee, "Annals of the Former World," *The New Yorker* (Sept. 7, 1992; Sept. 14, 1992; Sept. 21, 1992).

25. A developmental treatment of celibate chastity has been released recently in a series of videotapes entitled *Men Vowed and Sexual: Conversations about Celibate Chastity* by the Conference of Major Superiors of Men (Silver Springs, MD: 1993).

26. Reprinted from *The New York Times Magazine,* Sept. 13, 1992 in *Haversack: A Franciscan Review* (Dec. 16, 1992) 2.

27. Jn 3:16.

28. Marie McCarthy, "Celibacy as Possibility," *Review for Religious* 51 (Sept. 1992) 775.

29. T.S. Eliot, *Four Quartets* (New York: Harcourt, 1943) 59.

Heroes Seldom Ask Permission

Joseph F. Martin, FIC

Fortunately, heroes seldom ask permission from the authorities.
Sam Keen

The entire Earth is undergoing turbulent changes that have never before been experienced. This transformation includes the planet and all existing life forms that have emerged on it. The human community is involved in scientific, political, religious, moral, medical, social, industrial, technological, and educational upheaval. Cultural and racial diversity are global issues. The world and human civilization will never be the same.

The fall of the Berlin Wall was as unexpected as it was dramatic. The dissolution of the Soviet Union was rapid and tumultuous. Ethnic violence plagues Germany, the former Yugoslavia, and India. Artificial insemination and surrogate motherhood continue to be controversial procedures as does the suicide machine of a Michigan doctor. Sexual harassment and child abuse

---

BROTHER JOSEPH F. MARTIN, FIC, a Brother of Christian Instruction, lives in Cincinnati, Ohio. A native of Detroit, Michigan, he joined the Christian Instruction Brothers in 1962 and professed final vows in 1969. He earned his BA in English (1967) from Walsh University in Canton, Ohio, an MEd (1977) from St. Michael's College in Winooski, Vermont, and an MA in Creation Spirituality (1987) from Holy Names College in Oakland, California. Brother Joseph is the Associate Director of Program Development at Fatima Retreat House in Indianapolis, Indiana. Previously he taught high school English and religion, worked in vocation ministry and public relations, and served as a campus minister at three Ohio universities. For seven years he served on the national board of the National Assembly of Religious Brothers, including one term as president (1987 to 1989). Brother Joseph has written numerous articles, co-authored a textbook, *British Literature* (William C. Brown, 1979), and published the book, *Foolish Wisdom* (Resource Publications, 1990). Brother Joseph may be addressed at 417 West Vine Street, Cincinnati, OH 45215.

in North America appear more prevalent than ever suspected. Abortion and capital punishment divide opponents and advocates. Banks and small businesses fall into bankruptcy. Drug abuse and violent crime increase daily. The US military is sent to Somalia to feed the starving. These and other major world and national events are changing the human psyche.

One major change being documented as it happens is a global shift in consciousness. Scientists talk now about the unity of all life, an idea previously relegated to religion. The new story of the universe describes Earth as a living organism and humans as the means by which Earth reflects on itself in self-conscious awareness.[1] For many, this is a totally new understanding of what it means to be human. In what is now called a "time developmental" universe, everything is in constant change and evolution. Around the world people realize that humans are reshaping the chemistry of the planet and shutting down Earth's life support system. Given this new consciousness, all previous definitions and categories fail. As humans seek to reinvent themselves, every aspect of life and language will be transformed in a time of unprecedented change. Ultimately, it is necessary to understand the changes in order to create solutions. Living through a time of major transition poses its own challenges. Cultural historian Thomas Berry, CP, has accurately described the tension.

> A person has, in some manner, to smash the existing situation in order to arrive at the new situation, and that transformation has to have the historical realism that we cannot create anew simply out of nothingness, but that we must work with the materials that we have, and the existing historical conditions in which we live. The wisdom is how to carry it through, a disintegrating-integrating process. [We] have to survive the present while creating a viable future.[2]

Changes in the Church

In the midst of this global transformation, the Catholic Church struggles with these challenges and attempts to meet people's needs. John Paul II has traveled to more countries to visit the local church than any other pope in history. Women religious are accepting appointments to diocesan offices traditionally held by clerics. Over 300 US Catholic parishes now have nonordained administrators. Lay Catholics are involved in church ministries where sisters, brothers, or priests are no longer available. An annual collection in the United States supports retired men and women religious. On issues like capital punishment, abortion, war, and nuclear weapons, Catholics find themselves more and more at odds with their society's cultural values. One third of the US Catholic church population is now Hispanic. Young Catholics are not so active in church as their ancestors were. The church, too, is undergoing major transformations.

Recognizing that the present unfolds from the past, religious brothers also contend with the challenges of transformation in the church and in the world. Given their major investment in and commitment to the spiritual life, men (and women) religious will necessarily do the most "letting go" in grappling with what are called "paradigm shifts." The old paradigms or models of religious life are gone, never to return. New models are still being birthed. Living in a time of major changes, brothers today are in what Dutch anthropologist Arnold van Gennep has named the "neutral zone" when the old is not yet dead and the new is not yet born.[3] It is a difficult but hope-filled period; changes cut to the very heart of religious life. These times call for heroic and courageous pioneers who will risk new ventures in community living and who will not shrink from new challenges in ministry.

New Models of Religious Life

Much has been written about "refounding" religious life. Gerald Arbuckle, SM, in *Out of Chaos* challenges leadership to foster creativity among members. Patricia Wittberg, SC, author of *Creating a Future for Religious Life,* suggests that communities contain elements of three models: intentional, bureaucratic, and associational. Mary Jo Leddy, NDS, examines the impact of culture on religious life and proposes radical refounding in *Reweaving Religious Life.* In *New Wineskins,* Sandra Schneiders, IHM, addresses specific issues of religious life in a series of essays that reflect the evolution of her thinking. These works attempt to give some direction to the future of religious life.

The recent Future of Religious Orders in the United States (FORUS) project surveyed 10,000 women and men religious to search out directions for the future. According to researchers David Nygren, CM, and Miriam Ukeritis, CSJ, some signs appear clearer than others. Some religious suggested that individual commitments in ministry must acquiesce to a renewed corporate mission. Others felt that role clarity is an important issue. Certainly, religious life cannot and will not continue as it has in the past. Given the current state of flux in the world, nothing will remain unchanged. So, brothers find themselves in search of new identities, new models of community, and new roles in ministry. Twenty-five years after the renewal mandated by Vatican II, religious orders have merely scratched the surface of returning to their roots (founder's charism) and have not yet been radicalized (rooted) in the gospel message of Jesus for a new age.

Men religious in this new age must pursue the challenge to recreate brotherhood by examining the signs of the times and discovering a direction for the future. The major changes that will occur do not indicate that the past was without value. Rather, the fruitfulness of the past has brought brothers to an exciting moment of opportunity: to create a renaissance in religious life. The major issues facing humanity deal with a new identity and a new function. Given the fundamental shifts occurring in the world, brothers are challenged to transform their identity and their ministry. A key to that transformation may be found in some insights from the men's movement and in other elements from creation spirituality.

Men's Movement

In the quest for new identities and new roles for men, some authors have provided signposts for the journey. In his book, *Iron John*, the poet Robert Bly approaches the issue from the perspective of male initiation rites and the role of the mentor. Robert Moore and Douglas Gillette have researched four prominent masculine archetypes in *King, Warrior, Magician, Lover*. In *Wild Man's Journey*, Richard Rohr, OFM, and Joseph Martos offer men new ways to understand themselves as fathers, brothers, husbands, lovers, and friends. After noting that the traditional ideas of manhood no longer work, Sam Keen, author of *Fire in the Belly*, details an alternative vision for strength, virility, and passion for a modern age. These works offer men new role models, new masculine identities, and new elements for creating a masculine spirituality.

The men's movement is exploring the crisis in masculine identity caused in part by dramatic cultural shifts, by the compelling influence of feminism, and by the disappearance of male rites of passage. The focus is on men healing men, and men's soul work is "nonprofessional and community based—common and available to all."[4] Men are examining who they are and what roles they have in society and in families. Roles and role models for men are in transition. The "new man" or the "new Adam" is emerging as a post-feminist man and has been featured in *Newsweek* and other periodicals. Literature in the men's movement addresses three important areas: a redefinition of male spirit, new role models for men, and a renewed masculine spirituality. These three areas parallel the crisis among brothers and suggest an approach to the radical renewal of brotherhood.

New Identity for Brothers

Part of that radical renewal will be the claiming of a new identity for "brother" just as new definitions for men are evolving from the men's movement. Many are puzzled by the identity of brothers in the church. Some brothers are undoubtedly confused about their identity in these changing times. So a new definition may be pertinent. Previously, brothers were described by what they "do" (ministry). A new approach might balance that with attention to who brothers "are" (relationship), since most describe their calling as being available "to brother" those in need as Jesus did. The very word "brother" suggests a relationship. A brother, therefore, could be defined as "a male Christian who is called by God to commit himself by vows to a personal relationship with God, to fraternal relationships with others, and to action on behalf of those in need." Since brotherhood presupposes community life, a prophetic ministry, and the following of Jesus, these elements need not be part of the definition. This, or another, new description would assist in clarifying the identity of brothers and prompt them to renewed roles for themselves.

The confusion of roles for brothers probably evolved as they (and sisters) gradually became a work force for the church. At the 1992 convention of the National Association of Church Personnel Administrators, Saginaw Bishop Kenneth Untener noted that he was not concerned about religious vocations. He feels that religious life will thrive as it becomes more of a prophetic witness, free to do good works, instead of being a labor force. "Religious life is the poetic, prophetic expression of what we believe and love in our baptismal commitment lived out in a marvelous, unusual, and prophetic way."[5] One challenge for religious brothers, then, is letting go of the work force model and uncovering new prophetic possibilities.

New Role for Brothers

In the past brothers were role models for young men. As teachers, administrators, nurses or pastoral associates, they inspired and assisted young men in their growth to maturity. This modeling remains critical as men continue to search for appropriate masculine roles in society. Most men have been deeply wounded by an absence of their father or a healthy father figure, or they have suffered a severe deficiency in their relationship with their father.[6] As a result, they feel a profound, and perhaps unconscious, longing for affection and affirmation from their fathers or from another male authority figure. In a North American society suffering from the impact of this "father wound," religious brothers can recover a position as role models for men. Well-balanced and well-integrated male religious can contribute significantly as mentors in the church and in society. An appropriate archetype for this role is Mentor, the wizened teacher of Telemachus in Homer's *Odyssey*.[7]

When he left Ithaca for Troy, Odysseus chose Mentor to take charge of his household. An aged friend, Mentor acted as an adviser to Odysseys' son, Telemachus. Hence, his name is used to describe a trusted counsellor. Athena, the goddess of wisdom and warfare, assumed Mentor's form when she accompanied young Telemachus in his search for his father, absent for 20 years. After journeying to Pylos and Sparta, Telemachus returned home where he found his father. Initially, Telemachus lacked his father's energy and resourcefulness. But in the end, he astonished his mother by taking command of the household and fighting against her suitors. This is the archetypal story of the young man searching for his father energy and his own masculine identity. After a long excursion "outward" led by a wisdom figure as a companion and guide, Telemachus finds the answer "within" himself at home.

While the men's movement has not embraced this story as part of male mythology, mentoring offers an appropriate model for recovering some role clarity for religious brothers. Christian Instruction Brother Charles St. James consciously made mentoring part of his ministry during 13 years as a campus minister at Loyola University in Chicago. Men still need role models. In an estranged and violent society young men seek both community and spirituality. Most go about the search in the wrong way. Street gangs are a clear manifestation of the deep felt need for community. Drug abuse is an example of the search for ecstasy and communion, a relationship with God, gone awry. Brothers who are healthy masculine role models could assist in healing some of these unhealthy situations.

New Spirituality for Brothers

Healing their own father wounds has some implications for brothers. Courage is required, and the risk of traveling an inner journey that few men have pursued. This requires men who can open themselves to transformation and make what Joseph Campbell has called the "hero's journey," based on the archetype of the hero. It is a journey that all men must take in order to achieve wholeness, a journey that requires heroic men. There is no clear path, each man finds his own. Sam Keen writes:

> Cautious men will say that it is foolhardy to begin without a Triptik, a cost analysis, or a feasibility report from a committee of experts and the promise of cooperation from appropriate governmental agencies. But official sanction for radical departures is seldom given. Fortunately, heroes seldom ask permission from the authorities.[8]

While traveling the hero's journey, brothers can gain much by integrating aspects of mature male archetypes into a new masculine spirituality. The four powers of the masculine psyche that have been suggested—king, warrior, lover, magician—offer distinct energies that all men can access within themselves. The king energy provides order; the warrior defends the boundaries; the magus promotes transformation; the lover fosters passion. From the king energy comes caring, and from the warrior comes courage. The magus offers wisdom, and the lover creates joy.[9]

These archetypes have their place and their lessons for brothers. Yet the mentor archetype best provides an authentic role for brothers. The mentor energy provides guidance and counsel. The mentor is a confidant, teacher, friend, and, as in the case of Mentor, a male role model and an elder. Authentic male role models are important where children have fathers who are absent, deceased, divorced, alcoholic, workaholic, or emotionally distant. The "father wound" is deep in North American culture; brothers can bring healing to others by taking the gospel journey of love and compassion, and by creating a masculine spirituality that aims at promoting justice and acting to serve others.

On the other hand, brotherhood has something to offer the men's movement. Religious life provides an historical model of holistic living.[10] The paradigm is clear—men living together in community and sharing prayer, ministry, recreation, education, and possessions. Lived rightly, brotherhood offers a holistic lifestyle. Each day is balanced with the necessary components of prayer, work, and play. Brothers can be examples to men whose lives are unbalanced with heavy work loads and hectic schedules. Some brothers have skills in community building that would be invaluable to the men's movement. The spiritual life has allowed many brothers to embody some of the so-called feminine qualities needed for an integrated masculinity: receptivity, nurturing, patience, vulnerability, humility, and trust. This balancing of the masculine/feminine polarities is one of the goals of the post-feminist men's movement and something brothers can bring to it. Richard Rohr, OFM, is addressing this new male consciousness in challenging and exciting ways.

Important elements for the renewal of religious brotherhood can be gleaned from the insights and archetypes of the men's movement. The redefinition of "brother" and the clarification of appropriate roles will allow brothers to move into the future with renewed vigor and a clear identity in the church: authentic men dedicated to a holistic lifestyle, personal growth, prophetic mission, and generative leadership. A clearer vision of their ministry can be discovered by examining brotherhood from the perspective of creation spirituality.

Creation Spirituality

Over the past 15 years, creation spirituality has spread dramatically through Christian churches of many countries. A fundamental insight is that Earth is the primary revelation of the divine, the planet being significantly older than Scripture. Author of over a dozen books, Matthew Fox lays out the tenets of creation spirituality in *Original Blessing.* Thomas Berry, CP, in *The Dream of the Earth,* noting the loss of the old world view, maintains that humans must view the natural world as a sacred community to which they belong. Charlene Spretnak makes the necessary connections between the emerging ecology movement and spirituality in *The Spiritual Dimension of Green Politics.* In *The Universe Is A Green Dragon,* physicist Brian Swimme explains the new cosmic creation story and the relationship between humans and nature. Following their personal transformation, these and other authors explore the implications of a spirituality based on the sacredness of all creation. Some insights for a renewed ministry for brothers can be found by examining religious life from the perspective of four prominent themes in creation spirituality: blessing, emptying, creating, and transforming.

Blessing

One blessing that men religious experience is their tradition of prayer, solitude, and spirituality. These are gifts to men in search of a new masculine spirituality. Brothers have a wealth of experience in solitude, contemplation, and prayer. Sharing and teaching the techniques and practices of meditation and contemplation and the value of solitude is a promising new ministry for brothers. A revival of Western mysticism in the Catholic tradition would take contemplation out of the elitist model of being a practice for only men (and women) religious. Contemplation is an important element in a justice-making spirituality for a new age. In his article, "Creating a Just Heart," Maurice Proulx, MS, connects the contemplative attitude with the promotion of justice in the world.

> One needs a contemplative attitude in the presence of people and the human condition to possess a just heart. Being contemplative means being empty, helpless, open to what lies before us rather than doing something or having to be

involved in an activity to make it happen. It means losing control. . . . Being caught by a contemplative moment requires a contemplative attitude. Contemplation is being at risk, to be open to what lies out there and to be willing to let it affect me.[11]

A second blessing of brotherhood can be found in the generation of older brothers, the "wise men," the heroes in religious orders. These men are an asset to those on the journey since they have traveled their own paths, and as wise elders they mirror another male archetype. With the graying of US society reflected in religious life, these brothers have important gifts to offer. At 72, Christian Instruction Brother Philip Drouin left retirement and moved to a small village in Alaska. In the absence of a priest he frequently leads prayer and communion services, baptizes children, and buries the dead. Other older religious can offer gifts and wisdom if they are provided opportunities to share. Retired men can still make significant contributions in part-time mission work or in the pursuit of the creative arts. Letting go of previous images of retirement would allow brothers many active years ahead.

Emptying

Emptying or "letting go" is a second theme from creation spirituality. Brothers need to let go of some ministries in which they are not meeting the needs of the economically poor. The church has called us to a "preferential option" for the poor, yet many brothers (and sisters) continue in middle class (or better) ministries. Some find themselves in parish ministry or in diocesan offices having been taken in by "parochial assimilation," pursuing ministries not related to their founding charism. The FORUS study indicates that while most religious assent intellectually to having a ministry with the poor, few are actually engaged in such ministries.[12] It means changing lifestyle, locale, status quo, neighborhood, and ministerial activity. It means challenging the system both in church and in society on behalf of the *anawim:* all creatures great and small. It clearly means taking the Gospel of Jesus seriously, becoming radicalized, and possibly being persecuted, as in Latin America. If brothers are not meant to be a work force for the church, then they need to "refind" the prophetic and heroic ministry with the poor that inspired their founders' vision.

Another manner of letting go poses a more difficult choice: that is, allowing an order or a province to die. A Dutch province of one men's congregation decided to discontinue all recruiting efforts and to allow the province to come to a peaceful end. "Faced with dwindling numbers and aging communities, some British religious congregations are considering closing their doors and allowing the orders to fade away."[13] What freedom those men enjoy, released from anxiety and pressure to control their future. Their decision places them squarely in God's hands, prepared to follow God's will. Some women's communities have made similar choices, accepting death with a pro-active stance. The Shakers evidence this remarkable quality since they have no reluctance to let go or to put away a gift at the end of its proper time. They live by the conviction that "there are two kinds of gifts—gifts forever and gifts for a season—and very few are gifts forever."[14] Only a few Shakers remain at one active community in Maine. Perhaps a given province or congregation of brothers is a gift from God for a season. Some Shaker-like letting go may be in order.

Creating

A third theme for evaluating religious brotherhood is creativity. Using the imagination and skills they have, potential refounding brothers can lead the way in creating what Sandra Schneiders calls a "community of friends," that is, a group of brothers who join together to live genuine community and to be co-disciples in ministry.[15] Talented and creative men religious can tap their potential and create alternative models of adult communities. Mindful of the gospel imperative not to put new wine in old wineskins, Gerald Arbuckle notes that the first principle of refounding should be: "The new belongs elsewhere."[16] New members, potential candidates, and refounding brothers must live in new community situations and create new lifestyles. This need is reflected in the comment of one young religious who said, "I am so tired of hearing about the way it was!" Creativity has implications for ministry where a new and prophetic stance moves away from a mentality of "circling the wagons" and maintaining institutional commitments. These new communities could have the freedom to explore new corporate commitments rather than to survive minimally through fear or inertia. In some instances, tradition, or the attitudes of a few older members, or the pressures of province leaders may have prevented or crushed creativity. Arbuckle notes this point.

> My hunch is that brilliant, creative, and innovative ideas of potential refounding persons do not just fade away; instead they are crushed to death by highly analytical, logical, and rational problem-solving major superiors and by their administrations over-burdened by the demands of maintenance.[17]

Next, brothers can create sustainable communities where a bioregion's web of life can survive and flourish indefinitely. Presupposing that men religious are no longer a church work force, they can be pioneers in promoting a "mutually enhancing human-Earth relationship."[18] Education for this venture includes the new universe story and the three R's for a new age: Reduce, Reuse, and Recycle. Religious communities might be examples of a sustainable lifestyle by modeling such practices as composting, high fiber diets, gardening, alternate energy sources, conservation, and carpooling. By word and by example brothers could teach responsibility to care for Earth. Their simple lifestyle would lower expenses and reduce consumption, thus increasing their ability to serve the poor.[19] Creating sustainable communities can be a prophetic mission for brothers who seek to promote geo-justice, a preferential option for Earth. In Dayton, Ohio, Marianist Brother Donald Geiger has established a Center for Environmental Education with a dual purpose: to create a community of interested people and to make people aware of their appropriate place in Earth systems. The work of the Center focuses on organic gardening, low maintenance orchards, and the restoration of natural habitats.

Recreating their ministries is also an important task for brothers. Using the male model of mentoring, intrapreneurial brothers can develop new rites of passage for young men. Adolescent boys in this country have no appropriate rite of passage to adulthood. For some, the military provides this experience, but the training to kill and the humiliating realities of boot camp make this a rite of questionable value. For others, the first sexual experience becomes an initiation into manhood. However, fraught with anxiety, fearful of being caught, and concerned about AIDS or unwanted pregnancy, the young man finds this also pales as an appropriate rite of passage. Brothers can devise retreats, workshops, and reflection days that include discussion, lecture, prayer, rituals, and chants. Young men could be taught stories that embody male values and the importance of sacred sexuality where the human expression of sex is seen as part of the divine power of the universe. The value of meaningful work and the history and consequences of war could be taught from the perspective of masculine archetypes. High school students might be required to attend these programs. Experienced and healthy single and married men would be invited to lead appropriate aspects of these sessions. In Plano, Illinois, Dominican Brother Joseph Kilikevice and Sufi teacher Hal Dessel have already instituted Creating Male Spirit, a retreat program which provides similar experiences for men.

Another approach to ministry for brothers would be to return to their foundational myths to uncover their prophetic mission. US school systems are in trouble, and teaching brothers might address the educational needs of the new age with alternative schools. The Jonathan House near Montreal is a one-family residence which takes in 16 youths daily for classes in English, French, and mathematics, and workshops in woodwork, leather, glass, cooking, and tailoring. Owned by the Brothers of Christian Instruction, the house serves as a nontraditional school with a single purpose: getting students back into secondary schools. In Bonita Springs, Florida, three Irish Christian Brothers opened Los Hermanos, an educational ministry for migrant workers. Its unique approach offers tutoring in English, the basics of adequate documentation, and biblical lessons for uneducated adults. Brothers can develop other models of education for a new age, models that educate for bioregions, for cultural diversity, for celebration, and for the new universe story. Creativity and sensitivity to tradition will allow brothers to revision their ministries and meet the needs of changing times.

Transforming

The final theme for brothers to examine in recreating forms of religious life is transformation. One transforming and prophetic mission for brothers could be to live and teach the sacredness of the universe and of Earth. This is the good news for modern times. No longer can Christians defend the biblical injunction to "subdue the Earth." Respect for the planet, for air, water, and soil have become primary in human consciousness. This respect is best achieved by teaching and by example: two areas with obvious connections for brothers. One aspect would be to teach about Earth as a sacred planet and to examine the ecological issues as part of a spiritual dilemma that is becoming more apparent with time. Vice President Albert Gore has refocused the ecological crisis in his comprehensive work, *Earth in the Balance*, where he claims:

> The more deeply I search for the roots of the global environmental crisis, the more I am convinced that it is an outer manifestation of an inner crisis that is, for lack of a better word, spiritual. . . . What other word describes the collection of values and assumptions that determine our basic understanding of how we fit into the universe?[20]

Another avenue of transformation for brothers would be providing new opportunities for celebration. In a society racked by violence and consumerism, genuine celebrations would offer a potent antidote and would counteract cultural values. Genuine celebration means being in communion with others, risking intimacy, and creating sacred space. Communal sharing of holidays, holy days, birthdays, and national events would be a natural starting point. Brothers could create new festivals for Epiphany, Mardi Gras, Pentecost, Assumption, Thanksgiving, and other feasts. Parish prayer life could be enhanced by paraliturgical services for morning and evening prayer, especially in churches where a priest is not available for Eucharist. Religious liturgies, church festivals, first communions, weddings, and funerals could be enriched with music, dance, and other visual and performing arts. Earth-based celebrations could be developed for Earth holy days—solstice and equinox times—honoring the planet. Traditional Earth celebrations like Brigid, Beltane, Lughnasad, and Samhain could be revived. The use of Earth elements—soil, air, fire, water—could be complemented by incense, drums, dance, flowers, bells, and chants. Celebration draws people together and creates opportunities for sharing, for intimacy, for community, and for transformation. In the new universe story the role of humans is to celebrate the sacredness of the cosmos and the presence of divinity in all things. An exciting new ministry for brothers could be found in creating and re-creating the art of celebration.

Future Possibilities

After experiencing many years of change in religious life, brothers are still only beginning to return to their roots and be radicalized by the good news of Jesus. As men religious continue the journey of transformation, the men's movement and creation spirituality can contribute to brotherhood. A renewed identity, appropriate roles, and a masculine spirituality will give direction to brothers intent on meeting the needs of a society in transition. While no one can claim to have the answer, the signs of the times offer some hints toward a possible future. Brothers need to be open to receiving messages from unexpected places as they renew their lives and their mission. The Spirit continues to move in new and original ways.

Fresh approaches to the traditional vows are being explored and may provide other directions for the renewal of religious life. In her article "Reflections on the Vows from a Cosmic/Ecological Perspective," Alexandra Kovats, CSJP, examines the vows in light of the governing principles of the universe, and renames them "reverence, creativity, and solidarity."[21] Diarmuid O'Murchu, in his *Religious Life: A Prophetic Vision,* claims that celibacy can be lived authentically only in mixed communities of men and women. In *Living the Vision,* Barbara Fiand, SNDdeN, examines the meaning of the vows in the context of a holistic spirituality. These and other works demonstrate fresh currents of thought moving among men and women religious. More books are certain to follow.

Other aspects of religious life will be challenged in the process. No doubt totally new religious communities will evolve, some including both men and women as members. Other groups will opt for new religious vows. Ordination may be removed from some men's congregations and returned to diocesan ministry, thus clarifying the role of priests and alleviating current problems of jurisdiction in communities of priests and brothers. Celibacy may be relegated to those in monastic communities. Given the current crisis of sexual abuse cases involving priests and brothers and the number of religious still leaving congregations, mandatory celibacy may have outlived its time. Sam Keen points out an inherent paradox that befalls some virtues.

> The conditions of a certain age call forth some new virtue. But after a time, adherence to that virtue becomes counterproductive, and its opposite or corrective is called forth.

Ivan Illich called this the principle of "paradoxical counter-productivity." In time, educational institutions paralyze our ability to learn, medicine produces as much suffering as it alleviates, and freeways hurry us elsewhere at an ever diminishing rate of speed.[22]

The church and the world are in crisis, a time of danger and a time of opportunity. The transformation of Earth and of human society will continue and will impact every aspect of life. In a time developmental universe, that transformation cannot be controlled: it can only be guided. New definitions and new role models are emerging for men and women with implications for those in religious life. Creative and intrapreneurial brothers who will lead their congregations into the future have their work cut out for them. While there are no clear answers, signposts along the way will guide those courageous brothers on the journey. Prophets and heroes will not ask permission to recreate religious life. That precedent was set when founders (and foundresses) created new congregations during previous disintegrating-integrating eras. The key is to survive the present while creating a viable future. With God's Spirit hovering over the chaos, a new creation is being birthed.

Notes

1. Thomas Berry, CP, *The Dream of the Earth* (San Francisco: Sierra Club Books, 1988) 132.

2. Bernard Connaughton and Jo Roberts, "Thomas Berry: Dreaming of a New Earth," *The Catholic Worker* (March/April 1989) 6.

3. William Bridges, *Transitions: Making Sense of Life's Changes* (New York: Addison-Wesley, 1980) 87.

4. Aaron Kipnis, *Knights Without Armor* (New York: Jeremy P. Tarcher, 1991) 145.

5. Most Rev. Kenneth E. Untener, *2005 A.D.: Do You Know Where Your Priest Will Be?* NACPA Convocation (Louisville, KY: Veranda Communications, Nov. 5, 1992, audio cassette).

6. Richard Rohr, OFM and Joseph Martos, *The Wild Man's Journey* (Cincinnati: St. Anthony Messenger Press, 1992) 85.

7. Insight gleaned from a discussion with Edmund Knighton.

8. Sam Keen, *Fire in the Belly: On Being a Man* (New York: Bantam Books, 1991) 122.

9. Richard Rohr, OFM, *Finding our Fathers: Being a Brother* (Albuquerque, NM: Center for Action and Contemplation, Dec. 1991, audio cassette).

10. Insight gleaned from a discussion with Steve Torma.

11. Maurice Proulx, MS, "Creating a Just Heart," *Church Personnel Issues* (NACPA, Nov. 1989) 2.

12. David Nygren, CM, and Miriam Ukeritis, CSJ, "Future of Religious Orders in the United States," *Origins* 22:15 (Sept. 24, 1992).

13. "ADDENDA," *National Catholic Reporter,* 29:15 (Feb. 12, 1993) 7.

14. Pam Robbins and Robley Whitson, "Gift from the Shakers," *Sign* (Nov. 1979) 11.

15. Sandra M. Schneiders, IHM, *New Wineskins: Reimaging Religious Life Today* (New York: Paulist Press, 1986) 247.

16. Gerald Arbuckle, SM, *Out of Chaos: Refounding Religious Congregations* (New York: Paulist Press, 1988) 134.

17. Ibid., 40.

18. Berry, *Dream of the Earth,* 145.

19. Insights gleaned from a discussion with Steve Torma.

20. Albert Gore, *Earth in the Balance: Ecology and The Human Spirit* (New York: Houghton Mifflin, 1992) 12.

21. Alexandra Kovats, CSJP, "Reflections on the Vows from a Cosmic/Ecological Perspective," *InFormation* 146 (Silver Spring, MD: Religious Formation Conference, Nov.–Dec. 1992).

22. Keen, *Fire in the Belly,* 89.

Change and the Future:
A New Paradigm For Religious Life

Louis DeThomasis, FSC

Change and the future! These words can conjure up much exhilaration or fright for anyone with a stake in the future of religious life. Certitude about the future is very easy to grasp: change will occur. How exhilarating! What that change will entail for religious life in the third millennium is a bit more problematic, since we know it could mean our own demise. How frightening!

Professional psychologists David Nygren, CM, and Miriam Ukeritis, CSJ, recently completed their five-year research study sponsored by the Lilly Foundation entitled, "The Future of Religious Orders in the United States."[1] The purpose of this study is "to provide information that will help religious understand the choices before them, and to orient them toward their possible futures." It is not hyperbole to wonder whether the "possible future" Nygren and Ukeritis discuss could, indeed, be our own demise. Thomas H. Stahel captured this stark reality when he observed that the FORUS study, "though based on present perceptions of this history of the past 25 years, since Vatican II, . . . it

---

BROTHER LOUIS DETHOMASIS, FSC, is a De La Salle Christian Brother who is a native of Bethpage, Long Island, New York, and presently is President and Professor of Interdisciplinary Studies at Saint Mary's College of Minnesota in Winona, Minnesota. He entered the Christian Brothers in 1968, and was formally professed in 1973. He has a BSFS degree from the Edmund A. Walsh School of Foreign Service, Georgetown University, and a PhD from The Union Institute, Cincinnati. Brother Louis is active on several boards in the not-for-profit and for-profit sectors. He has also written several books, monographs, and articles involving the integration of the complex and seemingly disparate worlds of faith and finance. Brother Louis may be addressed at Saint Mary's College of Minnesota, 700 Terrace Heights, Winona, MN 55987-1399.

aims at learning from these troubled times what the future could and ought to hold if religious life is to survive."[2]

Those of us who have experienced religious life know how it can be shaped into patterns of behavior which defy even the most simple changes. We were all partners in a "dance" of standard phrases and actions which were a kind of procrustean bed that molded each of us to a form compatible with community life. The community captured our imaginations and gained this power over us because we had a common set of beliefs about our apostolate and shared experiences drawn from our years in novitiate and scholasticate. We committed our imaginations to a mythology which held that schooling made anything possible.

As an example, the mythology of those in educational apostolates went hand in hand with another myth at the core of religious life. We believed that a rigorous application of the content and methods of Catholic education would not only save our students, but it would also guarantee salvation for each of us. Driven by these important and constructive myths, we faced each new group of students with confidence and created community with symbolic support, and perhaps with only superficial friendship. We asked no questions, secure in the patterns of thought and behavior that had stood the test of generations of religious before us.

What was hidden from our imaginations during these years was the fact that we were living a life that was not only unrealistic—it was dead! The "awakenings" occurring in late twentieth century society, which enlightened us about the centrality of holistic and integrated interpersonal relationships, have not effectively permeated the imagination of many post-Vatican II religious men and women who did not join the, then, mass exodus from religious life. Post-Vatican II religious did not have a support system, or a mythology, that enabled them to interiorize in a healthy and sensitive manner that they, too, had personal and intimate needs which required attention. Until this day, systemically, even the most astute post-Vatican II men and women religious have not eradicated the subdued, yet pervasive, sense of guilt associated with caring for their personal needs while still serving others. We have not developed an effective infrastructure or imagination which integrates for men and women religious their personal need for continual transformation into a healthy, sexual, and holy celibate who can still serve others and the church.

This is not to say that in the past we did our work poorly. Far from it! We educated our young people to levels that made them competitive in the careers they selected. We spoke to the needs of their parents and gave them comfort in knowing that their children were in the hands of committed religious. We also believed that we were responsive to the deepest concerns of others in our communities and that all aspects of our lives were coming together in living testimony to the validity of our vows.

In effect, the paradigm of religious life was reinforcing a paradigm of religious education—and both were failing the test of modern society. The religious community was an island in a sea of change where many of the real issues affecting our members were not faced and resolved.

However, with the demise of these paradigms there is hope. It is the thesis of this article that the death of these traditional paradigms provides an opportunity for a resurrection of Christ's charism in new forms which can infuse modern day religious with the spiritual and physical energy required in ministering to the needs of a new global society, without neglecting their own personal, church, and spiritual needs.

Paradigms and the Religious Experience

The use of the term "paradigm" to describe religious life is expressive of a growing interest in the ways people pattern their lives and give structure to their organizations. When Thomas Kuhn [3] brought paradigms to our attention in the 1960s, he was primarily interested in how shared values and points of view shaped the behavior of scholars and scientists. It was his contention that commonly-held paradigms determined all aspects of intellectual life.

An excellent and thorough treatment of paradigms can be found in the book by Joel Arthur Barker, *Future Edge*. In it he defines a paradigm as a set of rules and regulations (written or unwritten) which establish or define boundaries, and tell us how to behave inside those boundaries in order to be successful.[4]

Paradigms gain impressive power over what we think and do for several reasons. First, they are rooted in our deepest wants and fears which we shape through mythology. For most religious, the role of myth is at the core of how we define our faith in action.

These myths are generally drawn from the charisma of the person who founded our order and defined its apostolate. The founder's work is summarized in a saga or story which illustrates how obstacles facing the apostolic vision were overcome. This story provides psychic energy for us when we face the challenges of our own work.

Second, paradigms are firmly rooted in our minds in the form of metaphors which capture the essential elements of life under the paradigm. Metaphors serve this purpose by capturing the essence of myth in a succinct summary which contains a core picture or image familiar to everyone. As we share in these metaphors, we get a sense of "singing out of the same book." The religious community is one example of a metaphor experienced by nearly all religious, implying a group of like-minded men or women living and working together with shared goals. Each religious is committed to the community and is sustained by it.

Third, paradigms become institutionalized as models which channel our daily work and our use of human and material resources. In religious life, models take root in the Rule, a document which translates the charism of the founder into specific guidelines for action. Models become reality in the shape of schools, churches, hospitals, contemplative houses, or wherever religious live out their apostolic commitment. Furthermore, it is in these working models that traditional paradigms of religious life are put to their most severe test.

It is important to recognize that the social organizations where many religious live and work are shaped mainly by the myths and metaphors of professional life, not by those of a religious nature. Thus, the religious following an apostolate to the sick in a modern hospital confronts a medical model that defines a view of the client and the healing professions quite at variance with the apostolic vision of the religious community.[5]

The effect of professional models on modern religious cannot be overemphasized. Individual religious at work in institutions shaped by professional models are under heavy pressure to fit their behavior to professional molds. The result is clearly seen in generations of religious who are often professional educators, social workers, or nurses first, and religious second.

Thus, when we speak of a "ruling paradigm," we are talking about shared myths and metaphors which exist within an institutional model that limits what we will do and how we will do it.

Failed Paradigm of Religious Life

As I look back on life experiences in my former school communities, I can see how we were attempting to order our lives by an outmoded paradigm. The myths and metaphors at the core of our thought and experience were not translatable into a lexicon that would enable us to speak to the problems and challenges we found in our community and classrooms every day. The model of community life was also drawn from another time. We replaced meaningful, useful rituals with superficial patterns of behavior that isolated us from authentic communal experiences. Our paradigm failed us, and we in time failed one another.

It is my contention that there is more than enough evidence to conclude that the traditional paradigm of religious life no longer speaks to us in a vital way in the present or for the future. Even though it was "right" for many generations, the older, traditional paradigm cannot be bent to the circumstances of our times. Yet the demise of our old paradigm can lead to a resurrection of apostolic spirit. It can translate our frustration into creative energy, but only if we approach the task of paradigm redefinition with open minds and an abiding faith in and love for the church we are called to serve.

The Paradigm Is Dead. Long Live the Paradigm!

Since the time of Peter, the church has been at the center of forces that would change its form and mission. In virtually every challenge, the church has been successful in resisting these forces while channeling the energy of believers in accord with its own doctrines. The church has accomplished this by refining a basic paradigm, one which continues to draw on the charism of Christ to excite the imaginations of the faithful. The powerful myth of Peter as the rock on which the church is built is a timeless justification for the institutional metaphors that have evolved over the centuries.

Our longing for the founding myth is a force which has changed the paradigms of the church and religious life many times in the past. This process of paradigm change is cyclic and set in motion by problem-solving failures of the ruling paradigm. When the *monastic* paradigm was introduced in the middle ages, it slowly gained adherents until it reached its greatest influence in modern times. But if a paradigm fails to evolve, it will begin to prove inadequate as a problem-solving tool. When this occurs, we see that anomalies increase, calling the ruling paradigm into question.

Consider a typical apostolate within the monastic paradigm—that of educational service to poor children. When this apostolate was carried out within secular communities where families were committed to the paradigm of parish education, there were few anomalies. Virtually every child, rich or poor, was able to obtain a quality educational experience along with the spiritual values which made him or her a productive citizen and church member.

However, as these parish communities became the victims of urban change, they were subject to major alterations in family and community structure. The poor were no longer committed to the paradigm of parish/community and they brought problems of increasing complexity to the doors of the parish school. When faced with these new problems, and with the lack of funds to remedy them, religious educators began to experience anomalies: student problems could not be resolved and the parish school began to fail some of its clientele. These experiences called the paradigm of schooling into question.

For religious involved in education, the failing of many parish schools as a community problem-solver occasioned the rise of a new paradigm. The paradigm was modified to one which cast the apostolate into a new form, essentially defining the anomalies of the poor out of existence. Instead of educating all comers in a parish school, many religious became professional developers of talent in what might be called "Catholic magnet schools" designed to attract mainly the more easily educated children. The Catholic magnet school paradigm rapidly gained adherents. As this paradigm shift took place, many religious became, foremost, practitioners of their professions and, incidentally, persons who lived in traditionally defined communities. At the same time, apostolates were also reformed along professional lines. Master educators practiced their craft at ever more sophisticated levels.

Breaking the Paradigm

Following the above example, one could argue that the new professional paradigm has not really addressed the anomalies of the past, but instead, has defined them out of existence. Given these changes, it is reasonable to ask whether the process of paradigm shifting can go in any other direction. Of course it can. Many religious, and some religious communities, have faced up to the anomalies of the traditional paradigm. These people are what I would call "paradigm breakers": men and women with a vision of a new paradigm which accepts the anomalies and finds new myths, metaphors, and models to deal with them.

Sister Jean is, in my experience, the prototypic "paradigm breaker." She was one of the lead administrators in our school. In 1984, she drew our attention to the now famous report, "A Nation At Risk," and challenged us to shape our apostolate to the reality of a generation of children in need. Unfortunately, her call went unheard by most of us. When we took time to listen to her, we found ways to rationalize our contributions to this national problem within the traditional educational paradigm of our school.

Fortunately, our lack of response did not deter Sister Jean from her vision for the educational apostolate. She entered a graduate program where she studied learners at risk and made herself an advocate for their cause at national conferences. She also took direct action to live out her apostolate by becoming the principal of a Catholic high school in one of highest risk areas of New York City. Her school was formerly a "white gloves" school for Catholic girls interested in careers in office practice, but in recent years the school has changed from an all-white clientele to a multi-racial mix of children at risk. Along with this change, Sister Jean found that staff members had lost confidence in their ability to educate their students and the school was gradually losing its ability to train and graduate its students. Against these enormous odds, Sister Jean was amazingly successful. Her school now graduates 95 percent of its students, and all become employed in office positions where each young woman has a potential career.

How did Sister Jean accomplish all these things? She did so by breaking the traditional paradigm of religious education. She centered her training on the children's needs rather than on honing narrow professional skills. In the language of paradigms, Sister

Jean observed the anomalies posed by at-risk students and recognized them as direct challenges to the educational apostolate. She also instituted a new paradigm for religious education by altering the conventional patterns of operating which had been in place within her order for generations.

The Paradigm Is Dead!

Alas, our religious orders need clones of Sister Jean. There are too few paradigm-breakers who can share their visions of new apostolates and patterns of living. We have lost great numbers of religious and find it very difficult to recruit their replacements. If we are to rebuild the vitality of the religious life, we must think through the process of catastrophe-recovery.

I use the word "catastrophe" to suggest that not all paradigm shifts follow a smooth progression; they are often under strains created by opposing forces. These strains can be in precarious balance so that ruling paradigms are at risk of catastrophic failure. Consider the effects of Vatican II on religious life.

The 1960s began with a relatively high level of commitment by men and women religious to their apostolates. However, by proposing a legitimate lay apostolate, the Council immediately increased the attractiveness of this option to both lay and religious members of the church. It was clearly the Council's intention to offer this option to lay persons only; it was expected that religious would remain within the bounds of the vows they had taken. But as time passed, religious leaders began to see a gradual erosion of their communities as religious opted to pursue their apostolates as lay persons. There was no smooth, limited paradigm shift toward modest changes in religious life. Clearly, the tension between the lay and religious apostolates was more fundamental than the Council had realized, and most orders experienced a catastrophic loss of membership. Two competing forces—lay and religious apostolates—caused abrupt, catastrophic changes in belief and behavior.[6]

Relative to this phenomenon, let us look at a few general principles of catastrophe theory as guidelines for our own life and work.[7]

1. Paradigm shifts. Various forces underlie people's commitment to any ruling paradigm. When these forces are in competition abrupt paradigm shifts can take place.

2. Irreversibility of paradigm shifts. When catastrophic changes of paradigm occur, they cannot be directly reversed. In no way can the traditional religious life be recovered by simple reaffirmation of vows or recourse to the Rule. The old paradigm must undergo drastic changes if it is to attract committed followers.

3. Inaccessible levels of attractiveness. Paradigms cannot co-exist without one assuming a ruling status. Thus, Vatican II set the stage for severe stress between the traditional paradigm and the ascendancy of the lay apostolate.

4. Divergence of commitment. At some points on a commitment "continuum" small changes in relative attractiveness of competing paradigms can move behavior to different levels where divergence can take place. However, the religious and lay lives of the 60s were not near any point of "cusp" and the loss of commitment to religious apostolates was catastrophic instead of gradual.

5. Splitting commitment. When a new paradigm comes on the scene, its problem-solving ability "splits" commitment and draws adherents away from its ruling adversary.

There are three concrete steps we can take to energize the discovery of a new religious paradigm.

1. Abandon ideology. We have seen that paradigms rise or fall based on their capacity to solve problems. They cannot be held in place by ideology which clouds perception and makes the perceiver even more irrelevant.[8]

2. Study attractive alternatives. In other words, know the competition. The personal and social problems of the needy will call ever more innovative paradigms into being. To the extent that these paradigms are successful problem solvers, they will be competitors that merit our close attention.

3. Adapt the ruling paradigm. Adaptation is what breathes life into our paradigms. Once the ideological underbrush has been cut away and our paradigm is exposed to the light of social change, we have set the stage for adaptation. But, more importantly, we have preserved a foundation for our work which enables each of us to draw on the institutional strength of the church and the magisterium, helping us to shape our lives and works in an adaptive mode.

Transformation of Religious Life

The reason paradigms are so important for men and women religious is due to the close link between paradigms and organizations. Every religious community, each school, and the church itself—all are organized according to the tenets of a ruling paradigm.

Men and women religious are bound to the ruling paradigm by the Rules of their orders or congregations. In the past, many changes in the paradigms of the church and religious life have been brought about by studying such information. Men and women have examined the scriptures and the documents of the church to ascertain how the church's core values could be given appropriate organizational form.

The contrasting approach I advocate here is one which emphasizes the social psychology of religious life rather than its documentary foundations. If we are to recruit able and energetic men and women to the life, we need to have a clear view of the capacity of our paradigms to liberate their problem-solving abilities. This, I argue, can only be done by knowing how the social relationships of the life affect the psychological dispositions of each member.

The psycho-social perspective I am advocating can best be understood by focusing on several key dimensions of the life. These dimensions are shown in Table 1, titled "Alternative Paradigms for the Religious Life," in which comparisons are drawn between the traditional paradigm of religious life and a new transformal paradigm.

Alternative Paradigms for Religious Life[9]

Organization Dimension	Alternative Paradigms	
	Traditional	Transformal
Purpose	Apostolate/Ministry	Transformation
Control	Congregation	Stakeholders
Mode of Organization	Bureaucracy	Symbiotic
Performance	Rituals	Social Justice
Direction	Administration	Leadership
Resources	Divine Providence	Human Potential
Dynamic	The Rule	Imagination
	Social Ecology Foundation	

Table 1

The dimensions offered in this Table are put in place to give some concrete shape to our discussion of paradigms. Each dimension refers to an aspect of religious life which has a direct effect on how religious think about what they do; how they take care of their personal need for continual transformation into an integrated, healthy, sexual, and holy celibate; how they interact with one another and their clients; and how they organize and direct their activities toward the goals of their communities. These aspects are familiar to all of us as we reflect on our experiences as religious. In the "Traditional" paradigm, we find much that is familiar. These are the aspects of the life which have both sustained and frustrated us, the critical defining features of the paradigm which put it at risk in the turbulent environment of contemporary times.

With this thought in mind, I have tried to select words which will draw clear distinctions between the alternative paradigms. To do this, I have used two metaphors: Traditional Community versus what I call Transformal Ecology. In using the metaphor of ecology, I am thinking of religious as small frogs in a complex world-sized pond. We can no longer be isolated in self-sufficient communities. Instead, we must take the plunge into a world society where our destiny is shaped by waves of change that originate from dimly seen shores. Thus, the whole issue of paradigm change is based on Transformal Ecology; all dimensions of these thoughts rest on this ecological foundation in which each individual religious must not only give to others, but must also receive from others.

Metaphors—such as community—and associated words and thoughts are the "stuff" of organizational life. The words collected under the Traditional Paradigm express the ways religious have come to view their world. These ways facilitate work and life within the community model, but they prevent us from seeing future threats and opportunities.

As you read down the column of words describing the new ecology of religious life, you will get a sense of the way each dimension of life is affected by forces outside church and order. Take, for instance, the dimension of control. In the past, control was vested in the congregation. Religious men and women ordered their affairs according to the Rule and sometimes paid little attention to the opinions of people outside the community. In contrast, the ecology of contemporary religious life is one which is controlled by stakeholders who have an interest in the purpose of the order. This makes the lives of religious interdependent with those of their clients and brings all activity under the sway of global social and economic forces.

The paragraphs that follow draw the distinctions between the Traditional and the Transformal Paradigms more clearly.

Purpose: No organized human activity can exist without purpose. When purpose changes, organizations must adapt or go out of existence. This is abundantly clear as we examine the contrast between purpose within the competing paradigms of the religious life.

Traditional Apostolate/Ministry: In the Traditional life, purpose is manifest as the personal commitment of each individual religious to the apostolate or ministry defined by the order to which one belongs. A familiar example of the Traditional purpose at work is the elementary or secondary school operated by a religious order. These schools give concrete form to purpose through the curriculum offered where secular and spiritual issues are balanced according to the views of religious superiors. The visibility of the apostolate in these schools draws clients who hold similar views with the result that the apostolate is reinforced and nurtured by the joint commitment of religious and clients. Tradition breaks down when clients no longer conform to familiar patterns of thought and behavior. The religious school that suddenly receives large numbers of at-risk learners is a case in point.

Transformation: The Transformal paradigm effectively turns the above relationship on its head. By transformation, I mean that the client defines the relationship between those who are served and the religious who would provide needed services rather than vice versa. From this new view of purpose comes a new organization, one which is mutually determined by the interactions between religious and those they serve. Unlike old apostolates and ministries which accept only a defined role in society, transformation seeks new opportunities to serve.

If we accept the challenge of a new *Ministry of Transformation,* we are committing ourselves to action. We are saying that religious may walk the corridors of power and directly influence the decisions which influence the lives of the powerless. By taking up this new Purpose, we become an integral part of the solution to human problems.

Transformed Purpose: Men and women religious are engaged in the ministry of action. They are actively involved in making economic, political, and moral decisions where they define the message of Christ by the human consequences of what they do.

Control: Organized pursuit of purpose implies control. Organizations must be able to issue authoritative commands and directions that will be followed by both members and clients. It is the source of authority which gives leaders the capacity to control the organization; their actions are effectively legitimized by the foundations on which control rests. At the same time, control gives form to purpose.

Traditional Congregation: Religious organizations have traditionally controlled the activities of members through their congregations. In the history of each religious order, there are events which, when taken together, make up the memory of the organization and provide a powerful rationalization for the patterns of our lives. When we took our vows, we were essentially "buying into" this congregational "memory" and accepting its rituals and controls as molds for our lives and work. The same can be said for the beneficiaries of our work. Those whom we serve have also bought into the congregation, and their behavior is controlled by its patterns and rules as they form relationships with us. But it is in these relationships that the Traditional Paradigm loses its capacity to control. Our clients are no longer drawn from a single ethnic group, one parish, or even from one set of beliefs. Instead, they come to us in need from all segments of an ethnically-diverse society, bringing with them cultural perspectives and experiences unfamiliar to us. When their demands and needs are filtered through the control of the congregation, there is little room for the flexibility and innovation called for by their condition.

Transformal Stakeholders: In the Transformal Paradigm, control penetrates the organization from the outside. Religious are no longer insulated from their constituencies by the congregation. Instead, those who have a stake in the purpose of the order are drawn into a relationship which gives them a substantial degree of control over the activities of men and women religious. This makes it possible for a mutual adaptation between the client's condition and the Transformal purpose that has drawn that person to us.

Control: All stakeholders are involved in defining the organizing paradigm for a living church, one which energizes people to pursue self-actualization and provides a safety net for those who falter in their quest.

Mode of Organization: As organizations mature, control practices become institutionalized in roles and procedures so that everyone involved senses control and responds to it. These institutional forms become part of the metaphors and models which drive the organization and characterize it to those outside its boundaries.[10] Thus, when a religious characterizes life as a "family" experience, that person is calling on our memory of a mode of organization which is paternalistic (or maternalistic) where an older authority takes our needs into account and protects us from the mistakes we might make, were we to determine our actions ourselves.

Traditional Bureaucracy: We are very much under the sway of our written rules. We accept the bureaucratic environment in which we live because it guarantees our place in the organized pursuit of the apostolate. It removes any pressure we might feel to find alternative ministries or to serve different stakeholders. Bureaucracy breeds complacency and a false sense of security.

Transformal Symbiosis: I have taken the ecological term symbiotic to describe how religious groups need to organize for the future. This choice indicates that we are interdependent with our clients and the social/economic environment. We cannot exist without interacting with them, nor can we continue our work without their support.

Mode of Organization: The transformed religious organization is a learning social system which draws the energy to do its work from symbiotic exchanges with people and organizations in its environment.

Performance: The purpose of any organization must, in the final analysis, be measured so that its use of resources can be weighed against what it has accomplished. The measures of performance must also reflect how individuals and groups within the organization have contributed to the attainment of common purpose.

Traditional Rituals: Performance in the Traditional Paradigm is measured by the extent to which religious engage in the ritualistic behavior mandated by the congregation and the larger church. If one accepts this view of ritualistic performance, it is easy to see why it is not a particularly effective way to assess the working of the modern religious organization. The very nature of Ritual ensures that the organization will be unable to adapt to changing circumstances.

Transformal Social Justice: In the Transformal Paradigm, we are taking a much wider view of performance. It is measured not only in ritual or in the narrow professional views of educators, nurses, and administrators. Quite the contrary! The gauge of performance is the extent to which religious organizations contribute to social justice.

But isn't this what we always have been about? Perhaps not. Many orders have strayed from their original charism to serve in more convenient ways. When our work is viewed under the light of social justice, it often fails on the ground that it does not benefit persons sufficiently.

Performance: The performance of the transformed religious life is measured by the extent to which the involvement of men and women religious increases social justice for all people.

Direction: If an organization of any size is to fulfill its purpose, it must devise means for making decisions and coordinating the many activities of its members. This is the role of management, one familiar to all of us. This acquiescence to management has stood in the way of countless paradigm changes in the past. By failing to consider new approaches to direction, those who advocate a paradigm change will inevitably come up against decisions and policies designed to preserve older models of organizational life.

Traditional Administration: In the bureaucratized environment of the Traditional Paradigm, direction is a matter of administration. Each order has its hierarchy of officials who interpret rules and assign priorities to apostolic activities. The power of administration is enhanced within religious communities by the de facto hierarchical nature of the church.

Transformal Leadership: These are people who have a visionary picture of the working of their purpose and a capacity to excite clients, religious, and candidates toward achieving its goals. This shift of emphasis in direction means that a very different sort of person is needed in the Transformed community. The man or woman who would direct his or her order will be, first of all, a person who has the capacity to imagine new ministries and ways to pursue them. But, this individual will also be a highly skilled manager who knows the ins and outs of modern organizational activity. At the center of an effective leadership style is the ability to see how resources can be acquired and orchestrated to enable the Transformed apostolate to sing out to those in need.[11]

Direction: Transformed religious communities are led by individuals who utilize interpersonal and pragmatic processes which assist all those involved in moving toward self-actualization.

Resources: At issue here are the raw materials, goods and services, and energies of an organization. The capacity to "perform" the mission becomes a significant concern.

Traditional Divine Providence: God will provide!

Transformal Human Potential: The miracle is within each of us. We have the human potential to energize our work at the practical level. Let God provide our spiritual strength so that we can get about the business of acquiring and using resources in pursuit of God's purpose.

In the call for Transformed religious life, the challenge is for every religious to examine all facets of the self. The Transformal Paradigm is like a set of tools which the individual can use to break down the barriers which have compartmentalized religious life in the past. Once these barriers, and those in our own minds, are leveled, we can look to the unique power each of us has to carry the message of Christ to the people of God.

To be self-actualized is to be an individual: a person whose vision of the ministry is unique. As we find our identities in service, we become part of the self-actualization of the people we serve. Here is the essence of the Transformal paradigm shift from Divine Providence as a resource, to human potential. It is a turning away from the notion of a religious community as a definer of the identities of its members in favor of organizations which offer options and help each person develop individual human potential. Insofar as we are able to transform our organizations in this direction, we will harvest the fruits of tremendous human potential in our congregations.

Resources: The transformal religious organization is vitalized by the creative use of human potential in the application of physical and financial resources to the attainment of God's purpose.

Dynamic: There is, as I see it, a mystic force which energizes the members of any successful organization. This force is not the same spiritual energy we associate with religious life, although it is similar. In most organizations, the dynamic derives from a founding person or concept and retains its vitality to the extent that the organization has achieved its goals.

Dynamic is not, alas, itself invincible. Like people and organizations, dynamism can be weakened by changing circumstances and organizational failure. We all know about organizations like US Steel where international competition effectively destroyed a powerful labor dynamic. We have also experienced the erosion of our own dynamics, although we have trouble admitting to their failure. In my judgment, this is the most serious impediment to the Transformation I am calling for in these pages.

Traditional Rule: The historical continuity expressed in our Rule can be a source of both strength and weakness. The considerable success we have achieved in the past can be ascribed to the balance between the Rule and the social and economic circumstances in which we work. These successes strengthen us and make it difficult to call the Rule into question. However, when circumstances undergo the cataclysmic changes now under way, the Rule may prevent adaptation. It is then a failed dynamic which must be replaced, else we lose relevance and become dying vestiges of the past.

Transformal Imagination: The paradigm shift here is one from documents to mind. Augmenting written Rules, a dynamic of imagination unleashes the creative abilities of all religious. Imagination forges the link that ties all stakeholders into one body, sharing in the charism of Christ and of the founders of our orders to feed our spiritual needs. This same imagination has its practical side which visualizes the relationships among the religious life, the church, and its surroundings; it is a unique blend of the spiritual and the mundane. If we have the courage to set imagination free, I believe that we will see countless innovative approaches to religious life. These approaches will greatly appeal to our stakeholders who will join with us in transforming our historical institutions.

Metanoic Experience

Global dynamics have raised several fundamental ethical issues. Who may earn even a subsistence level of living? Who may work with human dignity free of prejudice? Who may live on the land and take responsibility for stewardship over it? These issues of social justice face everyone who has a measure of control over the goods and services of modern society. They bear most heavily on the consciousness of men and women religious who have the unique capacity to affect the decisions of the powerful as well as the life chances of the unfortunate.

If we concerned religious are to take up this burden and succeed, we cannot in addition carry the weight of traditional religious life. We must transform our lives and organizations to accommodate global reality, so that our energies can be directed at an ever-expanding apostolate. The Transformal Paradigm I am proposing is a framework on which new lives can be constructed; it is a radical shift of ground with the potential to shake loose our imagination. Thus we will attract new vocations and experience a vibrant new life for our religious orders.

But the Transformal Paradigm is more than a modification of our Rules and rituals. It is a metanoic experience which alters our spirituality and refocuses our commitment. As the word metanoia suggests, embracing the ideas underlying the Transformal Paradigm involves a fundamental shift of mind.[12] We no longer think of religious life in the same terms. What was once a personal relationship between each of us and God, is now a network of social interactions in which spirituality brings God among us. It is a means to unleash the forces of creativity that reside in all religious. Imagination is the energy—the dynamic—that will position religious life for a productive transition to the new millennium. The imagination dynamic differs from other Transformal Principles in that it must be stated as a challenge. Because imagination is not static, it continues to suggest new visions of religious life which can keep the church alive in whatever ecology may evolve in the years ahead.

Dynamic: Let us, individually and together, set our imaginations free to discover transformed religious lives that meet the challenges and opportunities of the new millennium while preserving the essential charisma of Christ.

Notes

1. David Nygren, CM, and Miriam Ukeritis, CSJ, "Future of Religious Orders in the United States," *Origins* 22:15 (Sept. 24, 1992). Also referred to in this article as the FORUS study.

2. Thomas H. Stahel, "Whither Religious Life?" *America* (Sept. 26, 1992) 180.

3. Thomas Kuhn, *The Structure of Scientific Revolutions* (Chicago: University of Chicago Press, 1968).

4. Joel Arthur Barker, *Future Edge* (New York: William Morrow, 1992).

5. M. Ferguson, *The Aquarian Conspiracy* (San Francisco: Tarcher, 1980)

6. A. Woodcock and M. Davis, *Catastrophe Theory* (New York: E.P. Dutton, 1978).

7. E. Zeeman, *Catastrophe Theory: Selected Papers* (Reading, MA: Benjamin, 1977).

8. Louis DeThomasis, *Monasteries on Wall Street: The Ten Commandments of Doing Ethics In Business* (Winona, MN: Saint Mary's College Publications, 1989).

9. The term "alternative" here does not imply that the two paradigms are mutually exclusive; that the Transformal Paradigm should replace the Traditional Paradigm. Thus, imagination does not *replace* the Rule as the organizational dynamic; imagination is a new way of transforming the Rule so that it becomes an effective dynamic for religious communities.

10. G. Morgan, *Images of Organization* (Newbury Park, CA: Sage, 1986).

11. Louis DeThomasis, *Faith, Finance, and Society* (Memphis, TN: Christian Brothers College, 1987).

12. C. Kiefer and P. Stroh, "A New Paradigm for Developing Organizations," in Adams, ed., *Transforming Work* (Alexandria, VA: Miles River Press, 1984).

An Epilogue:
Brotherhood—A Renewed Vision

Thomas More Page, CFX

> *Write down the vision clearly upon the tablets so that one can read it readily. For the vision still has its time, presses on to fulfillment and will not disappoint. If it delays, wait for it; it will surely come; it will not be late.*
>
> Habakkuk 2:2-3

BROTHER THOMAS MORE PAGE, CFX, is a member of the Brothers of Saint Francis Xavier, commonly known as the Xaverian Brothers. He was born in Baltimore, Maryland, and entered the novitiate at Old Point Comfort, Virginia, in 1935. He is a graduate of the Catholic University of America, with a BA and an MA in English. In his congregation, he has been a teacher, principal, provincial, and superior general. In Louisville, he was a member of the local National Council of Christians and Jews, and also of the Louisville Catholic Poetry Society. He was active in the National Catholic Education Association, where he served on the Secondary School Committee. As a member of the Conference of Major Superiors of Men, he served on the Executive Committee and chaired the Latin American Committee. In Rome he was chairman of the Justice and Peace Committee of the Union of Superiors General, a member of the Pontifical Commission on Justice and Peace, director of AGRIMISSIO (a Vatican office with liaison to the United Nations' Food and Agricultural Office), and a member of SEDOS (a mission-orientated organization). Upon returning to the United States, Brother Thomas served as executive secretary of the United States Catholic Mission Council, and later of the Conference of Major Superiors of Men. He was on the Board of Directors of the Division of Overseas Ministry of the National Council of Churches, and also of Divine Word College, Epworth, Iowa. For ten years he was Director of the Institute of Theology and Spirituality at Santa Barbara, California. He was a member of the Religious Life Committee of the Pontifical Commission on the Religious Life. He is presently retired in Washington, DC. Brother Thomas may be addressed at 941 Perry Place, NE, Washington, DC 20017.

I prefer the word *brotherhood* to describe the life and the mission of brothers in the church because it has about it a quality not only of being a brother, but also a sense of relationship, companionship, friendship, and communion. So rich is its meaning, so fully satisfying a calling is it, that any attempt to define it fully is bound to fail. Only one who has lived brotherhood in all its richness and who continues to plumb the depths of its meaning knows that his life, his calling, cannot be captured fully in canonical definitions, nor yet in Constitutions or Chapter documents. The brother knows that his continuous encounter with his vision of brotherhood shapes the inner landscape of his soul and gives him a voice that is only an echo of what lies at the deepest level of his being, where he finds a companionship with his fellow brothers that enables him to bond so readily with all men and women.

This ability of brotherhood to bond readily with all others was seen and grasped by a black woman in southern Maryland who summed up in six words what brotherhood is all about: "You brothers are with the folks!" Being at home "with the folks" has always been a characteristic of brotherhood. Brother Kirby Boone, CFX, writing from Ruby, Alaska, where he ministers to the Iniutes in the Yukon territory, gets to the source of his brotherhood: "As in my previous locations, the word Brother gives me a wonderful calling card, one that Jesus initiated at the last supper." Recently a third-grader asked me: "Are you a Preacher-Man?" "No. I am your brother in Jesus."

Called by Name

I have known many brothers who have been called by name in their bonding "with the folks." Let me cite but a few examples. Brother Peter Donahue, CFX, director of the Department of Detention Ministries for the Archdiocese of Los Angeles, while working at a large prison in Maryland, introduced some radical education reform programs which eventually enabled some of the inmates to receive a high school education. With evident feeling, he recalled that he was never prouder of bearing the title brother than when the black prisoners finally called him by that name. "That word," he said, "has a special meaning to the Blacks. Knowing that, I treasured it all the more."

Brother Nivard Scheel, CFX, had a somewhat similar experience when he was Vice President for Student Affairs at the Catholic University of America, where he was instrumental in establishing a special center for black students. Early in the year a black student told him quite frankly that she could not call him brother. At the end of the year, she invited him to a farewell party at the center, where she welcomed him with the words, "Now we can call you brother."

Then there was Brother Peter Celestine, CFX, a genuinely simple religious who practiced ecumenism before the word became fashionable. At his wake, Joe Berg, his Jewish friend at whose Newton Market in Newton Highlands, Massachusetts Peter had shopped for the orphanage, approached the casket, withdrew a prayer from his pocket, and, putting on his yarmulke, prayed:

> May the death of my brother Peter, for whom I now mourn, cause me to reflect and repent. My brother has been an inspiration, example, and guide during his life on earth. I know no purer spirit, exponent of love, and man among men. May I be as positive about my salvation as I am about my brother.

After completing his term as provincial, Brother Nilus Cullen, CFX, volunteered to go to Bolivia, where he opened the first school in that country exclusively for the *compesinos*. He soon became known in all the tiny villages in the Alto Plano high in the Andes, and whenever he came into a village, he was greeted everywhere with the simple words,*"Hermano! Hermano!"*

These brothers, and more, have borne the title brother for a lifetime among and "with the folks." In bonding with all whom they have met in their varied ministries, they have had no need to explain who they are.

Personal History

Having lived brotherhood in the congregation of the Xaverian Brothers for 57 years, I now want to sketch briefly my own odyssey that led me to a new vision of brotherhood. Then I want to end with what I believe to be the mission of brotherhood today.

As I look back over the past 57 years, I realize now with greater clarity than ever before that the dream I had as a novice was one of brotherhood. I had set out on this journey carrying the beautiful title of brother. A "fair portion" was allotted to me by the church when first I heard the words, "You shall henceforth be known in religion as Brother Thomas More." On that day when I was first named brother, I could repeat the words of the chorus in *Murder in the Cathedral:* "This is my land. This is my inheritance."

At every turn of the journey, this title took on richer meaning; and as I look back at this growing revelation, I see that at the heart of the call to brotherhood is a life of simplicity, a life uncluttered with ambition and power, a life infused with the gospel values of brotherly compassion, lived in solidarity among all people, especially those who suffer from want, neglect, and injustice: the poor, the weak, the oppressed of this world.

Turning Point

The great turning point of this revelatory understanding of brotherhood was, of course, the renewal of the religious life that followed on the heels of Vatican Council II. But in those heady and exciting days, I little realized how radical and earthshaking this phase of my journey was to become. The tumultuous days that burst upon the religious life in the 1960s turned my world upside down. As our ranks became thinner, as internecine battles raged throughout our provinces and opened wounds that took years to heal, as new expressions of community emerged calling for new ministries, as all this and more was happening, I often felt that the religious world in which I had lived and so ardently believed and to which I had dedicated my life, was falling apart. It was then that I experienced the haunting words of the Ghanian poet, Meri Nana: "There are times when even the air weeps a eulogy for days past, things passing." I also began to know what the poet Yeats meant when he wrote at another turbulent time that "the center was not holding."

New Reality

But later when I looked more closely at what was happening, I began to see that my alarm and my apprehensions were wrongly directed. Like the Jews of old I saw that I had placed my trust in "horses and chariots": numbers, growth, the preservation of institutions, the adoption of society's values, a smooth-running and highly centralized government, and tightly-knit communities. But more particularly, I had lost the original vision of brotherhood. It was this world that was falling apart.

There was pain in experiencing this world crumbling, but born of it were a deeper meaning and a greater commitment to my life now seen in the light of the Gospel and the yearnings of the world community for a more just and free world. This deeper meaning and these world wide yearnings evolved lowly, as with my brothers I began the journey back to our original foundation, and from there joined with my confreres in writing a new rule of life, *Fundamental Principles*. This document captured in a very personal and beguiling manner a new vision of who we were as brothers, and laid the foundation for commitment to manifesting a gospel witness to Jesus' compassionate love for "those who suffer from want, neglect, and injustice: the poor, the oppressed of this world."

It was this vision and this gospel commitment that impelled the brothers at their 1990 gathering to articulate what they felt was a more radical call to live the Gospel in the following ways:

1. to be prayerful people of faith who will develop a spirituality for justice and equality which is nonviolent, hopeful, courageous, and collaborative
2. to clarify and articulate a Xaverian response to the needs of the church and the world through an ongoing process of discernment
3. to be brother for and with those who cannot speak or hear: the poor, the marginalized
4. to speak and act collectively regarding specific peace and justice issues in the church and in the world

This statement reflects not only the brothers' prayerful response to the dramatic changes that were taking place in church and society, but also their conviction that in working to make the world more just, more humane, and more peaceful they were living out the spirit of their founder, James Theodore Ryken, who had great compassion for the poor of Belgium, England, and the United States in the early part of the nineteenth century.

Grace of Change

As the result of the high priority given by the brothers to creating a more just and peaceful world, the great pain that I had experienced at seeing my world falling apart, the feeling that "the center was not holding," was now replaced by a growing understanding of what brotherhood is called upon to do today. So with my brothers I became convinced that brotherhood will endure only when it can arise transformed by the grace of change. I experienced Newman's assertion that "in a higher world it is otherwise, but here below to live is to change, and to be perfect is to change often."[1]

But while retaining a memory that is linked with its past, this revised understanding of brotherhood constantly opens itself to the new that is always unfolding. Yet, change is not itself the promise of renewed brotherhood. Rather, it is the capacity to develop new visions that will make its past history and traditions come alive, passionately alive. As Sally Cunneen put it so clearly:

> We who are, or would be church, must deepen our identity in response to the reality and mystery of this world. We must shuffle off old scales, burn off the fog of assumptions and stereotypes that limit our receptivity to the world through which the Spirit tries to teach us. We need to develop new visions if we are to make old traditions alive in our minds and actions.[2]

We cannot foresee the parameters of a new vision of brotherhood today, and attempts to do so would be debilitating. What I do know, however, is that we are not inventing something new, as if we were disconnecting ourselves from our past. Rather, we are responding to the grace of change in order to see more clearly what brotherhood's commitment means.

Brotherhood's Commitment Today

Whatever parameters may be established for a renewed vision of brotherhood, one urgent commitment must be made. I believe that in the wake of Vatican Council II brothers were left more free to join their fellow men and women everywhere to participate in the co-creation of a new world community. In light of this experience, and moving toward a deeper understanding of the radicalization that took place after the Council, brothers must do all that is humanly possible to effect a change in those structures and mentalities that prevent this dream from becoming a reality. Whether these structures be in church or in society, they must be the deep concern of brotherhood since they prevent the coming of the kingdom

> which Jesus wanted his contemporaries to believe was a "kingdom" of love and service, a kingdom of human brotherhood and sisterhood in which every person is loved and respected because he or she is a person.[3]

I do not intend to give a bill of particulars for implementing this commitment. But what I would like to do is to isolate two areas where I think brothers can make a contribution within the church, and then propose a more global agenda, ending with what I deem to be the constituent elements of brotherhood today that flow from this global view.

Two Priorities

The journey toward the co-creation of a new world community begins at home, within the church. While brothers can take many actions, I believe they can address two specific areas today: brothers in clerical orders, and the empowerment of the laity.

The long-standing question about the place of brothers in orders which canon law defines as clerical has seen much thoughtful progress. However, resistance to allowing brothers to participate in the governance of their religious institutes continues. If religious institutes are to remain true to their charism brothers should not only hold an honored place, but they should also be empowered to participate fully in all decision-making bodies at every level: local, provincial, and general. If a religious order eventually became all clerical, an essential element of community life and the charism of the order could be lost, and professionalism at its worst would easily creep in.

This problem within religious orders and the larger church links with the greater imperative of empowering the laity, key to fulfilling the church's mission to transform the world. The declericalizing of religious communities, then, needs to be viewed as a dimension of the larger declericalization of the life of the church to which we are all called through our common baptism. Philip Land, SJ, pleads that we have to get away from the belittling definition which says that a lay person

> is a "non-cleric" and [rather] name lay persons . . . [for] what they have in common with all others in the church. That commonality, stemming from baptism, is one of the common life—community—together with a mission that is one and the same for all: to evangelize the world in the full meaning of evangelization expressed by Paul VI in *Evangelization in Our Times*.[4]

One group in the church who can resonate with this "commonality" are brothers who, under the impetus of Vatican Council II, now see themselves as very much part of the life of the men and women among whom they live and minister. Brothers have a long history of not being concerned with power and status. Besides, their experience with clericalism in the church on the one hand, and their association "with the folks" on the other, make them uniquely fitted to contribute toward the laity's full participation in what John Coleman calls the "ministry of governance."[5]

Global Vision

However important these internal goals are, they must be subsumed under the larger global vision which aims at refashioning a broken world into a new community: the solidarity of the human family, where there is no longer poverty, and where the unity of the human family becomes a gospel imperative.

All evidence points to the fact that we are in a new global civilization. According to Bede Griffith, OSB:

> We are entering a new age. The European civilization which we have known for the past two thousand years is giving way to a global civilization, which will no longer be centered in Europe but will have its focus more in Asia, Africa, South America. Christianity will no longer be a separate religion but will be seen in the context of the religious traditions as a whole.[6]

The logo for this impending global civilization is the stunning photograph of Earth which astronauts took from their spacecraft. This picture of our fragile planet caught our imagination and made us realize that we were indeed a human family. As the poet Archibald MacLeish wrote:

> To see the earth as we see it, small and blue and beautiful in that eternal silence where it floats, is to see ourselves as riders on the earth together, brothers and sisters who now see they are truly brothers and sisters.[7]

As a part of this global civilization, brothers cannot help but be intensely involved in the yearning for universal justice and peace as the prelude for the co-creation of a new world community. In response to this yearning, brothers also see themselves as "riders on the earth together" with all men and women. They keep in mind that whatever vision they may fashion for the future, whatever they may set up as priorities, however they may go about refounding their orders—all will be "sounding brass and a tinkling cymbal" if they do not ground their efforts in cooperation with all men and women of good will to create a new global family.

Brotherhood Today

Within this global vision I see brotherhood today as an enterprise through which

1. the church is enriched by commitment to the mission of continually transforming religious life, enabling it to participate in the movement of refashioning a broken world into a global family groaning to be born;
2. brothers live on what Juan Sobrino calls "the frontier": where there is a need for prophetic activity which denounces sin more energetically and shakes the whole church out of the inertia which petrifies it;[8]
3. all the "hues and cries of existence"[9] are taken into its gospel net as Jesus did;
4. a passionate voice speaks out against injustice; a community to wounded spirits is forged; and a holy conspiracy is brought about in a world where there is "neither Greek nor Roman, Jew nor Gentile, slave nor free, male nor female," but where all are free.

Brotherhood's Quest

The ability of brothers to bond with all peoples, the solidarity and fraternity they have nourished in their ranks, the purification they have experienced in the fires of change, their dream of participating in the refashioning of a broken world into a global family where justice and compassion reign instead of oppression and racism—here may be found the seeds of brotherhood for tomorrow. The task may seem formidable, quixotic, beyond reach. But like a candle burning at the edge of dawn, let us dream, and let the dream intoxicate us into believing that it is possible.

The eye must have a vision, the heart a quest, if we are to make brotherhood ready for tomorrow's dawn. Come, my brothers, begin the quest. To follow it is to live; to shirk it is to die.

Notes

1. Quoted by John Tracy Ellis, *The Critic* (Winter 1985) 32.

2. Sally Cunneen, "God's Maternal Presence," *Commonweal* (Sept. 11, 1992) 18.

3. Albert Nolan, *Jesus Before Christianity* (Maryknoll, NY: Orbis, 1992) 101.

4. Philip Land, SJ, "Report on the Synod of the Laity," *Center Focus*, Center of Concern, 82 (Jan. 1988) 4.

5. John Coleman, SJ, "The Future of Ministry," *America* (March 28, 1981).

6. Bede Griffith, OSB, "A New Consciousness," *The Tablet* (London, Jan. 16, 1993) 70.

7. Quoted by Judy Mayotte, *Mission Update*, US Catholic Mission Association (Jan.–Feb. 1993) 8. The quotation has been altered slightly for inclusive language.

8. Quoted in *Brothers in Lay Religious Institutes*, (Rome: Union of Superiors General, 1991) 67.

9. Daniel Berrigan, SJ, "The Face of Jesus."

Summary of the Discussion

Michael F. Meister, FSC, Editor

The purpose of this summary is to give the reader an inside view of what we called the "Brotherhood Seminar." The richness of a seminar like this one is found not only in the final product, but also in the discussion among the participants. So, while the articles you have read in this book represent the finished work of the Seminar, this summary will give you a view of the articles as we discussed each of them in their initial form during the weekend of April 1 to 3, 1993, at the Christian Brothers Conference Center at Mont La Salle in Napa, California.

The schedule we used during this Seminar began with a general discussion of the articles on opening night, followed by two days of discussions on the separate articles. Each author had time to make introductory remarks; these were followed by a discussion which involved reactions to the article, related insights and perspectives, questions, clarifications, and editorial comments. All this was designed to help the author as he went home and put his article into its final form.

BROTHER MICHAEL F. MEISTER, FSC, is a De La Salle Christian Brother. He is a native of Ferndale, California, and presently lives in Moraga, California. He joined the Christian Brothers in 1963 and professed final vows in 1970. He has a BA in English and Humanities from the University of Southern California, an MA in Theology from Saint Mary's College of California, and a PhD in Theology and Literature from the Graduate Theological Union in Berkeley, California. He is presently an Assistant Professor in the Department of Religious Studies at Saint Mary's College of California. Brother Michael's previous ministries have included high school teaching, formation work, and high school, college, and community administration. He is also the convener and editor of the Christian Brothers Spirituality Seminar, and has written several articles for that publication. Brother Michael may be addressed at P.O. Box 5169, Moraga, CA 94575.

First Night's Discussion

In September of 1992, the group had met in Chicago to present proposals and synopses for articles, so our meeting in Napa was very much like a reunion, and we were able to get right to work after dinner on the first evening. Unfortunately, Brother Edward Coughlin was unable to attend the Seminar because a major storm in the East grounded most westbound flights. Brother Louis DeThomasis arrived late on the first evening due to the same storm.

The discussion that first night centered around the twofold experience of writing our own articles and reading those of everyone else. I began by noting that after reading all the drafts, it was apparent that the original title we had chosen for this book—*Brothers in the Church: Who We Are Among the People of God*—was probably not the title we would leave with. It has been my experience with the annual Christian Brothers' Spirituality Seminar that we often make adjustments to our proposed title after we have read the articles and discussed how they work together as a unit. With this in mind, I urged the group members to "keep their own score" as we discussed each of the articles so that when we determined the shape of the book at the end of the Seminar, we would have a fairly good sense of how we wanted to title it.

Thomas Page, our "elder statesman," began by noting the remarkable nature of our coming together in a collaborative effort of several congregations to "let the voice of the brothers be heard in the land." Noting the various emotional "pitches" of the articles, Thomas spoke of varied experiences enabling us to speak out to each other and to the church with voices that were clear, passionate, determined, and strong, but voices that were also compassionate and sensitive. Above all, Thomas felt that our voices spoke with a love for who and what we are as brothers, even as we struggle with that identity—particularly those brothers in clerical orders.

Bernard Spitzley made us all laugh when he told us that his presentation to us in Chicago was "real safe." He shared an experience many of us had: that after that discussion he went home and changed everything in his article in light of the many new perspectives and paradigms we had explored at that meeting. He reminded all of us of the "complacent brothers" in our ranks who need to be re-inspired and set aflame, and he felt that what we were about here would do just that. We all resonated with Bernard's observation that the writing of these articles was, in one sense, a movement from "the safe world of biblical quotes to seeing what can really be done out there."

In addition to many other experiences, Joseph Martin found the writing and reading of these articles to be a wonderful educational experience. He also did what several others did: circulate his draft article among several confreres and friends. Their feedback and encouragement resulted in an even better piece of work. Joseph commented on the diversity among the articles as a sure sign of the wealth of resources and thinking among contemporary brothers.

Joel Giallanza was also fascinated by the spectrum of approaches to the topic we chose, but even more so by the linkages among them. He said that some of the linkages caused him to change his original thinking and take a different approach. What was perhaps most compelling for Joel was revisiting significant issues in the articles that the institutional church is simply not talking about. Thus, these articles do have a vital message to convey to the upcoming Synod, and this message is an exciting dimension of the Seminar. Joel also noted that, while the articles are specifically directed at brotherhood, many women religious will be touched by the work we are doing here. The issue is that our work has implications far beyond just ourselves.

At this point, Thomas Paige asked Joel—and the rest of us— an important question: "When you were writing your article, who did you consider your audience to be?" We kept this question before us throughout the entire weekend. Joel responded that, while religious brothers were his primary audience—mainly because of what he calls "the unfinished agenda"—he was concerned that people outside religious orders understand the world of brotherhood and some of the issues with which we struggle. In answering his own question, Thomas said that he felt he was writing simply for a Catholic audience—bishops included—and that he wanted people "to know and hear that this is something I have loved, something that has transformed my life."

David Werthmann responded to Thomas's question by saying that his audience was not so much bishops and the Synod as the major superiors, many of whom might find here statements they have not heard before. More than the bishops, David felt that major superiors are in a position to "do something." He also told us that his second audience was his own confreres. David shared something we all experienced: in writing his article he felt the need for discipline, and (with our approving laughter) shock at receiving Louis DeThomasis's article long before anyone else's arrived!

I told David that I was really moved reading some sections of his article because it was the first time I had seen some of the issues he addresses in writing, and a world of brotherhood I had not experienced opened dramatically before me. These and issues in other articles, I noted, were sure to have a similar impact on our readers because they are not fabrications. They are our experiences, we have embraced them, and that is our gift. "But sometimes," I quipped, "it's like embracing a porcupine!" Amidst laughter, I suggested the title of this book might be: *Brothers in the Church: Hugging the Porcupine!*

Francis Presto said he found himself in a situation similar to that of David relative to needing discipline in writing his article. But above all he needed to deal with some of the hurt he was feeling because of experiences he (and others of his confreres) encountered in ministry. Sharing his article with some of his older confreres, he was told: "Someone needs to say this." The result was that he came back to the article with a renewed vigor. As for audience, Francis told us that he was writing mainly for his sister whose question to him was one many of us have heard: "Why did you choose to be a brother rather than be ordained?" Noting the diversity of the articles, Francis observed that readers of this book will come away with a broader view of the church, not just brotherhood.

Sean Sammon noted that he found himself writing primarily for brothers. As he did so, he wondered whether readers not in religious life would be able to grasp the significance of, say, the tension between the communitarian (brotherhood) and the hierarchical (clerical) with the vigor and concern that we in religious life do. When he began to read the other drafts as they came in, however, he saw that there was quite a broad spectrum of approaches to the "tensions" that concerned him, which convinced him of the uniqueness and the richness of this enterprise. In the end, he said he had to agree with Joel that we might be tempted to *assume* that a lot of people know and understand the issues raised in these articles—but they don't or, if they do, they may not wish to talk about them.

As our discussion continued, it became apparent that Thomas Page's question about audience was also pointing to the breadth of our motivations in writing the articles. Thomas Grady added yet another dimension to this discussion when he reported that he wrote primarily for himself, in the sense that he wanted to nail down a series of ideas he had been thinking about for several years—but with this question in his mind: "What do these ideas have to do with being a brother?" His answer, he told us, was that he believes the brothers' vocation synthesizes much of what both the church and the world are searching for, but haven't yet grasped. In this sense, he said he wasn't really writing only for himself, or for brothers, but "for anybody who cares to make sense out of life." For Thomas, this posed quite a challenge, without which the experience of writing would have lacked a great deal.

Robert Berger added yet another perspective to the question of audience by saying that he felt that instead of writing for all brothers, he had particular faces before him—friends, colleagues, confreres—for whom the question of brotherhood in its many dimensions represented a quest, an ongoing conversation. For Robert, it was experiences with the "owners" of these faces that crystallized his article.

Thomas Maddix shifted the focus of the discussion from audience to our impact on that audience by means of several anecdotes and questions. He recounted a recent experience where the local diocesan newspaper did a feature on vocations without ever mentioning brothers. He called the paper and reminded the editor that "we do live, and if people are going to be making a choice, we should have a chance to say who we are." Shortly thereafter, a reporter and a photographer showed up at his office to do an article on brothers. The problem was that, taking Thomas's cue about choices, the paper featured two brothers at extreme ends of the spectrum from each other—the last state being worse than the first! The point of his story, Thomas remarked, was that most people are clueless about brothers. Furthermore, he noted, many brothers are clueless about some of the issues raised in these articles, content with being the way they are. For him, the question about audience was: "What are they going to carry away with them?" Noting the comparatively small number of brothers in the United States and Canada, for instance, and the trend toward "comfortability" among them, Thomas observed that right now it is hard for brothers to have an impact on the Church.

Another question Thomas raised was this: "Are we willing to speak from our experience, or do we prefer to speak from 'shoulds'?" If we want to have a voice, and we want to be heard, then we need to speak, and speak well. These articles represent a significant "leap" in the conversation. A further question: "In reading these articles, what will people learn about us that will really enhance their understanding of our unique role in the church?"

John Paige then recounted a bit of the history that led up to this Seminar, noting how the right constellation of organizers and sponsors came together in 1992, all of which resulted in this "impossible dream" coming true. "This is a graced opportunity," John stated, "it's proactive and positive." Joseph Martin added that ours is a prophetic venture, as well.

Thomas Grady suggested that while we may not have a great impact on the Synod, the importance of this venture lies in the fact that we are telling the world: this is what we think of ourselves, this is what we hope for. Rather than reacting *after* the Synod, Thomas, said, we are creating our own starting place, not waiting for someone else to point it out to us. To him, this is a breath of fresh air that we are offering to our readers for their consideration. The dialogue is open.

Bruce Lescher offered an important insight when he told us: "This project is all about who's going to define who we are as human beings." He said that there have been too few experiences where brothers dialogue about their identity as we have done here. In the area of scholarship, Bruce noted, practically nothing is being written about brothers. That is what makes this venture so exciting. Remarking that bishops often don't know who and what we are, Bruce expressed the view that if we can begin to talk among ourselves, raising the questions we raise here, then this book will have done its job.

Thomas Maddix echoed Bruce's views about our being defined by others, applauding the fact that though we are writing from our lived, and diverse, experience, ours is a powerful collective voice that stands in utter contrast to the "Silent Josephs" so many of us were advised to be in our formation. He noted that if we begin to have a better sense of ourselves in our own writing and reflection, then this will impact on how we present ourselves in the church at large.

Brian Henderson brought the first night's discussion to a close, remarking how "reader-friendly" he thought the articles were. Like Joel, he felt that the connections between articles opened a world of richness no single article possessed by itself. Brian remarked that he was impressed with the "honesty" of the articles as brothers addressed brothers, noting that this is one of the book's major qualities. Echoing an earlier thought, he said that while certain experiences are singular to brothers, much here is worthy of consideration by any reader, including women religious and clerics.

First Day

Morning Session

The first morning session was devoted to a discussion of articles written by Brothers Robert Berger, Joel Giallanza, Edward Coughlin, Louis DeThomasis, and Thomas Page.

Brother Robert Berger. Robert began by recalling the issue of our "audience" from our discussion the night before. He felt that his article was generally directed to brothers, but particularly the brothers of his (New York) Province. In introducing his article, he recalled an aspect of the Future of Religious Life Study, namely, the need for vision among us and the need to talk with one another about our vision. Robert told us that we don't need to share our vision with bishops or with nonbrothers as much as we need to share that vision with each other. His point was that if we articulate our vision among ourselves and work to achieve it, others will begin to understand what brotherhood is all about. But we must do this for and among ourselves first. Robert pointed to one issue that distracts us from our vision: our over-involvement. This led him to summarize the central focus of his article: we must face the uncertainty of the future and the need to let go of many of our projects. The other side of this letting go, however, is an openness in faith to a newness that God brings about in our lives and our ministries. It is easy for us to talk about the past, Robert said, because we have so very much invested in it. But brothers of vision need to test the uncertain waters of the present and the future—a difficult task indeed! Robert saw his article as a word of encouragement to brothers to begin to witness to the newness of God among them rather than spend their energies holding on to a fading past.

Louis DeThomasis opened the discussion on this article with remarks on a passage in Robert's article: "serious danger of becoming overwhelmed by ministry. . . ." He noted that many contemporary religious are overwhelmed in their ministries, not so much from a conviction that they are doing what is needed, but rather as a way of running away from not knowing what to do. He encouraged Robert to pursue this thought, especially since many modern religious feel they are not really "where the action is." Robert agreed, and quipped that when we see space, we just fill it up with more ministry. Louis said that it seems when we're not sure of our direction, we move twice as fast which tends to blind us into thinking that since we are working, we are doing God's work. Robert added to this our seeming inability to set boundaries in our ministries, and in our personal lives.

Sean told us that he was intrigued by the same issue as Louis, but from a slightly different angle. He wondered whether part of the reason we find ourselves so overwhelmed is because deep down we have not really accepted the necessity to share (even the leadership of) our ministries with our lay colleagues. He suggested that this happens because many of us tend to define ourselves by the tasks we are involved in, and if others can do those tasks. . . . The main issue for Sean, then, was identity. For him the question was what we hold on to when we identify ourselves: is it *what we do,* or *what we are supposed to be about?*

Thomas Maddix suggested that ministry can actually stifle the imagination, and that the question is: how do we free our imagination? He said that modern religious need flexibility in their lives in order to give their imagination room to work. If we and our orders are so geared to tasks, we leave no space in our organizations for creativity. He noted that we do have individuals in our orders who are creative and imaginative; what we are really looking for is a way of life that needs imagination in order to be born. Our organizations have to allow this birth to take place. Perhaps we need a collective imagination just as the Exodus story Robert refers to in his article is the story of a collective transformation. In the end, he noted, we all need to embrace this collective transformation if we are going to be renewed.

Bruce complimented Robert for his exploration of the images of brokenness and exile, and urged him to amplify how important these images are for contemporary religious life. What captured Bruce's attention here was that the events Robert wrote about have happened before in the history of God's people; these previous experiences can enlighten the present moment in which we find ourselves.

Thomas Maddix, noting several of Robert's quotes from Bruggemann, said that one way change can happen is through articulated grief. He wondered whether what is missing at times is the articulated grief of the brothers walking through the desert. We need to take this walk, and we need to articulate our grief. This does not mean being negative and blaming others for our situation. Rather, we need to own our own losses, our break-downs, to share these with each other. Our responsibility right now, Thomas noted, was to provide ways to articulate this grief.

Joseph noted that this is one of the issues the men's movement is exploring at the present time. He observed that men generally don't deal well with grief and anger. One of the significant themes he saw stemming from Robert's article was that in the midst of all the changes we experience today in society, in the church, and in religious communities, we are re-conceiving our idea of God: re-conceptualizing the whole world, our place in it, and our relationship with God. Joseph added that this can also be very threatening, and suggested that the significant rise of fundamentalism is precisely a negative response to this issue of the newness of God (which is also our newness!).

Sean said that all of this made the article very challenging to the reader, particularly Robert's treatment of the fact that we are in the desert, in exile, on a journey. For Sean, the most poignant Moses example he could think of was that, while Moses led the people there, he himself never entered the Promised Land. Sean expressed to us that he had no expectation that he would ever see the future: that ours is one of those transitional generations. Rather than be depressed by this, however, we need to see ourselves as leaders of the present generation and take responsibility for the future.

John Paige offered several insights that also pointed to the linkages between a number of the articles. He was impressed with Robert's warning that we not surrender our imaginative powers to any pretension of absoluteness, that we not absolutize the present. What John saw in several of the articles translated into a caution in how we define our brotherhood. While the *Lineamenta* seeks to have everything neatly tied together, John suggested that we really need to make clear that we are in a transition and that we need to have the time and the space to hope, to explore, and to discover.

Brian brought the discussion on Robert's article to a close with a sharp insight: as soon as the People of God get to a place where they think they can figure things out on their own, they foul everything up! To him, this pointed to the fact that part of our journey is a recognition that we are not in charge. Our struggle comes in seeing ourselves as instruments in God's hands rather than always trying to seize control.

Brother Joel Giallanza. In writing his article, Joel told us that he was influenced by concerns within his own order as well as the relationship of his order to other dimensions of life. He told us that he was more and more aware of unfinished conversations—often one-sided—within orders, and within the church, about the future of religious life. His hope, he said, was to write an article that would contribute to these conversations in a positive and open-ended way. Joel agreed with John Paige that religious life in the church, particularly brotherhood, can probably not be so easily quantified or put together as the *Lineamenta* might suggest. Of course the church recognizes this, and on the positive side says: "Let's continue to investigate." In light of this, Joel said that he wanted to raise a lot of provocative questions in his article because it appears that we are not being asked to consider these kinds of questions by the church and the *Lineamenta*. Pointing to the fact that religious sometimes engage in ministries at odds with the mission of their congregation, the issue of mission was central in his explorations.

Thomas Maddix asked several general questions sparked by Joel's introduction. His basic concern was: What (where) is the voice of the brothers in the midst of the church, and where is this voice in the context of apostolic spirituality? He observed that as he read Joel's article, he could see issues of planning, of mission, and of spirituality emerging as thematic categories. Another question he raised was this: Do we, as brothers, have a voice or an experience of apostolic spirituality different from that of the cleric or the lay person? If so, what is that voice, and what is that experience? He felt from his own life that, in fact, our perspective is quite different from clerics and lay persons. The problem he noted, however, was that in not articulating this difference we get lost, or worse, we are ignored. Following up on this, Bruce wondered just what *is* our experience of mission as brothers? How does this experience of mission affect the question of apostolic spirituality?

Voicing my own appreciation for Joel's prophetic challenge to the church to raise more provocative questions, I noted how all of us religious, in a larger sense, are touched by this challenge because it was Jesus' own methodology. His ministry was a constant challenge to institutions and to individuals. My point was this: Why, or how, do we continue to be brothers if the church, as Christ's body, fails to maintain the momentum of Jesus' challenges to us?

Joseph echoed this by recalling one of Joel's statements about Jesus: that we need to look up from our own concerns and see, instead, the world of needs around us. He said that we are often so obsessed with concerns about our own future that we miss the needs of those to whom we minister. Where do we strike a balance between the future direction of our ministry and the present needs of those to whom we minister? Brian had a similar question: While we strive for competence in our ministries as brothers, how do we preserve the special way brothers reach out to others in those ministries?

John Paige concluded the discussion of this article by observing the significance of Joel's use of the cross. He noted that no matter how we follow Jesus, we are going to deal with the cross. One can either despair and leave the work, or one can live in hope. Linking with Robert's article, John likened the present situation of brothers to the journey of the Exodus: we must wait in hope for the Day of the Lord though we may not live to see it come.

Brother Edward Coughlin. John Paige opened the discussion by commending Edward for a wonderful explication of holiness in the context of apostolic life. He said the article affirmed many of his own experiences in living religious life and living as a religious person.

Joseph applauded the phrase "blessed ambiguity" in Edward's title, saying that it redeemed so much of what brothers are presently experiencing. He observed that Edward's consideration of the need for a new self-image and self-understanding again gives better focus to issues contemporary brothers face. We are in transition, and this means a changing self-image both within the church and the world. Joseph also appreciated the element of (prophetic) risk-taking called for in our transitions. Noting that this sometimes takes religious outside of traditional church ministries, he gave an example of two sisters in Cincinnati who opened a pizza parlor. They teach their waitresses and cooks the elements of their jobs, then send them out to full-time employment.

Thomas Maddix asked about ways to break the inertia and fear to which Edward referred. Noting the presence of paradigm shifts, he was concerned to know what has to happen in order for brothers to open themselves to something different, something renewed. We need to develop new models for people to explore, a venture that borders on the prophetic. Once this is done, however, people have something tangible to look toward in their renewal.

Thomas Grady said that he also appreciated Edward's use of "blessed ambiguity" as a way to capture the direction of religious life after *Lumen Gentium*. Since brothers have chosen not to belong to the hierarchical structure of the church, one result is an ambiguity which is very much part of the shift in paradigms we are now encountering. Thomas Maddix amplified the ambiguity issue by remarking that we brothers are often the invisible people in the church. He (and others) noted how he continually hears speakers address "Reverend Fathers, Sisters, Ladies and Gentlemen," but never include brothers.

Thomas Page responded that this Seminar was certainly one way to make brotherhood more visible within the church. He stated that we do have a story to tell, but that we ourselves have to tell it. The problem has been that we haven't had the mechanism to tell our story: now is the time for collaborative (even revolutionary) efforts to be made among us, such as this Brotherhood Seminar.

Brother Louis DeThomasis. Louis took up the revolutionary theme as he introduced his article, saying that his explorations were revolutionary in the way he was handling his topic—using a sociocultural approach rather than one that was theological, spiritual, or doctrinal. He told us that our custom of frequently homilizing each other about our situations has often gotten us into more problems because we have failed to make use of the ordinary cultural and social dynamics that give substance to the kinds of explorations we are making here. To illustrate his point, Louis told a little story that provoked an outburst of laughter, but drove his point home. Little Johnny, a five-year-old, was in the kitchen with his mother and father; his teen-aged brother was outside with his friends. Johnny told his mother, "I want to go outside with the big boys." His father, however, turned to the mother and whispered, "Don't let him go out on the patio; the boys are talking about condoms." Johnny then asked, "Mommy, what's a patio?" "Talk about blessed ambiguity!" Louis said. The church, religious life, brothers—we often know nothing of what is happening on the patio because we insulate and isolate ourselves to such an extent that we fail to develop effective and imaginative infrastructures which would help us integrate our various life experiences both in the kitchen *and* on the patio. A major problem, Louis pointed out, is that we spend a great deal of time trying to pump life into dying paradigms, failing to acknowledge the necessity of creating new ones which will help both ourselves and "the world" come to a more wholesome understanding of who we are. Louis ended by saying that we tend to build walls with our old paradigms, but instead of being supports, these walls prevent us from seeing what is healthy and wholesome outside.

Thomas Maddix asked about the effectiveness of the founding myths of some congregations, noting that some are actually detrimental to a wholesome world view. Louis responded by saying that this point touched on an important function of paradigms. When your paradigm no longer embraces reality you have two choices: you can die, or you can see the situation as a signal to change. If the metaphors we use to describe ourselves do not change or adapt, then the paradigm or the central myth we live by is endangered. Louis pointed to the difference between the paradigm of congregational control and stakeholder control as an example. The former paradigm enforces control from above, while the latter generates control through those who commit themselves (have a stake in) the organization. Stakeholders, Louis noted, are not only the members of a religious congregation themselves. They can also be those who are served by the congregation, family members of those served, or former members, to name a few.

David offered a fascinating insight when he noted that our various founders responded to needs they saw with new paradigms within the church. Interestingly, though, those paradigms have frequently become solidified rather than remaining flexible and open to new and changing needs. Thomas Page suggested that the concept of "ownership" makes "stakeholder" more accessible and opens the way for continuing flexibility. Thomas Maddix also noted that stakeholders sometimes give us feedback that points to inconsistencies between what we say and what we do as religious. To Joseph's question about how he intended his audience to understand paradigms, Louis told us that we need to be cautious not to confuse paradigms with models. While models are concrete realities, paradigms are often pre-cognitive approaches to those realities.

Brother Thomas Page. Thomas introduced his article by telling us that he had just retired, thinking he would not have to do any more research, when he received an invitation to participate in this Seminar! He told us that anything he could do to encourage other brothers about the value of their brotherhood was well worth doing and that the passage from the prophet Habakkuk conveyed a great message about brotherhood today. Thomas recalled that when he was a provincial in the early 1960s, his primary goal was the renewal of religious life. He said he then began to move slowly from the renewal of religious life to the understanding of who we are as religious brothers. His concern at that time was to capture a vision that would make that understanding a reality. When he became superior general of his congregation, he continued with his goal of the renewal of religious life, but added a component of social justice to it. His energy became focused on this question: What is brotherhood, and how does it fit into the world in general? In striving to answer that question, he noted that in his article he hoped to expand the notion of what brotherhood is all about, seeing it as part of the creation of a new world community. Another aspect of Thomas's vision touched all of us. He said that the history of our brotherhood is an evocation not an obituary. It is a spring, not a winter; a story of things passing, yet vibrantly new. Yet we experience all of this in a world—to echo the poet Yeats—where the center is not holding. Talking about the "story" brothers have to tell, Thomas remarked that we must not lose our energy by engaging in explanations that drain us while ignoring our deeper convictions, the convictions that often form the foundations of our stories.

A statement in Thomas's article sparked much discussion. He wrote: "If a religious order should want to be entirely clerical, an essential element of community life could easily be lost." As we pushed this idea around, Thomas said he felt a powerful sense of community would be lost in the Franciscans or the Dominicans, for example, if they no longer accepted brothers. Thomas Maddix noted that some orders of clerics do have a strong community life, that community is also a matter of personalities, and that both communities and personalities have their own histories, which shape us differently. Brothers often connect differently from the way priests do because we all share part of a story as brothers. Thomas Page responded that what concerned him was the uniqueness of particular orders that would be lost because of the brothers' contribution to their communities. Bernard Spitzley added that the Constitutions of his order, a mixed congregation, speak of the impoverishment of communities that do not have brothers in them.

Afternoon Session

The afternoon session was devoted to discussion of articles written by Brothers Brian Henderson, David Werthmann, Francis Presto, and Bernard Spitzley.

Brother Brian Henderson. Brian told us that his remarks the previous evening really introduced his article, so we dove right into the discussion with an exploration of the distinctions between celibacy and chastity for religious and for lay persons. Brian told us that one of his concerns in his article was to grapple with the confusion between chastity and celibacy. He said he preferred not to dwell a great deal on celibacy because it is one particular choice in a larger "world" of chastity.

Remarking on Brian's general treatment of the vows, I said that the suggestion that all humans have a set of responsibilities coming under the headings of poverty, chastity, and obedience, offers much food for thought. Joseph added that Brian's dealing with the struggle to determine God's will was also thought-provoking, particularly since many communities are struggling with this issue right now. As we pursued this idea of determining God's will, I asked Brian about a statement he wrote relative to the vow of obedience: "At the same time I am listening, I am also challenged to ready myself to be heard." He responded by telling us that as part of the "hearing" process of obedience, we also need to be ready to speak and participate when we find ourselves involved in decision-making activities. The crucial point for Brian is involvement. Obedience that is simply a following of orders lacks the richness of dialogue and the deeper commitment that can result. Joel observed that a good way to put it would be to say "I am readying myself to respond."

We then explored some issues related to Brian's exploration of the vow of poverty. Brian felt that one of the values of the vow of poverty lies in the tension it creates in us, and he raised an interesting question: Do we use our possessions to keep people away or below us? He felt that society is not so interested in more poor people (ourselves) as it is in people who are willing to give of themselves for the sake of those who *are* poor. Perhaps poverty means we divest ourselves of everything that will separate us from those to whom we minister.

Thomas Maddix observed that part of the modern dilemma regarding the vows is that they mean so many different things to different people. Christian writers even talk of the vows as ordinary ways of Christian living, for everybody. For Thomas, this pointed clearly to the tension we are experiencing as our paradigms change and we struggle to make our commitment meaningful in new categories.

Brother David Werthmann. David introduced his article by saying that the force behind it was the giftedness that brothers bring to clerical congregations. Bruce agreed that giftedness was prominent among the attributes of brotherhood. He also urged David to amplify the sense of context in his article so that the giftedness would be highlighted. He noted that in mixed communities we do not want to let clerics "off the hook" of the religious life, since they take the same vows brothers take and have as much responsibility to them as we do.

Joseph said that the article opened many new perspectives to him as a member of a lay congregation. He particularly appreciated David's quoting from the documents of his congregation. Sean felt much the same, stating that David's examples made the article come to life for him.

Thomas Maddix wanted to investigate David's suggestion that the primary focus of the brother's life is not so much ministry as community. This raised the question: What *is* the life to which we are called? Thomas also noted the distinctions between monastic communities and apostolic communities. For him, one of the significant features of community is the shared relationships among the members, which also provide a strong support for them. This view was shared by Thomas Page who added that relationships are a vital part of modern community living. He particularly appreciated David's statement: "In community life we have a capacity to repair broken relationships."

Robert commended David for doing a fine job of telling the church about the difficulties relative to ministry and community among brothers. Joseph agreed, noting that we are often dealing with issues that do not have clear distinctions among them. He noted the distinction between the common life and community life, where the former was sometimes seen as having everyone under the same roof, but there was no community. He said that what has happened in recent times is that we have reacted against the common life, saying "That isn't enough. We're looking for more." One thing we are struggling with today, he concluded, is this: What is community? Can you live in different places and still be part of a community?

Brother Francis Presto. Francis opened the discussion on his article by pointing to one of its major features: the grappling with a new set of definitions for old theological terms. He admitted that this was liable to cause some confusion, but that his goal of rethinking and re-visioning these terms was worth the risk.

Much of the discussion of Francis's article was sparked by his endeavor to come at these new definitions, and many fine questions emerged. Louis addressed the question of how we recognize and deal with a long-established institutional church when and as we propose new definitions for it. Thomas Maddix raised the question of how the brothers' calling is different from that of the clerics in mixed congregations. He noted that distinctions based on talent or education are artificial; the real distinction has to do with choice and the answering of an inner calling. Bruce pursued the issue of brothers and leadership roles that have been traditionally appropriated by or relegated to the priesthood. He noted that there are many ways (and many people through whom) the sacred is mediated to us, and he pointed to the inadequacy of equating the sacred or sacred leadership only to ordained priests.

Thomas Page was both appreciative of and encouraged by Francis's search for a new language or a new paradigm which would breathe new life and understanding into old and sometimes forbidding theological terminology. He noted how so many contemporary theologians and social reformers are also struggling with an entirely new language to make sense of their experience and their vision.

Joseph told Francis that he admired the challenge that flowed out of his article. He encouraged Francis to amplify his perspective on prophecy to include the role of challenging the church as well as prevailing cultural and social attitudes. He also noted how we are coming to a new understanding of the (former) dichotomy between the sacred and the profane. By virtue of the fact that everything comes to us from God, who is the creator, is there anything that is really profane?

Bruce concluded the discussion by suggesting that Francis's article also raised the question of a problem in attitude that might underlie the ministerial conflicts to which Francis was pointing. Bruce wondered whether the way "the system" works—particularly in parish ministries—breeds a certain attitude that is ultimately unhealthy for the Christian community as a whole. This is not so much a matter of roles as much as it is how we view and describe or define our different roles.

Brother Bernard Spitzley. Bernard introduced his article by telling us that his audience was primarily brothers in clerical institutes, though it was applicable to brothers in other congregations as well. The point he was trying to communicate, he told us, was that we need to be active in creating right relationships not only in our communities, but wherever we minister. He said his article was a call to brothers to explore all their relationships. If there is an injustice—like clericalism, for example—brothers should name it and work to change it. Unless we strive for right relationships, he said, we cannot really call ourselves religious. We must guard against the contradiction of being institutes whose documents are filled with dynamism, but whose communities are lethargic. Each of us must strive to bring our communities to the dynamic level expressed in our documents; this means change from the bottom up, rather than from the administrative levels down.

Bernard used the example of NETWORK, where he presently works. This opened the discussion to several questions and perspectives. The issue of equal pay, for example, was explored by Joseph, who was curious how NETWORK personnel are administered and paid as opposed to religious community personnel.

In the context of right relationships, Thomas Maddix raised the issue of reverse clericalism in mixed communities, where brothers sometimes behave like the clerics they blame for being elitist. Thomas Grady noted that the Congregation of Major Superiors of Men (CMSM) study on clericalism notes that it is an *attitude* in brothers as well as in priests.

Bruce encouraged Bernard to pursue examples of brothers responding to injustices, with a particular emphasis on how we can bond together in our responses as we work for change. Bernard acknowledged that we do need to look for new models of response to injustice, in both how we live and how we minister. Asked how NETWORK might better demonstrate good management than IBM, for example, Bernard noted that NETWORK strives to integrate a spirituality into its labors for justice. This, of course, is where religious communities have an edge over "secular" organizations. As a fascinating contrast, Thomas Maddix noted the Taizé community, where some clerics function as brothers. He also remarked on how Taizé purposely chose not to be a part of the Roman Church in order to avoid the pitfalls of clericalism and hierarchialism. The result is Protestants and Catholics living together in brotherhood in various places in the world.

Second Day

Morning Session

Articles discussed on the second morning were those written by Brothers Thomas Grady, Joseph Martin, Bruce Lescher, Sean Sammon, and Thomas Maddix.

Brother Thomas Grady. Thomas opened his article for discussion with a concern whether it was "user-friendly." In responding, Thomas Maddix asked who the specific audience was and how the ideas presented would be integrated into the arena of brotherhood. Thomas Grady replied that he was writing for a broad audience, and that he found himself writing about a definite paradigm shift which left uncertain—at least for the moment—whether his cosmological views were to be integrated into brotherhood or vice versa. He told us that in the article he found himself describing his experience of being a brother with a language that goes beyond the traditional formulae.

Thomas Page noted that several authors in recent years have been striving to reframe the way we view ourselves in relation to the earth, the cosmos, and God. Robert added that a reader whose first encounter with Creation Spirituality was this article would find it a good introduction and a fine blend of both theory and narrative. Louis also applauded the article, stating that Thomas was giving us a good example of what a new paradigm is, right now, and how people are not realizing it. Thomas Page quipped that it was wonderful to have a Franciscan writing on Creation Spirituality.

John Paige mentioned that he did not know much about Thomas Berry's work but that this article was a good introduction to a new way of thinking about and articulating our experience of brotherhood in terms of new categories from different disciplines—some radically dissociated from religious life.

Sean said that what he particularly enjoyed about the article was the way it developed around the evangelical counsels because so much of what appears on the vows is dry and technical. What struck Sean most was that brothers, because they are not part of the power structure or the hierarchy of the church, have a kind of freedom to vision and stretch what is often dry and lifeless into something quite meaningful. He saw that happening in Thomas's article. Thomas noted that he strove as often as possible in his article to replace the word vow with counsel as a way of moving away from technical and canonical language.

Bruce asked whether Thomas's linkage between poverty, obedience, and chastity on the one hand, and differentiation, subjectivity, and communion on the other was arbitrary. Thomas responded that while there is an overlap among them, the linkage is not arbitrary. He noted that another author, writing on religious formation, independently found the same correspondence.

Joseph related that he was much affirmed in his own article after reading that of Thomas. Regarding Thomas Berry, Joseph told us how his work (and that of others like him) is having a profound effect on the way we see ourselves as humans, and how we approach the study of science and history. The "new story" that is emerging from these writers is one in which any person, any group or tribe, any culture can find its place. The result is a new kind of unity, a new kind of brotherhood and sisterhood.

Brother Joseph Martin. Joseph presented his article by telling us that it grew out of his own experience with and interest in the Men's Movement and Creation Spirituality. Joseph noted that the Men's Movement is raising significant questions, the answers to which will have a profound effect on the way we define what it means to be a man today. Older definitions of maleness and manhood, Joseph related, are no longer effective since men's roles have changed so radically in modern times. In addition, many involved in the Men's Movement are also interested in a spirituality that is applicable to men. With all of this as background, Joseph said that in his article, he was striving to listen to what the Men's Movement might have to say to brothers in religious communities. Likewise, religious communities of brothers have much they might offer to the Men's Movement. Joseph also indicated that his work in Creation Spirituality found a place in his article, especially that spirituality's four major themes: blessing, emptying, creating, and transforming.

As discussion began, several of us expressed appreciation for the title of Joseph's article. Robert said that one of the benefits of this article was that it introduced the reader to several fine sources that can be tapped into for further information and study. Sean noted that Joseph's definition of brothers by who they are rather than what they do was significant, and he urged him to include the idea of "call" in his definition. John Paige added that Joseph's definition created several linkages with that of Thomas Maddix.

Brother Bruce Lescher. Bruce began by recalling that his article grew out of collaboration and conversations with several of his confreres. He said that his aim in the article was to give his reading of the present situation of brotherhood while at the same time laying out some categories for further discussion of the future of brotherhood.

Sean said that the article presented an accurate picture on several fronts, and that it laid out many issues that must be faced. He noted that identity is an important feature underlying Bruce's discussion, adding that while many priests stake their identity on the sacramental dimension of their ministry, once the clerical culture begins to face the situation brothers now confront, it will have a great deal of re-evaluation and redefinition to do. Relative to the issue of gender differences, Sean took issue with men religious who talk about women religious being "so far ahead." He warned against a generic approach to religious life that glosses over gender differences and results in a failure to learn from each other.

Joseph told Bruce that he was impressed with the article's clarity, and that he particularly appreciated the way he spoke about "brotherhoods" instead of brotherhood. When Joseph urged Bruce to amplify certain points with examples—an urging, by the way, that we all gave each other—Thomas Page quite seriously began to speak about illustrations with one of his own, which brought the house down. He said that he read of an exchange between the theologian William Sloan Coffin and Secretary of State Henry Kissinger during the Viet Nam War. Coffin was attacking the US government's policy about the war, and Kissinger said to him something like this: "If you're so smart, why don't you tell us what to do?" Coffin, in a rather distant manner, responded: "Mr. Secretary, my job is to say to you: 'Let justice rain down like mighty waters.' Your job is to get the plumbing in place!"

Thomas Grady observed that Bruce's remarks about rebuilding meaning reminded him of Robert's comment the previous day about being overinvolved and overworked in ministry. He said he found it paradoxical that modern religious, so many of whom are well-educated and deal with ideas all the time, have such trouble addressing questions of meaning. Bruce added that once you have lost meaning, it is easier to throw yourself into all kinds of activities, a problem brothers urgently need to face.

Brother Sean Sammon. Sean introduced his article by telling us that from a consciously psychological point of view, he was trying to grapple with the issue of loss of identity. This loss of identity, he proposed, stems from a tendency to define ourselves by our work. He told us that while the cultural and paradigmatic perspectives were important for him, another motivation for the article was that he wanted to write from the context of individual journey. A central question asked at midlife is this: Who am I now, and how have I changed? In answering this question, he found that he had to look at various stages of personal development. In their "youth," brothers are heavily involved in their work; they struggle for autonomy and self-reliance, and they feel they need to prove themselves. Gradually, Sean noted, they develop a deeper sense of compassion as they begin to consider the generations who will follow them. Early on, prayer tends to be noisy and busy, whereas later it becomes more of a being with God, a listening, contemplation. Sean observed that in midlife, brothers often begin to face the fact that we have little power or status, and at times relatively little influence. But this experience can lead us to reflect on what we are actually about and who we really are. At midlife, Sean said, we tend to begin surrendering to the Lord's mission rather pursuing our own. This often involves journeying through a desert of abandonment, but it also signals a realization that God loves us in God's ways and not ours.

As the discussion began, Thomas Maddix wondered whether Sean's point about mutual and corporate dreams might not also be experienced by organizations in midlife. He noted that an interesting feature of Sean's framework was that it could be fruitfully applied to provinces and whole religious congregations. These organizations experience the need for restructuring and rediscovery. Noting that there has to be a shared dream among us, not just individual dreams, Sean agreed that his framework could also apply to institutions as well as individuals.

Joseph said that one of the reasons he appreciated the article was because its uniqueness nevertheless complemented the rest of the articles. He noted that the article will have a wide appeal since so many brothers are in midlife and experiencing the kinds of transitions Sean wrote about. Following on Thomas Maddix's observation, Joseph wondered what a *congregational* midlife transition means in the face of the midlife transitions among its own members.

John Paige added that Sean's article brought a certain sense of comfort and compassion to the reader who sincerely desires to live out his brotherhood for the rest of his days. This could be seen in what John called "guideposts" or "checkpoints" to keep us on track, to insure that we are doing the right thing, to ask whether we are listening well, or responding with integrity.

David commended Sean for what he called a direct address to brothers in the article. He noted that the sense of personal journey that plays throughout the article, as well as its spiritual dimension, gives it a great appeal. Robert agreed, saying that there is much in the article for young men who are thinking about our life.

Thomas Maddix raised an interesting question at this point: Is there a unique experience we, as brothers, face in midlife because of the nature of our way of life? Sean agreed that this is a significant question that can be developed out of the article. Midlife (mortality) faces all of us, but perhaps because we strive to live our lives without illusions or pretensions, the "crisis" of midlife affects us differently. He added, however, that this does not mean we don't have our illusions.

Thomas Page spoke from his own experience, saying that midlife for him was a time of fire, suffering, and struggle to find continued meaning to life, particularly the life he had committed himself to for so many years already. What got him through was the realization that we often need to wait in silence and prayer, that light does come at the end of the tunnel (though it could be a freight train!), that we are held tenderly in God's hands. He ended by saying that this midlife suffering can be tremendously regenerative and redemptive.

Brother Thomas Maddix. Thomas began by telling us that his article was an attempt to sort out who we really are as brothers, and why we exist. One of his basic questions was this: If we are brothers, what is unique about us, and where do we find this uniqueness? He told us that his concern for archetype grew out of his conviction that if we are going to continue as brothers, we need to have an archetype that nurtures us and makes sense out of our experiences. Thomas continued that while the cultic archetype serves priests, there is definitely one for those who are called to be brothers, to be married, and so on. He was concerned, however, that in the Christian tradition we have lost touch with the brotherhood archetype. So, in his article he wanted to explore history and ask the questions: what has happened to us? How have we gotten lost along the way? What factors have contributed to our getting lost? Can we break the bonds that often keep us invisible among the People of God? What is unique about the brothers' voice?

Sean remarked that the article was both exciting and inviting to read, and raised this question: Did brothers in the past feel the same urgency (or any urgency) to ask the questions Thomas was now raising? If not, why not? Why have these questions grown so urgent nowadays? Sean also said he was intrigued by one of Frank Houdek's categories that characterizes the brother/monk as anti-intellectual. Thomas responded that his first instinct was to reject that notion, but that in fact earlier brothers spent a great deal of time side by side with the ordinary working people.

Thomas Grady remarked that one can sometimes observe an intellectual laziness among brothers, and Thomas Maddix referred to a question Thomas Page (we had a lot of Thomases!) had asked the previous day about why more brothers were not writing about the brothers' vocation instead of choosing to be out of the mainstream. Thomas Maddix said: "If we're going to make change, we've got to be at the table!" But, he continued, we tend not to be at that table, though we sit in the back and complain. Sean and others agreed.

Joseph offered two other historical realities that feed into our being viewed as anti-intellectual. He first noted how brothers whose mission is education were often so totally involved in running schools that they failed to participate in the larger world of education. Second, he noted that brothers in mixed congregations often did the domestic work, while the "intellectual" work was done by the priests.

The discussion then focused on Thomas's definition of brother which included the term monk. This elicited several positive responses. Sean noted that it speaks to a larger sense of identity. David agreed, saying that something would be missing without the monk element. What was significant for him was the sense of the holy man among the laity. Thomas Maddix added a significant point: "As a brother, whether I'm in the boardroom or doing retreat work, my task is to make the holy present—any way I can."

This concluded our discussions on the articles. Following a much-deserved free afternoon, we celebrated the Liturgy of Palm Sunday. The evening session brought this "Brotherhood Seminar" to a conclusion with a discussion about the "shape" of the book: its title and the order of the articles. Having critically discussed each of the articles, this conversation was a fine complement to the discussion on opening night. We concluded by discussing the logistics of publication, marketing, and distribution.

A Final Note

It goes without saying that this Seminar was a graced occasion for all of us who participated. It marked the end of an intense process that began with an announcement of the Seminar and a call for articles in the summer of 1992. The articles presented here represent our wide and diverse experiences. What binds them together, however, is our zealous commitment to the calling of brotherhood, which, like a good mystery, defies explanation. We hope the articles will raise consciousness and spark conversation wherever they are read. If you are so inclined, please feel free to write to us.

We are deeply grateful to the Regional Conference of Christian Brothers (RCCB), the National Assembly of Religious Brothers (NARB), and the Conference of Major Superiors of Men (CMSM) for having supported and underwritten this venture.